Studies in Talmudic Logic

Volume 14

Philosophy and History of Talmudic Logic

Volume 4
Temporal Logic in the Talmud
Michael Abraham, Israel Belfer, Dov Gabbay and Uri Schild

Volume 5
Resolution of Conflicts and Normative Loops in the Talmud
Michael Abraham, Dov Gabbay and Uri Schild

Volume 6
Talmudic Logic
Andrew Schumann

Volume 7
Delegation in Talmudic Logic
Michael Abraham, Israel Belfer, Dov Gabbay and Uri Schild

Volume 8
Synthesis of Concepts in Talmudic Logic
Michael Abraham, Israel Belfer, Dov Gabbay and Uri Schild

Volume 9
Analysis of Concepts and States in Talmudic Reasoning
Michael Abraham, Israel Belfer, Dov Gabbay and Uri Schild

Volume 10
Principles of Talmudic Logic
Michael Abraham, Dov Gabbay and Uri Schild

Volume 11
Platonic Realism and Talmudic Reasoning
Michael Abraham, Israel Belfer, Dov Gabbay and Uri Schild

Volume 12
Fuzzy Logic and Quantum States in Talmudic Reasoning
Michael Abraham, Israel Belfer, Dov Gabbay and Uri Schild

Volume 13
Partition Problems in Talmudic Reasoning
Michael Abraham, Israel Belfer, Dov Gabbay and Uri Schild

Volume 14
Philosophy and History of Talmudic Logic
Andrew Schumann, ed.

Studies in Talmudic Logic Series Editors
Michael Abraham, Dov Gabbay and Uri Schild   dov.gabbay@kcl.ac.uk

Philosophy and History of Talmudic Loigc

Edited by

Andrew Schumann

ISBN 978-1-84890-254-1

College Publications
Scientific Director: Dov Gabbay
Managing Director: Jane Spurr

http://www.collegepublications.co.uk

Original cover design by Laraine Welch
Printed by Lightning Source, Milton Keynes, UK

CONTENTS

Andrew Schumann
Preface. Philosophy and History of Talmudic Logic……………………………8

Joshua Halberstam
Epistemic Disagreement and *'Elu We'Elu*……………………………………..14

Michael Chernick
Developments in the Syntax and Logic of the Talmudic Hermeneutic *Kelal Uferaṭ Ukelal*…………………………………………………………………..28

Mauro Zonta
Medieval Judaic Logic and the Scholastic One in the 14th – 15th Centuries Provence and Italy: a Comparison of the Logical Works by Rav Hezekiah bar Halafta (First Half of the 14th Century) and Rav Judah Messer Leon (Second Half of the 15th Century)……………………………………………...56

Sergey Dolgopolski
Suspending New Testament: Do the Two Talmuds Belong to Hermeneutics of Texts?…………………………………………………………………………70

Hany Azazy
The Genesis of Arabic Logical Activities: From Syriac Rhetoric and Jewish Hermeneutics to āl-Šāfi'y's Logical Techniques…………………………….98

Michael Nosonovsky
Connecting Sacred and Mundane: From Bilingualism to Hermeneutics in Hebrew Epitaphs…………………………………………………………...146

Ely Merzbach
Using Lotteries in Logic of *Halakhah* Law. The Meaning of Randomness in Judaism…………………………………………………………………..162

Moshe Koppel
Probabilistic Foundations of Rabbinic Methods for Resolving Uncertainty………………………………………………………………….174

Andrew Schumann
On the Babylonian Origin of Symbolic Logic.................................188

Authors..226

Preface. Philosophy and History of Talmudic Logic

Andrew Schumann

University of Information Technology and
Management in Rzeszow,
Rzeszow, Poland
Andrew.Schumann@gmail.com

The purpose of the workshop *Philosophy and History of Talmudic Logic* held on October 27, 2016, in Krakow, Poland, was to examine the meaning of Talmudic hermeneutics in the contemporary epistemology and logic. One of the main features of Judaism is that Jewish religious laws are not dogmatic but based on specific legal reasoning. This reasoning was developed by the first Judaic commentators of the Bible (*Tann'ayim*) for inferring Judaic laws (*halaḵah*) from the *Pentateuch*. Our workshop was aimed to consider Judaic reasoning from the standpoint of modern philosophy: symbolic logic, rhetoric, analytic philosophy, pragmatics and so on. On the one hand, we are interested in possibilities to import into the Talmudic study modern logical methods. On the other hand, we are interested in possibilities to export from the *Talmud* new logical principles which are innovative to contemporary logic.

The *Talmud* introduces a specific logical hermeneutics, so different from the Greek logic. This hermeneutics first appeared within the Babylonian legal tradition established by the Sumerians to interpret the law codes which were first over the world: *Ur-Nammu* (ca. 2047 – 2030 B.C.); *Lipit-Ishtar* (ca. 1900 – 1850 B.C.), and later by their successors, the Akkadians: *Hammurabi* (1728 – 1686 B.C.). In these codes the casuistic law formulation was used: 'if/when (Akkadian: *šumma*) this or that occurs, this or that must be done' – in the same way how it is formulated in the Bible. So, a trial decision looked like an inference by *modus pones* or by other logical rules from an appropriate article in the law code. The law code was founded in a stele or on a stone wall. It was considered a set of axioms announced for all. For instance, in the *Samaritan Pentateuch* it is claimed that the Israelites should have written dawn the law code of the *Pentateuch* on stones, too:

> And when *Shehmaa* your *Eloowwem* will bring you to the land of the *Kaanannee* which you are going to inherit it. You shall set yourself up great stones and lime them with lime. And you shall write on them all the words of this law (*Exodus* 20:14a-14b, tr. by Benyamim Tsedaka).

Then the trial decisions are regarded as claims logically inferred from the law code on the stones. One of the first law codes of the Greeks that were excavated recently is the *Gortyn Code* (Crete, 5 c. B.C.). It is analogous with the Babylonian codes by its law formulations; therefore, we can suppose that the Greeks developed their codes under the direct influence of the Phoenicians: the Code as the words of the stele and the courts as logic applications to these words. In this way the Greek logic was established within a Babylonian legal tradition, as well. Hence, we can conclude that, first, logic appeared in Babylonia and, second, it appeared within a unique legal tradition where all trial decisions must have been transparent, obvious, and provable. The formal logic appears first not in Greece, but in Mesopotamia and this tradition was grounded in the Sumerian/Akkadian jurisprudence.

The *Talmud* just continues the Sumerian/Akkadian jurisprudence tradition with a specific logic. So, the *Talmud* is closer to the Sumerian/Akkadian origin of logic, than the Greek logic developed by Aristotle and Chrysippus within the Greek legal tradition. Hence, the tradition of Talmudic hermeneutics is really oldest with the roots in the Sumerian/Akkadian culture with the oldest jurisprudence. Therefore this hermeneutics is so significant to be studied not only from the standpoint of *halaḵah* (Judaic laws), but also from the standpoint of logic, history of thinking, and history of law.

This volume, devoted to different philosophical aspects of Talmudic hermeneutics, includes a variety of contributions. The first of them, written by Joshua Halberstam and entitled 'Epistemic Disagreement and *'Elu We'Elu*,' is focused on the Hebrew notion *'elu w'elu divrey 'Elohim ḵayim*, according to that both sides of *halakhic* disputes can have 'heavenly' legitimacy simultaneously. It means that Judaism is not dogmatic in its nature and allows us to have opposite views.

In the paper 'Developments in the Syntax and Logic of the Talmudic Hermeneutic *Kelal Uferaṭ Ukelal*' by Michael Chernick, there is considered a logical rule from the Talmudic hermeneutics, called 'a general statement (*kelal*) is followed by a particular statement (*feraṭ*) that is followed in turn by another general statement (*kelal*)' – *kelal uferaṭ ukelal*. The author shows that this rule was understood differently by the early Talmudic commentators of the Bible (*Tann'ayim*) and by the late Talmudic commentators of the Bible (*'Amor'ayim*). It is evidence that the Talmudic logic was a life tradition that changed in the course of time.

Mauro Zonta contributed the paper entitled 'Medieval Judaic Logic and the Scholastic One in the 14th – 15th Centuries Provence and Italy: a Comparison of the Logical Works by Rav Hezekiah bar Halafta (First Half of the 14th Century) and Rav Judah Messer Leon (Second Half of the 15th Century),' where he compares the logical ideas of the two "Jewish Schoolmen:" Hezekiah bar Halafta, who wrote in 1320 probably the first text on Peter of Spain's *Summulae Logicales* in Hebrew, and Judah Messer Leon, who lived in the 15th century also in Provence and Italy. At that time the Rabbinic logic was influenced by the Medieval tradition of the Aristotelian logic.

Sergey Dolgopolski wrote the paper 'Suspending New Testament: Do the Two Talmuds Belong to Hermeneutics of Texts?' to show that the Christian hermeneutic idea of the suspension of the Old Testament in the New Testament can be articulated within the Rabbinic literature as a suspension of any new testament to the divine or any other version of law. It is so important that in the Christian hermeneutics the Aristotelian logic was applied to suspend the 'Old' Testament, while in the Talmudic hermeneutics there was an own logical tradition and the Talmudic logic was regarded as a way to preserve the borders of Judaism to suspend any 'New' Testament.

The contribution written by Hany Azazy and entitled 'The Genesis of Arabic Logical Activities: From Syriac Rhetoric and Jewish Hermeneutics to āl-Šāfi'y's Logical Techniques' shows some Judaic roots of the Islamic logic appeared at āl-Šāfi'y'*s Risāla*, the work on *'uswl āl-fiqh* or methodology of law. So, the Hebrew logical rule called *heqqeš* for inferring by analogy was transformed into the rule called *qiyās* in Arabic (this word is with the same Semitic root as *heqqeš*).

The Tamudic logical rule *qal wa-ḥomer* (in Arabic: **أقل و أكثر**) was considered by āl-Šāfi'y as the *argumentum a minore ad maius*:

فإما أن يثبت أنه إن كان الذى هو أقل، كان الذى هو أكثر

Demonstrating that if it was the less then it would be the more.

and the *argumentum a majori ad minus*:

وهذا الموضع هو أنه إن لم يكن ذلك الأمر للذى هو أحرى أن يكون، فواضح أنه
ليس للذى هو أقل أو أنقص

This topic is if it was not the case for what is more likely to be, then it is obvious that it cannot be the case for what is less or from what something is missing.

These Judaic roots of some Islamic hermeneutic rules are evidence that the Islamic hermeneutics continues the Sumerian/Akkadian legal tradition as well as the Talmudic hermeneutics does. It distinguishes the Islamic logic from the Christian traditional hermeneutics established within the Hellenistic philosophy with completely eliminating the Babylonian tradition.

The paper 'Connecting Sacred and Mundane: From Bilingualism to Hermeneutics in Hebrew Epitaphs' contributed by Michael Nosonovsky analyzes complex hermeneutic mechanisms of indirect quotations in the epitaphs and shows that the methods of actualization of the Bible are similar to those of the Rabbinical literature. It means that the Talmudic hermeneutics is applied even in the Hebrew traditional epitaphs.

The contribution 'Using Lotteries in Logic of *Halakhah* Law. The Meaning of Randomness in Judaism' by Ely Merzbach examines a philosophical meaning of lottery in the *Talmud* and in the later Rabbinic tradition as not a blind process, but as randomness that is a form of logical determinacy. It shows the Sumerian/Akkadian roots of the Talmudic hermeneutics as well, because according to the Babylonian tradition of omens there is grounded the idea that the future is fully logically determined by our choices. Randomness is not accidental in essence. We remember that according to Aristotle, there exist accidental events (like the 'sea battle tomorrow') which cannot be foretold and there is no logical determinacy in any way. However, in Judaism, any accidental event is a sign from the Lord. So, it is not accidental in the pure meaning.

Moshe Koppel wrote the paper entitled 'Probabilistic Foundations of Rabbinic Methods for Resolving Uncertainty' about the meaning of the Talmudic logical rule 'to follow the majority'. This rule is treated in the following two ways: as (i) *rub'a d'it'a qaman* ('a majority which is in front of us') and as (ii) *rub'a d'leyt'a qaman* ('a majority which is not in front of us'). As the author shows, the first way corresponds to the classical interpretation of probability, while the second way corresponds to the frequentist interpretation of probability. When the first way is applied, a random object taken (*pariš*) from a set, a majority of the members of which have property *P*, may be presumed to have property *P*. However, in some cases (*qavu'a*) the object is regarded as being a mere fragment of a mixed set and hence is regarded as "mixed," neither *P* nor not-*P*.

In the paper 'On the Babylonian Origin of Symbolic Logic' contributed by Andrew Schumann there are analyzed many examples of difficult logical schemata as results of applications of some inference rules to law codes. The Talmudic hermeneutics grew up from the Sumerian/Akkadian legal tradition.

Thus, this volume is devoted to different aspects of *Philosophy and History of Talmudic Logic*. I am thankful to all the authors for the valuable contributions and the brilliant presentations at the workshop.

In this volume the following transliterations of Hebrew and Arabic letters have been used:

Hebrew transliterations

א בּ ב ג ד ה ו ז ח ט י כּ כ ל מ נ ס ע פּ פ צ ק ר שׁ שׂ ת

t ś š r q ẓ f p ʻ s n m l k̲ k y ṭ ḥ z w h d g v b ʼ

Arabic transliterations

ا ب ج د ه و ز ح ط ي ك ل م ن ص ع ف ض ق ر س ت ث خ ذ ظ غ ش

š ḡ ẓ ḏ k̲ ṯ t s r q ḍ f ʻ ṣ n m l k y ṭ ḥ z w h d j b ā

Epistemic Disagreement and *'Elu We'Elu*

Joshua Halberstam

Department of Communication Arts and Sciences,
BCC/City University of New York,
the United States of America
joshua.halberstam@bcc.cuny.edu

1. Introduction

You look out the window and announce that it's raining. I look out and say with equal assurance that it isn't. I know you have excellent vision, I'm sure you haven't been drinking, and I have no reason to think you would declare it to be raining if you didn't think it was. You, in turn, have every reason to believe that I, too, meet the usual criteria for holding to my belief: adequate perceptual ability, lack of bias, sobriety, rationality, seriousness etc. That is to say, in this instance, we are epistemic peers. Should I therefore reconsider and substantially reduce my confidence in my belief – as should you?

In recent years, epistemologists have engaged in a robust discussion on how we ought to proceed in instances of peer disagreement: *S* has rationally and critically considered the evidence and concludes that *P* but now confronts an epistemic peer *R* whose opinion *S* values in matters concerning *P*, but who, having reviewed the same evidence *S* relied on, concludes that ~*P*. Various responses have been forwarded on how to proceed in these cases.

The broad division in this literature is between advocates of so-called conciliatory views (sometimes called conformist views) and those who favor so-called steadfast views. According to conciliationists, when faced with a peer disagreement one should reduce one's confidence in one's own belief or abandon it altogether; according to steadfasters, one is epistemically warranted in maintaining confidence in one's own view.

Does the treatment of Talmudic arguments support the conciliationist or steadfast position? It does seem, at first glance, that the Talmudic attitude toward peer disagreement favors the latter view. Although the opposing rabbis are accorded parity of intellectual ability and are recognized as supporting their respective viewpoints on relevantly equivalent sources and argumentation, neither disputant is urged to relinquish or minimize his own opinion. To be sure, adversaries are generally expected to not implement their judgments in deference, say, to an opposing majority rule, or, in one instance, in deference to a heavenly judgment. But the reason to yield is the non-epistemic requirements of the *halakhic* process, and not because the rejected view is deemed epistemically unwarranted.

This assumption concerning Talmudic disputes needs, of course, to be examined more precisely. Why shouldn't the reality of a disagreeing peer not reduce one's confidence in one's own view in Talmudic disputes as it might elsewhere? Why is not judicial compromise, when possible, the preferred solution in the usual cases of Talmudic peer disagreement? Moreover, how can a third party choose between a dispute between two peers, especially when the disputants are the epistemic superiors of the third party, as is commonplace in *Talmud* arguments? One might suppose that these epistemic concerns are largely inapplicable here as these disagreements are primarily, though certainly not exclusively, directed to issues of law and its practice, to the determination of *quaestio juris* (legal truth) and not *quaestio facti* (factual truth). But one needs to show why, if such is the case, the appeal to conciliation is not operative in this legal domain as well.

The Talmudic decree *'elu we'elu divrey 'Elohim ḵayim hen*, 'these and these are the words of the living God,' is regularly appealed to as providing the underlying support for preserving the equal epistemic status of Talmudic disputants. But, as we shall see, the principle does not provide this presumed support for steadfastness and our question about the lack of conciliation remains.

In addressing these issues, I first will highlight some key arguments for and against the conciliatory view and then note how these arguments do or don't apply to Talmudic disagreements. This, in turn, directs us to a closer look at the principle of *'elu we'elu* and why, contrary to a prevalent presumption, the notion does not justify the steadfast viewpoint. Finally, I will note some particular difficulties with epistemically inferior third party judgments of peer disagreements.

2. Conciliation or Steadfastness?

Peer disagreements occur when two persons who disagree with one another also recognize that they are equally qualified to have an opinion on the matter in question. In these circumstances, peers cannot appeal to their differences about the particular issue as favoring their own respective views without begging the question about whose evidence or reasoning is the better, since both their evidence and reasoning is under reciprocal investigation. This principle of independence stipulates that in evaluating a disagreeing subject's epistemic credentials, one may use only *dispute-*

independent reasons [1]. What is sought is an explanation for the disagreement that is independent of a first-person perspective, an explanation that is determinative from a third-person perspective. Inasmuch as no such first-person privilege manifests here, some form of skepticism is warranted. So according to proponents of the Equal Weight View, compromise is mandated.[1] Others, especially those favoring a uniqueness thesis such that there is a uniquely warranted rational belief given the body of evidence, conclude that when confronted by peer disagreement one must relinquish one's belief entirely. Whether we ought to compromise or suspend judgment entirely, all conciliationists agree that peer disagreement necessitates a substantial revision of belief.

Steadfasters, on the other hand, argue that we are warranted in relying on our own conclusions in cases of peer disagreement. Although it might seem prima facie reasonable to reduce one's credence in these situations – after all, why should you presume your belief is better than your peer's? – steadfasters have defended maintaining one's prior belief on a number of grounds. Some contend that conciliation fosters intolerable epistemic weakness. The Equal Weight View is 'objectionably self-abasing' and 'servile,' exhibiting 'spinelessness' and 'lack of self-trust' [2]. Conciliatory views have also been criticized as leading to skepticism and 'it would be bad to have to suspend judgment on just about any controversial question' [11]. Steadfasters also sometimes deny that peer disagreement is actually genuine or frequent. Perhaps one might be willing to grant an Equal Weight View in minor, narrowly constrained cases, such as when two peers disagree over what is an 18% tip for a lunch bill but, they contend, most of our controversial differences are embedded in a cluster of larger issues, often with regard to values about which we don't really judge our opponents to be our peers. Still other steadfasters submit that conciliatory views are self-refuting. Since epistemologists are in deep disagreement about whether to support conciliation or steadfastness, conciliationists should rescind their advocacy of their position or, at least, be willing to compromise in the direction of steadfastness.

But perhaps the central defense of the steadfast view allows that genuine peer disagreements do obtain, but insists one is still entitled to one's own view because the first-person perspective *does* break the symmetry of peer disagreement. You can rely on your own judgment more than on your peer's because you have greater intimacy with your own evidence and reasoning. And some steadfasters acknowledge that the egoist perspective is insufficient to destroy peer symmetry, but propose a doxastic value in holding to one's own opinion that is independent of rationality… a doxastic value that tips the scale in one's own favor in cases of peer disagreement.

Defenders of conciliation have, in turn, offered rebuttals to these steadfast challenges. They reject the notion that conciliation promotes a genuinely deleterious 'spinelessness,' inasmuch as there is nothing spineless in willing to alter one's level of credence when faced with serious contrary evidence. And rather than promote skepticism, conciliationist note that their view proceeds precisely because they recognize there are genuinely knowable truths which happen to be in question in a peer disagreement. Furthermore, the self-refuting objection can be parried, they argue, by distinguishing between second-order and first-order propositions in the manner many other meta-epistemic claims avoid self-refutation such as in defenses of induction and ethical relativism, and especially recursive epistemic or semantic propositions. (The outcome of a self-referential conciliation is a particularly complicated business: If the conciliationist adopts more of the steadfast view, that directs her to be more steadfast in her original judgment… i.e. conciliation! This renders the 'self-undermining' refutation 'self-undermining' in turn.) Conciliationists, therefore, see no convincing reason why a personal perspective should trump that of an opposing peer and, they also emphasize, this symmetry is especially salient when a third party must choose between the rival peers.

As one might imagine, this debate between conciliationists and steadfasters has invited a complex literature of fine distinctions and nuanced applications.[2] Nonetheless, with this admittedly broad outline of the divide, we can turn for a look at how the *Talmud* seems to treat peer disagreement.

3. Talmudic Disagreements and *'elu we'elu*

The *Talmud* is a repository of thousands of disputes, disagreements that often turn on the valuation of evidence based on original interpretation versus tradition, as well as disagreements about the correct applicable tradition itself.[3] Rarely, however, do we read of one Rabbi offering to relinquish or compromise his view *purely* because his rabbinic colleagues disagree with him.

This presumptive support for steadfastness does not appeal to the usual concerns with conciliation noted above. Genuine symmetry is recognized: a *Tann'a* is a qualified peer when arguing with another *Tann'a* as an *'Amor'a* is a qualified peer when arguing with another *'Amor'a*. Nor do we find attributions of 'spinelessness,' toward those abdicating their view. Worries that conciliation is self-refuting do not appear to be a concern either. Rather, a standard justification for steadfastness in Talmudic commentaries and in *halakhic* literature in general is the notion that when the appropriate conditions obtain, each of the disputants has the authority of divine approval: *'Elu we'elu divrey 'Elohim k̲ayim.* All arguments 'for the sake of heaven' are thought to attain 'divine' legitimacy and though one rival view must yield with regard to practice, generally neither side is called upon to desist from retaining its opinion. But, in fact, on closer examination, the precept of *'elu we'elu* does not endorse such steadfastness.

The phrase *'elu we'elu divrey 'Elohim kayim hen* actually appears only twice in the *Babylonian Talmud*, once with regard to a factual dispute and the other with regard to *halakhic* rulings.[4] We should notice, at the outset, however, that in both instances, the phrase is employed by a third party adjudicating arguments between peers – it is God (or His representative Divine voice) that renders a judgment about a dispute between his human epistemic inferiors. As we shall see, matters are more problematic when the principle is used to decide between an argument of peers, both of whom we recognize as our epistemic superiors.

The occurrence of *'elu we'elu* in the *Maseket Gittin* (*Babylonian Talmud, Gittin* 6b) is infrequently referred to as it concerns a disagreement about an obscure historical fact with no practical implications. Still less often noticed, rather than affirming the legitimacy of genuine disagreement, the phrase is used to deny that we are dealing with a genuine disagreement.

The immediate preceding discussion in that text concerns the establishment of authority of Rabbi Abiathar. Support for his standing derives from the following episode:

> Commenting on the text, 'And his concubine played the harlot against him,' (*2 Judg.* 19:2) R. Abiathar said that the Levite found a fly with her, and R. Jonathan said that he found a hair on her. R. Abiathar soon afterwards came across Elijah and said to him: 'What is the Holy One, blessed be He, doing?' and he answered, 'He is discussing the question of the concubine in Gibea.' 'What does He say?' Elijah replied: '[He says], My son Abiathar says so-and-so, and my son Jonathan says so-and-so,' R. Abiathar asked: 'Can it be that the Almighty is uncertain?' He replied: Both [views] are the word of the living God (*'elu we'elu divrey 'Elohim kayim hen*). He [the Levite] found a fly and excused it, he found a hair and did not excuse it. Reb Judah explained: He found a fly in his food and a hair in *loco concubitus*; the fly was disgusting, but the hair was dangerous. Some say, both {the fly and the hair} were in his food but the fly was not her fault, while the hair was.

When Elijah is asked how God could have any doubts about who is correct in these contested opinions, he replies that both views are consonant with the 'words of the Living God,' for they do not, in fact, contradict one another but refer, respectively, to two different instances, one concerning a fly, the other a hair. So, in this case at least, *'elu we'elu* not only does not support the legitimacy of both opposing views, but also reformulates the dispute so that there is no genuine disagreement. The implication is that a genuine disagreement would entail that at least one view was false and thus be unacceptable; this case does not present such a disagreement.

It is, however, the far more famous appearance of the term *'elu we'elu* in the *Babylonian Talmud, 'Eruvin* 13b that is regularly enlisted as supporting the view that both sides of a *halakhic* controversy are warranted in being steadfast about their respective opinions.

Rabbi Abba said in the name of Shmuel: For three years, the House of Hillel and the House of Shammai (*Beit Hillel* and *Beit Šammay*) were in dispute. One said, 'The *halaḵah* is like us,' and the other said, 'The *halaḵah* is like us.' A heavenly voice descended, and declared: 'These and these are the words of the living God,' (*'elu we'elu divrey 'Elohim ḵayim hen*) and the *halaḵah* is like the House of Hillel.' The question arose: Since the heavenly voice announced: 'Both these and those are the words of the Living God,' why is the *halaḵah* in accordance with the views of *Beit Hillel*? It is because the students of Hillel were gracious and humble. They taught the ideas of the students of Shammai as well as their own ideas; indeed, they went so far as to consider Shammai's opinions before considering their own opinions.

Here the principle of *'elu we'elu* does seem to presume that we are dealing with a genuine conflict yet both sides have equal validity with regard to warrant, and it is only for extra-legal reasons that the law abides with *Beit Hillel*. The positions of *Beit Hillel* are favored, we are told, because of their superior moral qualities: they were *noḵin* – gracious (or calm) and *'aluvin* – humble. We might think that the third quality mentioned, *Beit Hillel*'s intellectual virtue of open-mindedness toward opposing points of view encouraged a more balanced examination of the evidence and therefore a reason to think they were more likely than *Beit Šammay* to reach the truth.[5] If so, then peer symmetry is not sustained here, so this would not serve as evidence in support of steadfastness in genuine peer disagreements. However, there is no evidence that *Beit Hillel* considered their adversaries as less than their peers, albeit mistaken in their rulings. Indeed, the *Talmud* suggests elsewhere (*Babylonian Talmud, Yevamot* 14a) that, if anything, *Beit Šammay* was the *m'ḵadadidey tfey*, intellectually sharper than *Beit Hillel*. Nor should we deduce the converse, as some commentators recommend we do: we follow *Bet Hillel* because they were the more conciliatory (followers of peace as modeled by Aaron rather than Moses – see the *Babylonian Talmud, Sanhedrin* 6-7) and not steadfast as was *Beit Šammay*. Rather, the *Bat Qol*'s declaration of *'elu we'elu* does seem to straightforwardly assert a genuine disagreement between equal adversaries. Nonetheless, this dictum cannot be relied on as supporting steadfastness.

4. Three Interpretations of *'elu we'elu*

The central, immediate and obvious challenge to *'elu we'elu* is that it appears to violate the law of non-contradiction: *X* cannot simultaneously and in the same respect be both *Y* and not *Y*. How, then, can both sides of the

Talmudic disagreement have equal validity? One renders the cow *košer*, the other *treyf*, one side claims the vessel is pure, the other impure, one says the lighting of the *ḥanukah* menorah should begin with one candle and increase to eight, the other says we are to begin with eight candles and decrease to one. At least one view must be false.

Over the millennia, numerous responses have been proposed to address this challenge. We can profitably cluster these responses into three broad categories.

An analogy to these categories can be drawn to three perspectives on the role of a sports referee, a baseball umpire, say, calling balls and strikes.

(A) Umpire 1: 'I call them as they are.'
(B) Umpire 2: 'I call them as I see them.'
(C) Umpire 3: 'They aren't until I call them.'

4.1. Disagreement as Case-Dependent

This response to the non-contradiction challenge turns on a distinction between the reasons for ruling *P*, the *ratio decedendi*, and the ruling of *P* itself. The arguments posited for claiming ~*P* might be as compelling as those offered in support of *P*, but those arguments happen not to be conclusive in particular case *C*. They might be persuasive, however in some similar case *C*1. This is the perspective, for example, proposed by Rashi (commentary to the *Babylonian Talmud, Ketubot* 57a, s.v. *ka mašm'a lan*). Rashi acknowledges that when two decisors pose contradictory positions about the attribution of a doctrine to an individual authority, one of these disputants must be mistaken, but when the debate is over a matter of permissibility or prohibition, or a matter of civil law, neither reasoning need be wrong: '[I]t is appropriate to declare *'elu we'elu divrey 'Elohim ḵayim*. There are times when one reason is applicable, and times that the other reason is, because what is the appropriate reason can change with a change of circumstances, even if the change in circumstances is only slight.'[6]

This case-dependent approach grants that there is, indeed, one unique correct ruling, some single 'truth out there' with regard to each circumstance, although the reasoning that supports that truth might apply in one instance but not in another similar circumstance. As a consequence, it follows that we should allow the retention of dissenting opinion in the corpus of *halakhic* discourse. Dissenting opinions not only help clarify the correct opinion, but should be preserved for their own integrity, and as the *Mišnah* asserts, they might later be used as a precedent (*Mišnah, 'Eduyot* 1:4-5).

So as does umpire *A*, the decisor aims 'to call them as they are.' Therefore, when a third party asserts *'elu we'elu* about some peer disagreement, he is only claiming that the disputing parties are equally reasonable, but as there is only one way 'they are,' one of the disputants fails to make his case. With regard to the dispute between *Beit Hillel* and *Beit Šammay*, God knows who has the correct rulings and so declares the victorious party, but between the peers themselves there is no such knowledge and therefore no apparent reason to maintain steadfastness. The appeal to *'elu we'elu* does not suffice.

4.2. Disagreement as Tracking Multiple Truths

This approach evokes the perspective of legal pluralism and also has a distinguished and continuing pedigree in explanations of *'elu we'elu.* According to this view, the problem of contradiction is resolved by stipulating there are 'multiple truths' to which each side of a 'heavenly dispute' respectively and accurately corresponds. As a result, no contradictory propositions are averred – the claims are, therefore, compatible. It is reasonable, therefore, to maintain one's own view, as one's peer is not in genuine disagreement.

A reference to a discussion in the *K̲agigah* (*Babylonian Talmud, K̲agigah* 3b) is sometimes alluded to as an endorsement of this perspective:

> The masters of assemblies' refer to the disciples of the wise who sit in the assemblies and occupy themselves with Torah, some pronouncing unclean and others pronouncing clean, some prohibiting and others permitting, some declaring unfit what others declare fit. Should someone ask: How then shall I learn Torah? Therefore the text says: 'All of them are given from one Shepherd. One God gave them; one leader repeated them from the mouth of the Lord of all creation, blessed be He; for it is written: (*Exodus* 20:1) 'And God spoke all these words'.

In an influential comment, the well-known Talmudist, Ritva (Yom Tov ben Avraham Asevilli 1260s – 1320s) refers to the 'the French rabbis' who understand *'elu we'elu* as expressing this notion of multiple truths:

> When Moses went up to receive the Torah, they [the angels] showed him on every issue 49 views to forbid and 49 views to permit. When he asked God about this, he was told that these decisions will be handed to the sages of Israel of each generation and the ruling would be like them.

As this pluralistic view is often expressed: God showed Moses many possibilities within every matter and there is no single, original Truth.

Therefore, the decision procedure by which *halakhic* decisions are reached can non-defectively conclude with two incompatible rulings.[7]

The notion of *'elu we'elu* as indicating 'multiple truths' is an especially popular theme in *Qabbalah*, where a plethora of *midrašim* and Talmudic passages are alluded to in support of the pluralistic thesis. So, as does Umpire (*B*), the decisor calls them as he sees them. His judgment tracks a truth, the one he perceives. That is enough inasmuch as there is no single Truth which defeats other reasonable perspectives.[8]

This understanding of *halakhic* judgments has its epistemic parallel in alethic or, as it is sometimes called, semantic relativism. This relativist view is motivated by the observation that facts about the world appear in different ways to different people and nothing makes it true that they, in fact, are one way rather than another. More specifically: we should not construe *S*'s claim in the form '*P* justifies belief *Q*' as the claim *P justifies belief Q* but rather as asserting: According to the epistemic system *C* that I, *S* adopt, information *P* justifies belief *Q*.

Epistemic relativism admits of some serious criticism and unpacking the concept of multiple-truths is no easy task, but, thankfully, not a task that need detain us at present. We should recognize, however, that in this explication as well, *'elu we'elu* sidesteps the problem of non-contradiction, by reformulating disagreement so as to diffuse it: the two views are compatible. Consequently, each side is justified in retaining its viewpoint. But this will not serve as a justification for steadfastness when there is genuine disagreement.

4.3. Disagreement as Performative

This explication of *'elu we'elu* also enjoys a distinguished and continuing advocacy and has affinities to the legal pluralist tradition.

Halakhic judgments, in this view, are not propositional assertions that aim to correspond to outside facts or meet criteria of coherence to other legal rulings. They have no 'truth value' as such. That is, nothing is intrinsically *košer* or non-*košer*, pure or impure but that an appropriate legal ruling makes it so. As umpire *C* avows, 'they aren't until I call them.' The *halakhic* declaration is a kind of performative speech act – it does not discover facts but creates them: the judge pronounces you husband and wife and you are thereby married, you say 'I promise to buy you a new sweater,' and you are now under an obligation to do so.

A Talmudic *locus classicus* for this view is the well-known story of *Aḵnay*'s oven (*Babylonian Talmud, Bab'a Meẓy'a'* 59a-b). Here, a *Bat Qol* in favor of Rabbi Eliezer's opinion is rejected in favor of the view of the majority because '*Torah lo bašamyin he*,' Torah is not in heaven, i.e. law is decided here in earth, by majority as stipulated in the Bible.[9] Note that the rabbis here invoke scripture, the Word of God, to justify their rejection of the Word of God in His support of Rabbi Eliezer's minority pronouncement.

The challenge of non-contradiction is thereby parried: undecided *halakhic* claims lack truth-value and therefore cannot present genuine contradictory propositions. *Halakah* is procedural not propositional. *'Elu we'elu* therefore grants standing to both sides as they are only provisional judgments. Again, this does not establish the justification for steadfastness in cases of genuine peer disagreements (as certainly might occur in non-*halakhic* Talmudic disagreements).

5. Questions Remain

As we have seen, the standard interpretations of *'elu we'elu* avoid the charge of permitting contradiction by diffusing actual opposition: only the reasoning process has equal validity, not the specific application; both sides of the dispute advocate for truths, but aim for different, compatible truths; or *halakhic* judgments are propositions that are true or false, but have legitimacy only as acceptable legal process. That each of these approaches will support maintaining one's opinion – *'elu we'elu* – is not surprising since, on each account, we are not dealing with a genuine disagreement.

If *'elu we'elu* does not explain why Talmudic arguments seem to favor a steadfast view, what does? Why do we not see systemic support for a conciliatory process? The problem is even more pronounced when we consider how Talmudic rabbis (and later *halakhists*) choose between disagreeing superiors.

The philosophic literature about disagreement has been largely devoted to disagreements between epistemic peers, far less so to disagreements with one's superiors. Presumably, that is because even the most extreme steadfasters would agree that when one is confronted by an epistemic superior – noting the usual caveats with regard to bias, access to special information and other relevant distortions – conciliation, complete or partial is mandated. If I am sitting with an expert on, say, Akkadian logic – a field I have little to no knowledge of – it would be obnoxious for me to submit my own contrary ideas about the subject with any sort of confidence: I lack the requisite epistemic standing. I should reasonably assume that the expert arguing for a particular thesis *P* is well aware of my elementary arguments for ~*P* and has superior reasons for rejecting ~*P*. Matters are no different if I'm sitting with two authorities in this field who themselves differ about *P* – my evidence for ~*P* has clearly been defeated by the expert who asserts *P*. Nor should it matter whether those experts are sitting across me or live on the other side of the globe. Of course, there is a possibility that I might be lucky and have alighted on some hitherto obscure evidence in support of ~*P*. Yes, and I might also guess this week's lottery number. I'd be utterly irrational to count on either development. I don't have the epistemic warrant to assert a point of view with confidence when my epistemic superior disagrees with that point of view.[10]

'Amor'ayim, traditionally, do not argue with *Tann'ayim*, allowing that they are their *halakhic* superiors. (One common reason for this deference is that *Tann'ayim* were a closer link on the chain to original transmission and therefore their testimony is more likely to reflect that original transmission). But how then can the *'Amor'a* choose to adopt claim *P*, the position of *Tann'a Q* when another *Tann'a K* argues ~*P*? After all, by stipulation, the *'Amor'a* is the inferior of *K*, and should acknowledge that his own evidence for *P* is defeated by the likelihood that this evidence has been considered and rejected by his *halakhic* (epistemic) superior, *Tann'a K*. Now there might be extra-rational reasons for following in practice one *Tann'a* rather than another, reasons, say, of familial or pedagogical legacy, but there would be no grounds for this *'Amor'a* to assert with confidence that his own view has any more chance of being true than that of the opposing view. Through His *Bat Qol*, God can pronounce who is right in a *Tann'ay*itic peer dispute, for, after all, He is their epistemic superior. But how can their *'Amor'a*ic inferiors make this decision? Here one would suppose, conciliation would seem particularly apt.

To conclude: Why, indeed, is conciliation not recommended with regard to Talmudic peer disputes? On what grounds can inferiors choose between disagreeing superiors? *'Elu we'elu* doesn't provide the requisite answers. I'm not sure what does.

References

1. Christensen, D. Epistemic Modesty Defended, *The Epistemology of Disagreement New Essays*, 2013, pp. 76-97.
2. Elga, A. Reflection and Disagreement, *Nous*, 41 (3), 2007, pp. 478-502.
3. Enoch, D. Not Just a Truthometer: Taking Oneself Seriously (but Not Too Seriously) in Cases of Peer Disagreement, *Mind*, 119 (476), 2010, pp. 953-97.
4. Halberstam, J. *With All Due Epistemic Humility*, Presentation, Athens Institute for Education and Research, Annual International Conference on Philosophy, 2016. Athens, Greece.
5. Halbertal, M. *The History of Halakhah, Views from Within: Three Medieval Approaches to Tradition and Controversy*', http://www.law.harvard.edu/programs/ Gruss/halbert.html
6. Hidary, R. *Dispute for the Sake of Heaven: Legal Pluralism in the Talmud*, Providence, Brown Judaic Studies- 2010.
7. Kramer, D. *The Mind of the Talmud: An Intellectual History of the Babylonian Talmud*, Oxford, Oxford University Press, 1990.

8. Rosensweig, R. M. *Elu V'elu Divrei Elokim Hayyim*: Halakhic Pluralism and Theories of Controversies, *Tradition*, 26/3, 1992), pp. 4-23.
9. Sagi, A. Both are the Words of the Living God, *HUCA LXV*, 1994, pp. 105-136.
10. Sokol, M. (ed.) *Rabbinic Authority and Personal Autonomy*, Northvale, New Jersey: Rowman and Littlefield, 1992.
11. Sosa, E. The Epistemology of Disagreement, In A. Haddock, A. Millar, and D. Pritchard, *Social Epistemology*, Oxford: Oxford University Press, 2010, pp.278-297.
12. Zion, N. Elu V'Elu: Two Schools of Halakha Face off on Issues of Human Autonomy, Majority Rule and Divine Voice of Authority, Jerusalem, Shalom Hartman Institute, 2008.

Notes

1. The impetus toward compromise when dealing with peer disagreement is even more compelling when one is confronted by two competing 'truthometers,' non-human peers. For example, one consults his two watches, both of equal reputable, reliable status, but one says it's 10:10 and the other 10:20. On this view, it's most reasonable to go with 10:15.
2. The literature on this topic is, as noted, already vast. This is even so for the various subtopics of epistemic peer disagreement including religious disagreements, moral disagreements, and aesthetic disagreements.
3. A *Talmud* fault line of justification is sometimes suggested dividing those *Tann'ayim* who favor tradition as crucial support for one's position, a view ascribed to Shammai, Rabban Yokanan ben Zakai and later represented by Eliezer ben Hyrcanus, as opposed to *Tann'ayim* who leaned more toward creative interpretation, a view ascribed to Hillel and represented later by Reb Yehoshua (as in his confrontation with R' Eliezer). For a useful explication of this divide see [12].
4. The occurrence of the phrase *'elu we'elu* in the *Talmud Yerushalmi*, *Berakot* 1:4 refers to the *Bat Qol* announced with regard to the rivalry between *Beit Hillel* and *Beit Šammay* as it does in the *Bavli*.
5. The *Talmud Yerušalmi* (*Sukkah* 2:8 53 b) offers two reasons why *Beit Hillel*'s views were implemented. The first, that *Beit Hillel* considered *Beit Šammay*'s opinion before considering their own is rejected; neither House considered the other's first. Rather, the law was decided according to *Beit Hillel* because they were willing to change their opinion when convinced by the arguments of *Beit Šammay*. For the *Yerušalmi*, in keeping with its general negative attitude toward debate and its preference for a clear decision, this willingness to change one' s view is significant for it is more likely to lead to a correct ruling. Richard Hidary provides a thorough review of the history of, and the Talmudic attitude toward, the division between *Beit Hillel* and *Beit Šammay* [6].
6. Rambam grants rabbinic legislation authority as long as it doesn't claim to be 'from Sinai'; the Sinaic message is immutable. Rambam never mentions *'elu we'elu, as* he believes the primary purpose of one's study should be to reach *halakhic*

conclusions, not analyze arguments. Thus, he specifically omits all rejected opinions from his *Peruš ha-Mišna'yot* and *Mišneh Torah.*

7. A number of scholars have argued that a pluralistic attitude underlies the general bent of the *Bavli* authors, that 'truth is interminable and that alternative views can encompass different aspects of the whole truth' [7].

8. Avi Sagi (1994) similarly distinguishes between the 'discovery model' akin to the first approach to *'elu w'elu* and a 'creative model' represented in this second approach. Moshe Halbertal [5] proposes a division like this, describing one approach as 'the retrieval view' the other as the 'constitutive view.'

9. The laws of *zaken mamr'e,* the rebellious elder, described in the Bible (*Deuteronomy* 17:8-13) allocate full judicial power to the high court. The Talmudic rabbis have interpreted these laws to license their suppression of dissenting rabbis (*Mišnah*, *Sanhedrin* 11b). On the other hand, permission in some cases is granted to learned persons who believe the court has erred (*Babylonian Talmud*, *Horayot*). Rendering these two different attitudes cohesive has been a focus of much Talmudic commentary.

10. If this point seems to suggest that we are rarely epistemically entitled to hold to most of our opinions, given that we lack expertise about most things, this is the conclusion I do in fact embrace and argue for in [4].

Developments in the Syntax and Logic of the Talmudic Hermeneutic *Kelal Uferaṭ Ukelal*

Michael Chernick

Professor Emeritus of Rabbinic Literature,
Hebrew Union College-Jewish Institute of Religion in New York,
the United States of America
michaelchernick41@gmail.com

1. Introduction

In a book and article on the development of the hermeneutic called *kelal uferaṭ ukelal* I have shown that that hermeneutic used in *Tann'ay*itic *halakhic midrašim* and later in the *Talmud* changed in form from era to era [2], [3]. The changes take place in two main areas: in the syntactical format of the hermeneutic and in its logic.

Kelal uferaṭ ukelal uses phrases in a biblical verse that include an inclusive clause at the beginning of the phrase, a series of specifics that represent subsets of the inclusive clause in the phrase's middle clause, followed by a second inclusive clause at the phrase's end. An example of this kind of structure within a verse appears in *Exodus* 22:8,[1]

על כל דבר פשע על שור על חמור על שה על שלמה על כל אבדה אשר יאמר כי הוא זה

The first clause על כל דבר פשע, "Regarding all charges of misappropriation," includes all claims against an unsalaried bailee who avers that an item or items left with him for safekeeping were stolen. The middle clause provides information about the specific items that are typically left with a bailee which might have been stolen due to his negligence. These include oxen, donkeys, sheep, and clothing. The verse concludes with another inclusive clause, "about any loss regarding which (the bailor) will say, 'This (object) is it (i.e., one stolen by the bailee)."

Those who interpret *Exodus* 22:8 applying the *kelal uferaṭ ukelal* hermeneutic in order to take judicial action in a case where a bailor accuses a bailee of negligence or theft hold that the specifics in the verse do not represent the full range of items the law covers. Rather, items with the shared characteristic of all the specifics mentioned between the two inclusive clauses are those for which an unsalaried bailee who is negligent or a thief must pay. These include any things that are movable property not subject to the possibility of lien, not just animals.[2] Had clothing not been one of the specifics, the law would have been that the bailor could make a claim against the bailee only for lost or stolen animals.

One might rightly ask, "What logic explains why the bailee who stole or lost the item entrusted to him must pay for anything that has the shared features of all the specifics sandwiched between the inclusive clauses?" For example, why would a bailee who stole a chair have to repay double its worth if he was guilty? A chair is neither a sheep nor a garment. What extended the range of these specific items to "any movable property not subject to lien"? According to the rabbinic interpreters it seems that the superfluity of the second inclusive clause extends the range of items for which the bailor may sue the bailee. In a sense, the second inclusive clause seems to say, "Include even more than the mentioned specifics."

Proof of this logic is the case where the initial inclusive clause is followed only by specifics but lacks a second inclusive clause. In Hebrew, such a syntactical arrangement in a biblical verse is called *kelal uferaṭ*. *Leviticus* 1:2 provides an example of this form of hermeneutic and its result. The verse states,[3]

דבר אל בני ישראל
ואמרת אלהם אדם כי יקריב מכם קרבן לה' מן הבהמה מן הבקר ומן הצאן תקריבו
קרבנכם

The inclusive section of this verse is מן הבהמה, "from among class of ungulates." The specifics clause states, "from the herd and from the flock." According to the rabbinic interpreters this syntax produces the result אין בכלל אלא מה שבפרט, "the inclusive clause comprises only the specifics." Therefore, the animals fit for sacrificial purposes are not all cattle, but only bulls, cows, sheep, and goats. Despite the opening clause's inclusiveness, the specifics define the inclusive clause. This is because the second inclusive clause is not present to suggest that more than the stated specifics are implied by the verse. Had a second inclusive been present perhaps the shared features of the animals described would have allowed deer or ibex to be used as sacrificial animals since they too chew their cud and have split hooves and share other characteristics. That second inclusive clause, however, is not available in

Leviticus 1:2 and animals other than the ones listed are therefore excluded from serving as sacrifices.

2. The Second Inclusive Clause Must Be of Greater Scope Than the First

The form of the *kelal uferaṭ ukelal* that appears in collections of interpretations of the Torah called *Tann'ay*itic *halakhic midrašim* requires that the second inclusive clause be wider in scope than the first one. Each case of *kelal uferaṭ ukelal* in these collections includes the formula, כלל בכלל הראשון אמרת or כלל ככלל הראשון אמרת, "perhaps you are stating a (second) inclusive clause already included in the first inclusive clause," or "perhaps you are stating a (second) inclusive clause like the first inclusive clause." The implication is that if the second inclusive clause only repeats the first, it may not qualify as a second *kelal*. In that case, we may have only a *kelal uferaṭ* interpretation. If so, then the exact items listed in the specifics clause would define what is included in the inclusive clause.

A good example of this phenomenon appears in the following interpretation of *Exodus* 20:14, one of the so-called Ten Commandments. The verse states[4]

לא תחמד בית רעך לא תחמד אשת רעך ועבדו ואמתו ושורו וחמרו וכל אשר לרעך

The first part of the verse is an inclusive clause, "You shall not covet your fellow's house." The clause is inclusive because the term "house" in the Hebrew Bible implies the people, animals, and objects that are part of family's home [1, p. 111]. Indeed, the specifics clause lists some of these: one's neighbor's wife, his male or female slave, his ox and his ass. Had there been no second clause or had that clause been no more inclusive than the first clause, rabbinic interpretation would have prohibited coveting just what was specified in the specifics list: one's neighbor's wife, male or female slaves, or his ox or ass. Here, however, the second clause is indeed greater in scope than the first inclusive clause. It includes beyond the things that make up a man's domicile, "everything that belongs to your neighbor." It is hard to imagine what these might be beyond what is needed for his home, so the rabbinic interpreter provides a definition. As is the case with all *kelal uferaṭ ukelal* interpretations, this definition is based on the shared characteristics of all the listed specifics. These shared characteristics include things that one can sell or buy, movable property, and items that can only enter one's possession willingly.[5] The interpreter derived these characteristics from the commonalities between male and female slaves and oxen and asses all of which can be bought and sold. They also are all examples of movable property. A wife adds the characteristic of something that can enter one's possession willingly since according to Jewish law a woman cannot be forced into marriage against her will.[6] Hence, "you shall not covet" is defined by the rabbis as any attempt to pressure an individual to sell or give anything with the properties listed above against his will [4, p. 449].

3. Early Talmudic *kelal uferaṭ ukelal* Interpretations: The *kelal uferaṭ ukelal* with Equivalent Inclusive Clauses

While the classical *Tann'ayi*tic *halakhic midrašim* contain only examples of *kelal uferaṭ ukelal* in which the second inclusive clause is wider in scope than the first, the *Talmudim* preserve several examples of *kelal uferaṭ ukelal* with equivalent inclusive clauses. The Talmudic *kelal uferaṭ ukelal* may be the product of a school different from the one that required a difference in scope between the inclusive clauses. It is, however, more likely that these *kelal uferaṭ ukelal* interpretations emanate from a single school. That school accepted *kelal uferaṭ ukelal* with two equivalent inclusive clauses when the verses it interpreted allowed no other choice. In that case syntax was more determinative for applying the *kelal uferaṭ ukelal* hermeneutic than the fact that the inclusive clauses were the same in scope. The argument that two equivalent inclusive clauses meant there was actually only one doubled *kelal* could be easily countered by appealing to the theology that underlies rabbinic *midraš*, namely, that every word of the Torah is significant because it is the perfect word of God [5, p. 8], [6, p. 120]. Therefore, it might be argued that if God, the *Torah*'s writer, had meant a verse with a *kelal uferaṭ ukelal* sequence to be regarded as a *kelal uferaṭ* interpretation in which the specifics completely define the inclusive clause, He would have formulated the verse's syntax accordingly.

Let us now examine the two examples of *kelal uferaṭ ukelal* with equivalent inclusive clauses that appear in both the *Babylonian* and *Palestinian Talmudim.*

3.1. The kelal uferaṭ ukelal Interpretation of Leviticus 14:9

A *kelal uferaṭ ukelal* interpretation that appears in both the *Palestinian* and *Babylonian Talmudim* interprets this phrase in *Leviticus* 14:9:[7]

> והיה ביום השביעי יגלח את כל שערו את ראשו ואת זקנו ואת גבת עיניו ואת כל שערו יגלח

The two equivalent inclusive clauses, "all his hair," parenthesize the specifics: the hair of his head, beard, and eyebrows. The following is the formulation of the *kelal uferaṭ ukelal* in the *Babylonian Talmud*:

והיה ביום השביעי יגלח את כל שערו - כלל, את ראשו ואת זקנו ואת גבות עיניו - פרט, ואת כל שערו יגלח - חזר וכלל, כלל ופרט וכלל אי אתה דן אלא כעין הפרט, מה פרט מפורש מקום כינוס שער ונראה, אף כל מקום כינוס שער ונראה (סוטה טז ע"א)

"And it shall be that on the seventh day he shall shave all his hair" – this is an inclusive clause (*kelal*); "his head, his beard, and his eyebrows" – this is a specifics clause" (*peraṭ*); "and all his hair he shall shave" – the *Torah* repeats an inclusive clause (*kelal*). When we have a *kelal uferaṭ ukelal* arrangement, we apply the law to the anything with the shared characteristics of the specifics. Just as the specifics indicate a place where hair is thick and visible, so all places on the body where hair is thick and visible (must be shaved) (*Soṭah* 16a).

The *Babylonian Talmud* explains that this definition would excuse the leper undergoing his purification rites from shaving his underarms, which are generally not visible, and the majority of his body since arm and leg hair is scattered and not thick. The recovered leper would, however, have to shave pubic hair because it is thick, and when the recovered leper is nude, it is visible. The *Talmudim* note, however, that this is one of the places where R. Ishmael held that the actual law overrides the hermeneutic interpretation. Therefore, he requires that the leper's entire body must be shaved in order for him to complete his purification rites.[8]

3.2. The kelal uferaṭ ukelal Interpretation of Deuteronomy 14:26

The *kelal uferaṭ ukelal* interpretation that emerges from *Deuteronomy* 14:26 also contains two equivalent inclusive clauses. It deals with the law pertaining to money used to redeem what is called the second tithe. The first tithe of produce was given to the Levites, but the second tithe belonged to the owner of the produce. In terms of its use, the farmer had two choices. He could bring the actual produce to Jerusalem and consume it there. If, however, it was too abundant for the owner to transport to Jerusalem, he could redeem it with money and spend the redemption money in Jerusalem. The *kelal uferaṭ ukelal* defines what kind of goods the farmer could purchase with second tithe redemption money. The section of the verse that forms the basis for the *kelal uferaṭ ukelal* interpretation reads as follows: [9]

ונתתה הכסף בכל אשר תאוה נפשך בבקר ובצאן וביין ובשכר ובכל אשר תשאלך נפשך

The *kelal uferaṭ ukelal* interpretation makes it clear what constitutes the inclusive clauses and specifics clause: [10]

ונתתה הכסף בכל אשר תאוה נפשך – כלל, בבקר ובצאן וביין ובשכר – פרט,
ובכל אשר תשאלך נפשך – חזר וכלל. כלל ופרט וכלל – אי אתה דן אלא כעין
הפרט; מה הפרט מפורש – פרי מפרי וגידולי קרקע, אף כל - פרי מפרי וגידולי
קרקע (תלמוד בבלי מסכת עירובין דף כז עמוד ב)

> "You shall apply the money to anything you desire" – this is an inclusive clause (*kelal*); "cattle, sheep, wine, or other intoxicant" – this is a specifics clause (*peraṭ*); "or anything you may desire" – the *Torah* repeats the inclusive clause (*kelal*). When we have a *kelal uferaṭ ukelal,* one decides the law according to the shared characteristics of the specifics clause: Just as the specifics' shared characteristics are that they are fruits that come from fruits and are the produce of the earth, so too one may purchase foodstuffs that are fruits from fruits and the produce of the earth (*Babylonian Talmud*, *'Eruvin* 27b).[11]

It is obvious that there is no significant difference between the biblical clause "and apply the money to anything you want" and "or on anything you may desire." There is some doubt whether this interpretation is a product of the *Tann'ay*itic period. This is due to how the *Talmud* introduces the interpretation as part of the *Talmud*'s discussion. The *Talmud* usually introduces extra-*mišnah*ic *Tann'ay*itic sources (*barayt'ot*) with the terms תניא ("it was taught") or תנו רבנן ("our Rabbis taught"). In the case of our *kelal uferaṭ ukelal,* תניא introduces the interpretation indicating that our source is *Tann'ay*itic. However, Rashi, the eleventh century commentator par excellence, comments on our source thus: "Our version is this: 'as it is taught (דתניא): "and spend the money on anything you want."'" This implies that there were other versions of this source's introduction; and, in fact, this is the case.

Our *kelal uferaṭ kelal* appears in four different places in the *Talmud*: in *'Eruvin* 27b, *Nazir* 35b, and *Bab'a Qam'a* 54b, and 66a. In several manuscripts and incunabula the *kelal uferaṭ ukelal* under discussion either has no introduction or is introduced with דכתיב ("as it is written"). This latter is only an introduction to the biblical verse which serves as the basis for the *kelal uferaṭ ukelal.* As such, it says nothing about when this interpretation was created. Nevertheless, the overwhelming evidence of the Babylonian Talmudic versions is that this *kelal uferaṭ ukelal* is a *Tann'ay*itic source. The *Jerusalem Talmud*, which cites this *kelal uferaṭ ukelal* twice, also suggests that this is the case.[12]

4. The Talmudic Departure From the Syntactical Requirements and Logic of the Classical *kelal uferaṭ ukelal*: The Implied "Any" or "Anything"

As we move into the third *'Amor'a*ic generation and beyond, the requirements for a verse to serve as the basis for a *kelal uferaṭ ukelal* interpretation fall away and with them the logic of *kelal uferaṭ ukelal* changes radically. What follows are examples of these changes all of which are departures from the classical *Tann'ay*itic formats of *kelal uferaṭ ukelal.*

4.1. Palestinian Talmud, Sanhedrin 7:9

Mišnah Sanhedrin 7:9 distinguishes between idolatrous actions that are capital crimes and those which are prohibited but do not carry capital punishment. The Palestinian *'Amor'ayim*, R. Bun Bar Kahana (the 3rd – 4th generation) asked R. Hila (Palestinian *'Amor'a*, the 3rd generation) why the *Mišnah* exempts the actions it does from capital punishment. The source of his question is a *kelal uferaṭ ukelal* interpretation he formulates.

...רבי בון בר כהנא בעא קומי רבי הילא לא תעשון כן כלל זובח לאלהים יחרם פרט בלתי ליי' לבדו חזר וכלל כלל ופרט וכלל והכל בכלל וריבה את המגפף והמנשק (תלמוד ירושלמי מסכת סנהדרין ז, ט [כה ע"ב])

> R. Bun bar Kahana asked in the presence of R. Hila: "Do not do thus"[13] – this is an inclusive clause (*kelal*); "one who slaughters sacrifices to gods shall be destroyed"[14] – this is a specifics clause (*peraṭ*); "save only unto the Lord" – this is the repetition of an inclusive clause (*kelal*). This produces a *kelal uferaṭ ukelal,* and everything is included in the *kelal.* This encompasses kissing and embracing (an idol, which should be treated like sacrificing to other gods)."

It is clear that this version of *kelal uferaṭ ukelal* is unlike any interpretation using this hermeneutic that we have seen until now. Indeed, one wonders what makes the various components of this interpretation inclusive or specifics clauses. How is "Do not do thus" an inclusive clause? How is "one who slaughters sacrifices to gods shall be destroyed" a specifics clause? And how does "save only unto the Lord" repeat an inclusive clause?

While R. Hila responds to this question, his response is not germane to our issue. What is significant is that in the third-fourth *'Amor'aic* generation in Palestine this form of *kelal uferaṭ ukelal* presented a significant enough challenge to the *Mišnah* to elicit a response from R. Hila. Given the uniqueness of this form of *kelal uferaṭ ukelal* compared to anything we have seen heretofore it is important to analyze this interpretation and its understanding of its verse's syntax, its definition of inclusive and specific clauses, and its logic.

First, this *kelal uferaṭ ukelal* derives its inclusive clauses from phrases in different books of the Torah, *Exodus* and *Deuteronomy*. This in itself is not unknown since the *Meḵilt'a d'R. Yišma'el* and *Sifre Numbers*, which are clearly older, do the same in one case.[15] This is because the subject matter of the verses in the interpretation is the same, namely, redemption of firstborn sons. There are however no examples of *Tann'ay*itic *kelal uferaṭ ukelal* interpretations lacking a clear subject in the form of a noun or using the Hebrew word כל ("all") with a noun. "You shall not do thus" or even the fuller version of the verse, "you shall not do thus to the Lord your God" do not provide an inclusive noun. How then is this an inclusive clause? The answer is: the interpreter, R. Bun bar Kahana, understood this biblical clause to mean "you shall not do for idols anything done for the worship of God." This could be understood as any aspect of the sacrificial service, which understood this way would serve as a *kelal.* The phrase from the *Exodus*, "one who slaughters a sacrifice to other gods shall be destroyed" refers to only one aspect of the sacrificial service, namely, slaughter. As such, it can be viewed as a specifics clause. Finally, "save only unto the Lord" as understood by R. Bun bar Kahana means "all those forms of worship reserved for the Lord." Thus, he produces a second *kelal.* The shared characteristic of sacrificial slaughter is that it honors God and is forbidden on pain of death if directed to other gods. The conclusion that R. Bun bar Kahana reaches is anything done to honor a god should receive the death penalty, which would include such activities as kissing or embracing an idol. This conclusion contravenes the *Mišnah* which prohibits these activities, but not on pain of death.

It is clear that this *'Amor'a*ic *kelal uferaṭ ukelal* leaves much information to be filled in by the reader. It seems that R. Bun bar Kahana used the various biblical phrases in his *kelal uferaṭ ukelal* as signals pointing to subjects not specifically mentioned in his interpretation. In this case, the verb "do" refers to all activities that are directly part of the sacrificial service like slaughtering the sacrificial animal, receiving its blood, and the like. "Unto the Lord alone" refers to every action related to the worship of God such as prostrating oneself. This, too, is an innovation we have not seen before.

In sum, unlike earlier examples of *kelal uferaṭ ukelal* interpretations this Palestinian Talmudic *kelal uferaṭ ukelal* is anything but straightforward. The role of the verses' syntax in this interpretation, what constitutes an inclusive or specifics clause in it, and its logic are hard, indeed almost impossible, to define without a considerable overlay of inference applied to what is present in the *Palestinian Talmud*'s text. As we shall see, this may be the first case of its kind, but this form of *kelal uferaṭ ukelal* is a commonplace in the *Babylonian Talmud.*

5. Post-*Tann'ayitic* *Babylonian Talmud kelal uferaṭ ukelal* Interpretations: "The Second *kelal* is Not Similar to the First *kelal*"

There are two examples in the *Talmud* where the validity of a *kelal uferaṭ ukelal* interpretation is challenged by sages of the latest generations of the Babylonian *'Amor'ayim*. Both examples appear in tractate *Zebaḥim*, one on page 4b and the other on 8b. In the first case R. Aḥa of Difti, a sage of the final generation of Babylonian *'Amor'ayim*, challenges the validity of a *kelal uferaṭ ukelal* and receives a defense of it from Ravina, another seventh generation Babylonian *'Amor'a*. On 8b R. Ya'aqov of Nehar Peqod, a sixth generation Babylonian *'Amor'a*, strongly objects to the legitimacy of an anonymous *kelal uferaṭ ukelal.* The fact that there are named *'Amor'ayim* relating to these interpretations helps us date them.

Zebaḥim 4b

In *Zebaḥim* 4b there is a search for a source for the rule that the priest who receives sacrificial blood in a sanctified vessel must intend to receive it with the sacrifice's donor in mind. After rejecting several suggestions, the discussants propose that the application of the *kelal uferaṭ ukelal* hermeneutic to *Numbers* 6:17 might produce part of the needed prooftext.[16] R. Aḥa of Difti, a seventh generation *'Amor'a* (c. 455 – 485 C.E.), objects to this because the first inclusive clause is not similar to the last one. Ravina, a major figure of the sixth *'Amor'a*ic generation and a teacher of R. Aḥa, responds to this challenge and allows the formation of a *kelal uferaṭ ukelal.*

As we will see, this late form of *kelal uferaṭ ukelal* is similar in many ways to the one in the *Palestinian Talmud*, *Sanhedrin* 7:9. The Talmudic discussion in which this *kelal uferaṭ ukelal* appears is extremely complex. Therefore, I will limit my discussion of it only to what is pertinent to our issue, namely, the interpretation's form and logic.

> רבינא אמר: לעולם דנין, ולה' - חזר וכלל. אמר ליה רב אחא מדיפתי לרבינא: והא לא דמי כללא קמא לכללא בתרא, כללא קמא מרבה עשיות ותו לא, כללא בתרא כל לה', ואפילו שפיכת שיריים והקטרת אימורין! הא תנא דבי רבי ישמעאל בכללי ופרטי דריש כי האי גוונא, כלל ופרט וכלל אי אתה דן אלא כעין הפרט, מה הפרט מפורש עבודה ובעינן לשמן, אף כל עבודה ובעינן לשמן.

> Ravina said (accepting a *kelal uferaṭ* that other sages considered illegitimate):[17] We accept "he shall offer" as an inclusive clause; "a slaughtered sacrifice" as a specifics clause, then the phrase 'to the Lord" as another inclusive clause.
> R. Aḥa of Difti said to Ravina: But the first inclusive clause is not similar to the second one! The first clause includes only the rites directly related to sacrificing the offering. The last clause includes even those activities carried out on the sacrificed animals after the

> basic sacrificial rites have been performed. For example, disposing of excess sacrificial blood and burning those organs not required to be placed on the altar.
> (Ravina replied): Behold! The representative of the interpretive method of the School of R. Ishmael use this form of *kelal uferaṭ ukelal,* and when we have a *kelal uferaṭ ukelal* the law is determined according to the shared characteristics of the specifics clause. (In our case this means) just as the shared characteristics of the specifics refer to all aspects of the sacrificial rites performed with proper intention (for the sacrifice to be valid), so too (for the sacrifice to be in fulfillment of the donor's vow) all the sacrificial rite must be with proper intention (i.e., with the donor in mind)...

An analysis of the form of this *kelal uferaṭ ukelal* shows that Ravina, its creator, did not use the entire phrase ואת האיל יעשה זבח שלמים לה', "and he shall offer the ram as a *šelamim*-sacrifice to the Lord", in *Numbers* 6:17. Rather he used just these words from it: יעשה, זבח, לה', "he shall offer," "a slaughtered sacrifice," "to the Lord." As was the case in the *Palestinian Talmud*'s *kelal uferaṭ ukelal* it is difficult to see how any of these words would qualify as an inclusive clause, though "a slaughtered sacrifice" refers to a specific item. Therefore we are required to fill in the blank spaces as follows: יעשה, "he shall offer," we should understand to mean that he should perform all the עשיות. This term based on the same Hebrew root as יעשה in rabbinic parlance means all the basic rites the priest performs on a sacrifice: slaughter, receiving the sacrificial blood, bringing it to the altar, and sprinkling the blood on the altar. Hence, it is inclusive of all those rites.

The second inclusive clause is לה', "to the Lord." Initially this does not appear to be an inclusive clause. As Ravina understood it, however, its meaning is "all those activities done to a sacrifice offered to the Lord." These would include the basic sacrificial rites and further actions carried out on the offering. Some examples of these actions are disposing of sacrificial blood in excess of what was needed for sprinkling and burning those parts of the sacrificial animal not needed for the altar. Understood thus, לה' is an inclusive clause and together the terms יעשה, זבח, לה' form a *kelal uferaṭ ukelal.*

Like the *kelal uferaṭ ukelal* in the *Palestinian Talmud*, a verb without a noun as a subject can function as a *kelal*. There the Hebrew word לה', "to the Lord" was also understood as including all forms of rites used to worship God, though not strictly sacrificial ones. Nevertheless, it is possible to see how *Palestinian Talmud*'s use of this word could be a precedent for Ravina. Regarding the specifics clause in *Zebaḥim* 4b, it is a noun, as is the case in almost every *kelal uferaṭ ukelal* we have seen. Once one accepts the thinking guiding the formation of the inclusive clauses, the logic of this *kelal uferaṭ ukelal* is the same as any other interpretation of this kind. The one issue related to the logic of this *kelal uferaṭ ukelal* is R. Aḥa of Difti's concern is that the first and last inclusive clauses are not similar. The meaning of "similar" here is not related to the use of the same word or phrase as the first and last inclusive clause of a *kelal uferaṭ ukelal.* Rather "similarity" means quantitative similarity. That is, in this example of *kelal uferaṭ ukelal*, the first inclusive clause includes less than the final one. For R. Aḥa of Difti this raises the question of whether the two inclusive clauses are speaking about the same subject. If they are not, then how can an interpreter form a *kelal uferaṭ ukelal* out of two totally unrelated though inclusive phrases? Ravina's response to this query is that there is authoritative precedent for doing this emerging from the School of R. Ishmael's application of the *kelal uferaṭ ukelal* hermeneutic to the biblical text.

Zebaḥim 8b

In *Zebaḥim* 8b there is a *kelal uferaṭ ukelal* interpretation. Like the one in *Zebaḥim* 4b it appears in the midst of a complicated Talmudic passage. Also like the *kelal uferaṭ ukelal* in 4b it appears to be a product of the sixth *'Amor'a*ic generation because R. Ya'aqov of Nehar Peqod forcefully attacks it.

The issue at hand is what happens when one slaughters the animal he initially designated as a Passover offering with the intention for that animal to be another kind of offering. A *barayt'a* distinguishes between improper intention regarding the Passover offering when this occurs in its proper time on *Nisan* 14 toward the evening, in which case the sacrifice is invalid. If, however, one slaughters an animal with the intention of it being a Passover offering at any other time of the year, it is acceptable, but only as a *šelamim*-sacrifice. The passage in *Zebaḥim* 8b investigates why this is so.

As part of its investigation an anonymous interpreter proposes that sacrifices of one sort slaughtered with intention for another sort automatically become *šelamim*-sacrifices because of the following *kelal uferaṭ* interpretation based on *Leviticus* 3:6,[18]

ואם מן הצאן קרבנו לזבח שלמים לה' זכר או נקבה תמים יקריבנו

The interpreter uses the phrase לזבח שלמים, "as a *šelamim*-sacrifice," as follows:

לזבח - כלל, שלמים - פרט, כלל ופרט אין בכלל אלא מה שבפרט, שלמים אין, מידי אחרינא לא! (זבחים ח ע"ב)

"as a slaughtered sacrifice" – this is an inclusive clause (*kelal*); "*šelamim*" – this is a specification (*peraṭ*). When we have an inclusive clause followed by specification, the specification defines the content of the inclusive clause. (Therefore, a sacrifice designated as one kind of offering slaughtered with intention for another kind) becomes a *šelamim*-sacrifice and nothing else.

The anonymous interpreter continues and shows that if one uses *kelal uferaṭ ukelal,* an offering that the donor or priest slaughters with incorrect intention may become an offering other than a *šelamim*-sacrifice. The following is the interpreter's *kelal uferaṭ ukelal* with a rejoinder by R. Ya'qov of Nehar Peqod. The Talmud rejects the rejoinder and the *kelal uferaṭ ukelal* and its result stand, but only temporarily. I will include in the citation of the passage only what is germane to the *kelal uferaṭ ukelal.*

לה' - הדר וכלל. מתקיף לה ר' יעקב מנהר פקוד: הא לא דמי כללא בתרא לכללא קמא, כללא קמא מרבי זבחים ותו לא, כללא בתרא לה' - כל דלה', ואפי' לעופות ואפי' למנחות! הא תנא דבי רבי ישמעאל: בכללי ופרטי דריש כי האי גוונא, כלל ופרט וכלל אי אתה דן אלא כעין הפרט, מה הפרט מפורש שהוא שלא לשמו וכשר, אף כל שהוא שלא לשמו וכשר.

"To the Lord" is, however, another inclusive clause. R. Ya'aqov of Nehar Peqod vigorously attacked this *kelal uferaṭ ukelal:* "But the last inclusive clause is not similar to the first inclusive clause! The first inclusive clause ("as a sacrifice") includes only sacrifices that are slaughtered. 'To the Lord' includes all that is (offered) to the Lord, even offerings of birds and meal-offerings."[19]
(Anonymous response): But the representative of the interpretive method of the School of R. Ishmael interprets using this form of *kelal uferaṭ ukelal.* Hence, we have a *kelal uferaṭ ukelal.* Therefore, the shared characteristics of the specifics clause determine the law. Just as the specifics clause's shared characteristics imply an offering brought with the wrong intention which is nevertheless valid, so too all offerings brought with the wrong intention are nevertheless valid.

This passage is almost a replay of *Zebaḥim* 4b. True, the verses that the interpreters use come from different books of the *Torah* – the *Numbers* in the case of *Zebaḥim* 4b, and the *Leviticus* here in *Zebaḥim* 8b – but that is due to the difference in subject matter with which the passages deal. In *Zebaḥim* 4b the topic is failure to have the donor of the sacrifice in mind when the priest slaughters his offering. In *Zebaḥim* 8b the issue is what happens when one designates an offering for one sort of sacrifice but at the moment of slaughter intends it to be another variety of sacrifice.

The words that form the components of the inclusive clauses at first glance would not seem to be inclusive at all. In *Leviticus* 3:6 the words זבח שלמים, "a *šelamim*-sacrifice" refer to specific kind of sacrifice. Only when the interpreter sunders the connection between "sacrifice" (זבח) and *šelamim* can he form a *kelal* out of "sacrifice." Even then, the word "sacrifice" basically refers to something specific. Therefore, we are again called upon to read "sacrifice" as "any form of sacrifice," which then means all slaughtered sacrifices since the Hebrew root ז-ב-ח means "to slaughter." We are also expected to understand לה' as "everything that is offered to the Lord," which would include offerings that were not slaughtered. This is what calls forth R. Ya'aqov of Nehar Peqod's attack: the first and last inclusive clauses are not talking about the same thing if we understand them in this way. As was the case in *Zebaḥim* 4b the logic behind R. Ya'aqov of Nehar Peqod's objection is if the two inclusive clauses speak of entirely different things, how can they connect with each other to form a *kelal uferaṭ ukelal*? The response here is the same one that appears in the *Zebaḥim* 4b passage: Those who followed the interpretive method of the School of R. Ishmael accepted this form of *kelal uferaṭ ukelal* as perfectly legitimate.

In sum, this *kelal uferaṭ ukelal* brings us close to full circle with the early *Tann'ay*itic form of *kelal uferaṭ ukelal.* Those required that the second inclusive clause had to be different from the first for the interpretation to be acceptable. In the case of the *Tann'ay*itic *kelal uferaṭ ukelal,* however, the difference between the two inclusive clauses was usually quantitative. In Talmudic *kelal uferaṭ ukelal* interpretations the second inclusive clause is different from the first in subject matter, and the subject matter of the second inclusive clause is wider in scope in terms of the issues it includes than that of the first inclusive clause.

6. The Victory of the Post-*Tann'ay*itic Form of *kelal uferaṭ ukelal* in the "Anonymous Talmud"

Interspersed within most Talmudic passages is an anonymous stratum which creates the give and take that typifies Talmudic discussions. The academic consensus holds this stratum to be at least late or post-*'Amor'a*ic.[20] We have seen that we may date some of these anonymous passages to the sixth and seventh *'Amor'a*ic generations since *'Amor'ayim* like R. Aḥa of Difti and R. Ya'aqov of Nehar Peqod respond to them. This brings us close to the end of the *'Amor'a*ic period which lasted one more generation. The seventh generation's teachings appear with the names of their authors included, though there are more queries, challenges, and comments, usually formulated in Aramaic, than straightforward legal opinions or teachings. On one hand, the "anonymous Talmud" may be the product of the sixth and seventh *'Amor'a*ic generations since its contents consist overwhelmingly of the elements I described above. On the other hand, once the process of connecting *'Amor'a*ic traditions one to another by means of anonymous comments started, it likely continued beyond the last *'Amor'a*ic generations into what we might call the post-*'Amor'a*ic period.

One element in the anonymous Talmudic give and take is the use of *kelal uferaṭ ukelal* interpretations. As in the sixth and seventh generation examples we have analyzed, these usually function as support for some proposition in a Talmudic discussion. That support is usually undermined as the discussion proceeds. Our concern is less with the fate of a *kelal uferaṭ ukelal* interpretation in a Talmudic passage than with the form and logic of the late *kelal uferaṭ ukelal* interpretations. As we shall see they follow the syntactic pattern with which we are already familiar.

In completely anonymous Talmudic passages in which *kelal uferaṭ ukelal* interpretations appear there is no longer any concern expressed about the first and second inclusive clauses being dissimilar. In that sense, the post-*Tann'ay*itic Talmudic *kelal uferaṭ ukelal* is the victor in the battle over what constitutes a legitimate application of this form of the hermeneutic to a biblical source. That being said, let us turn now to some examples of the unchallenged post-*Tanna'y*itic Talmudic *kelal uferaṭ ukelal.*

Qiddušin 21b

Torah law demands that a Hebrew slave who refuses manumission after seven years of slavery must have his ear pierced with an awl.[21] In a Talmudic passage discussing this law R. Yosi, a 4th generation *Tann'a*, and Rabbi Judah Hanasi (from here forward, just "Rabbi"), compiler of the *Mišnah*, both deny that what one uses to pierce the slave's ear can only be an awl. R. Yosi argues that any sharp pointed object may be used. Rabbi requires that any pointed instrument made of metal like an awl may be used. The "anonymous Talmud" presents a *kelal uferaṭ ukelal* interpretation to explain how Rabbi arrived at his view. The interpretation is not preceded by any introduction that would indicate that it is a *Tann'ay*itic source.

> ולקחת - כלל, מרצע - פרט, באזנו ובדלת - חזר וכלל, כלל ופרט וכלל אי אתה דן אלא כעין הפרט, מה הפרט מפורש של מתכת, אף כל של מתכת (תלמוד בבלי, מסכת קידושין כא ע"ב).

> "And you shall take" – this is a general clause (*kelal*); "an awl" – this is a particulars clause; "in his ear and in the door" – this is another general clause (*kelal*). When we have a *kelal uferaṭ ukelal* arrangement the application of the law is based on the shared characteristics of the items in the specifics clause. Just as the specifics clause indicates a thing made of metal, so anything (used to pierce the Hebrew slave's ear) must be made of metal.

Like the *Palestinian Talmud*'s *kelal uferaṭ ukelal,* the differences in formulation between this Babylonian Talmudic *kelal uferaṭ ukelal* and the *Tann'ay*itic *kelal uferaṭ ukelal* are quite noticeable. The so-called *kelal* consists only of a verb, ולקחת, "and you shall take." It seems that the creator of this interpretation understood this to mean "and you shall take anything." As such, this would be an inclusive clause. The specifics clause follows a more normal pattern insofar as it is a noun, מרצע, "awl." According to the interpreter it would define the implied "anything" in the first inclusive clause.

The last phrase that the interpreter used to create a second inclusive clause is באזנו ובדלת, "in his ear and into the door," which describes the place on the Hebrew slave's body that the piercing takes place and the locale at which the piercing is done. In its present form, it is impossible to understand how this phrase could generate an inclusive clause. This, however, is not the only formulation of this *kelal.* In ms. *Vatican* 111 and an early Spanish imprint (c. 1480) the *kelal* is based on the phrase in *Deuteronomy* 15:17, ונתתה באזנו ובדלת, "and you shall put it through his ear into the door." This formulation would allow the verb ונתתה, "you shall put" to mean "you shall put anything" in the same way as the interpreter understood the verb ולקחת, "you shall take," to mean "you shall take anything."[22] It should be noted here that the interpreter did not need to apply the *kelal uferaṭ ukelal* hermeneutic to arrive at his conclusion. Had he applied *kelal uferaṭ* the *halakhic* outcome would have been the same since that hermeneutic's result is that the specific clause fully defines what the inclusive clause encompasses.[23] Hence it is clear that the form of his *kelal uferaṭ ukelal* is influenced by some other factor than hermeneutical necessity. That factor is the *midraš* the anonymous interpreter supplies to explain R. Yosi's position using what I will translate as the "extension-limitation-extension" hermeneutic which produces a more inclusive result than *kelal uferaṭ ukelal.*[24]

As is the case with most *Tann'ay*itic examples of *kelal uferaṭ ukelal* we analyzed, the interpreter in this case uses phrases from a single verse dealing with one *Torah* law. This, however, is where the comparison ends. First, we must accept that the implied word "anything" forms the first and second inclusive clause. In the *Tann'ay*itic interpretations the inclusive clauses are stated rather than implied. If the implied word "anything" forms the two inclusive clauses, then they are equivalent as is the case with some *Tann'ay*itic *kelal uferaṭ ukelal* interpretations. One cannot, however, be certain that the interpreter consciously sought to make the two inclusive clauses equivalent since the words that would form them are not actually present in the interpretation. Whatever the case, it is obvious that the form of the post-*Tann'ay*itic Talmudic *kelal uferaṭ ukelal* changed radically from that of its *Tann'ay*itic predecessors. Let us examine a few more examples of this kind of *kelal uferaṭ ukelal* in order to draw some conclusions about their construction and logic. We will also hypothesize about why their authors created them.

Sukkah 50b

We find a similar phenomenon to the one we just analyzed in *Sukkah* 50b. In that passage, Rabbi and R. Yosi ben Yehudah, both fifth generation *Tann'ayim* (c. 180 – 210 C.E.), debate whether a sanctified object used in the Temple may be made of wood. Rabbi says "no," and R. Yosi ben Yehudah says "yes." Neither of them give a reason for their opinions. In an attempt to explain the basis for their views, the "anonymous Talmud" constructs a *kelal uferaṭ ukelal* to explain Rabbi's view and another form of *halakhic midraš* to explain R. Yosi ben Yehudah's opinion. For our purposes an analysis of the *kelal uferaṭ ukelal* interpretation suffices.

The anonymous commentator fashioned his *kelal uferaṭ ukelal* from the following part of *Exodus* 25:31: מנרת זהב טהור מקשה תיעשה, "The menorah of pure gold: the menorah shall be made of hammered work...."[25] The following is the form his *kelal uferaṭ ukelal* takes:

> רבי דריש כללי ופרטי: ועשית מנורת - כלל, זהב טהור - פרט, מקשה תעשה המנורה חזר וכלל. כלל ופרט וכלל אי אתה דן אלא כעין הפרט, מה הפרט מפורש - של מתכת, אף כל של מתכת.

> (According to the opinion of the anonymous Talmud) Rabbi interpreted using the *kelal uferaṭ ukelal* hermeneutic: "And you shall make a menorah of" – this is an inclusive clause (*kelal*); "pure gold" – this is a specifics clause (*peraṭ*); "the menorah shall be made of hammered work" – this is a second inclusive clause. When we have a *kelal uferaṭ ukelal* arrangement the application of the law is based on the shared characteristics of the items in the specifics clause.

Here, too, the *kelal* is mystifying. The word used, מנורת, literally "a menorah of" in the construct state but without a connection to any noun must be understood as "a menorah of any material" to function as a *kelal*. This is basically the use of the implied "anything" we have seen in the *kelal uferaṭ ukelal* in *Qiddušin* 21b. "Pure gold" insofar as it is a specific material works similarly to the specifics clause in the classical *kelal uferaṭ ukelal* interpretations.

But what makes "the menorah shall be made of hammered work" a second *kelal?* It seems that the interpreter reuses the word "*menorah*" as a second inclusive clause because he already established that the first use of "*menorah*" suggested inclusiveness. If so, the verse containing the second clause would be rendered, "the *menorah* (made of any material) shall be made of hammered work." Since "pure gold" was the item making up the specifics clause in this interpretation, the law is that the Temple's menorah could be made of anything that had something in common with gold, namely, it was a form of metal. The possibility that the interpreter was consciously creating a *kelal uferaṭ ukelal* with equivalent inclusive clauses is greater here than in the case of *Qiddušin* 21. It is, however, just as likely that the syntax of the phrase from *Exodus* 25:31 forced him to us the word "*menorah*" as his two inclusive clauses.

Here, too, the interpreter could have arrived at the same *halakhic* conclusion he derived by using the *kelal uferaṭ* hermeneutic. As was the case in *Qiddušin* 21b the format of an "extension-limitation-extension" interpretation supporting R. Yosi ben Yehudah's view forced the interpreter to counter with an interpretation that included three elements. Hence, the use of *kelal uferaṭ ukelal.*

Bab'a Meẓi'a' 57b

The following example of a *kelal uferaṭ ukelal* interpretation in *Bab'a Meẓi'a'* 57b provides no new information about the use of elements as inclusive clauses that actually are not. Its logic, or better lack of it, in the *halakhic* conclusion the interpreter draws from the interpretation is a key to why the post-*Tann'ay*itic Babylonian Talmudic *kelal uferaṭ ukelal* developed as it did. Namely, the *kelal uferaṭ ukelal* no longer derives *halakhah* from a biblical verse but rather supports *halaḵah* that already exists. The post-*Tann'ay*itic Baylonian Talmudic *kelal uferaṭ ukelal* we will analyze uses as its source *Exodus* 22:9: [26]

> כי יתן איש אל רעהו חמור או שור או שה וכל בהמה לשמר ומת או נשבר או
> נשבה אין ראה

The following is the text of the Talmudic discussion in which the *kelal uferaṭ ukelal* in question appears:

> נושא שכר אינו משלם (וכו'). מנהני מילי? - דתנו רבנן: כי יתן איש אל רעהו
> כלל, - חמור או שור או שה - פרט, וכל בהמה לשמור - חזר וכלל. כלל ופרט
> וכלל אי אתה דן אלא כעין הפרט; מה הפרט מפורש - דבר המטלטל וגופו ממון,
> אף כל דבר המטלטל וגופו ממון. יצאו קרקעות שאינן מטלטלין, יצאו עבדים
> שהוקשו לקרקעות, יצאו שטרות שאף על פי שמטלטלין אין גופן ממון. הקדשות,
> אמר קרא רעהו - רעהו ולא של הקדש. (בבא מציעא נז ע"ב)

> *Mišnah*: One who is a salaried bailee need not pay (in the case of theft or loss of the deposit left with him for safekeeping) if the deposit consists of slaves, or promissory notes, or land, or sanctified items:
> *Talmudic comment:* Whence do we know this? As it is taught by our Rabbis (in a *barayt'a*): "If a man deliver" – this is an inclusive clause (*kelal*); "an ass, or an ox, or a sheep" – this is a specifics clause (*peraṭ*); "or any beast to keep" – this is a second inclusive clause (*kelal*). When we have a *kelal uferaṭ ukelal* arrangement the

> application of the law is based on the shared characteristics of the items in the specifics clause…

Just as the specifics' shared characteristics are that they are movable objects with monetary worth, so too (the salaried bailee only pays for items) that are movable objects with monetary worth. This excludes slaves who are analogized to land[27] and promissory notes (which are movable but have no intrinsic monetary value). Sanctified items are excluded because the Torah says "he (i.e., the bailee who stole what was deposited with him must pay twice its value) to his fellow" (*Exodus* 22:8) – to his fellow, but not to the realm of the sacred (which is God's).

This *kelal uferaṭ ukelal* supposedly functions as the prooftext for the *halakhah* that exempts a salaried bailee, who is normally responsible to pay for the loss or theft of the deposit left with him, from having to remunerate the bailor if he stolen the property is land, slaves, promissory notes, or sanctified items. This interpretation is presented as a product of the *Tann'ayim* since it has the marker תנו רבנן, "our Rabbis taught," which indicates the source is a *barayt'a.* However, the format of this *kelal uferaṭ ukelal* does not match the format of any *Tann'ay*itic *kelal uferaṭ ukelal* interpretation we have seen. I would reject the view that this is just a different form of *Tann'ay*itic *kelal uferaṭ ukelal* despite the fact that all the major manuscripts and incunabula presently at our disposal mark this *kelal uferaṭ ukelal* interpretation as a *barayt'a.*

What clinches this position for me is the *halakhic* result this *kelal uferaṭ ukelal* produces. Recall that the result of a *kelal uferaṭ ukelal* interpretation is that the shared characteristics of the specifics defines the situations to which the Torah's law applies. In the case of this *kelal uferaṭ ukelal* the specifics clause is חמור או שור או שה, "an ass, or ox, or sheep." One would therefore have assumed that the shared characteristics of the specifics would be "they are all animals." In that case, the salaried bailee would not have to pay for the theft or loss of an animal. According to the *Talmud,* however, the specific clause's shared characteristics are "they are movable and have monetary worth." While at a certain level this is true, these are not the primary characteristics of the items listed in the specifics clause of the *kelal uferaṭ ukelal.* Therefore, the activity the interpreter engages in is not hermeneutical in the sense that a hermeneutic's application is what generates a *Torah* law. Rather, in this case the existent *halakah* drives the interpretation and the hermeneutic called *kelal uferaṭ ukelal* is, in a sense, a ploy to make the interpretation seem to be the source of the law.[28]

We are left with question: If this *kelal uferaṭ ukelal* is not a true *Tann'ay*itic *kelal uferaṭ ukelal,* why is it introduced as one in every early manuscript and imprint we possess?

I would suggest that the *kelal uferaṭ ukelal* interpretations in this Talmudic passage are "recyclings" of another form of hermeneutic using a series of inclusive and specifics clauses. For example, the first *kelal uferaṭ ukelal* that appears in *Bab'a Meẓi'a'* 57b is parallel to a *kelal uferaṭ ukelal* in the *Mek̲ilt'a*, but the result it generates is completely different. This is the Talmudic form of the interpretation:

> על כל דבר פשע - כלל. על שור על חמור על שה על שלמה - פרט, על כל אבדה אשר יאמר - חזר וכלל, כלל ופרט וכלל אי אתה דן אלא כעין הפרט; מה הפרט מפורש - דבר המטלטל וגופו ממון - אף כל דבר המטלטל וגופו ממון.

> "Regarding every manner of negligence" – this is an inclusive clause (*kelal*); "regarding an ox or ass or sheep or garment" – this is a specifics clause (*peraṭ*); "regarding every sort of loss about which one says" – this is another inclusive clause (*kelal*). When we have a *kelal uferaṭ ukelal,* the law is decided in accordance with the shared characteristics of the items in the specifics clause. Just as the specifics have in common that they are all movable property with intrinsic monetary value, so the law covers only those things that are movable property with intrinsic monetary worth.

Compare this with its parallel in the *Mek̲ilt'a*:[29]

> על כל דבר פשע. כלל, על שור ועל חמור על שה ועל שלמה, פרט, או כלל ופרט, אין בכלל אלא מה שבפרט, וכשהוא אומר על כל אבדה אשר יאמר, חזר וכלל, או כלל ככלל הראשון, אמרת לאו, אלא כלל ופרט וכלל, אי אתה דן אלא כעין הפרט, מה הפרט מפורש בנכסים מטלטלין שאין להם אחריות אף אין לי אלא נכסים מטלטלין שאין להם אחריות.

> "Regarding every manner of negligence" – this is an inclusive clause (*kelal*); "regarding an ox or ass or sheep or garment" – this is a specifics clause (*peraṭ*); when we have an inclusive clause followed by a specifics clause the law follows exactly what is in the specifics clause. When however, the Torah says, "regarding every sort of loss about which one says" – this is another inclusive clause (*kelal*). Or is the last inclusive clause's content already included in the first one? You should say "No." Rather, we have a *kelal uferaṭ ukelal.* When we have a *kelal uferaṭ ukelal,* the law is decided in accordance with the shared characteristics of the items in the specifics clause. Just as the specifics have in common that they are all items that are movable and not subject to lien, so the law applies to any item that is movable and not subject to being liened.

It seems clear that the creator of the *Talmud*'s *kelal uferaṭ ukelal* reformulated an original *Tann'ay*itic *kelal uferaṭ ukelal* from the *Mek̲ilt'a*. He did so in order for the new "*barayt'a*" to function as proof that an unpaid bailee need not take an oath to the bailor when land, or slaves, or promissory notes have gone missing. Because the anonymous *Talmud* made use of original *Tann'ayitic barayt'a* material he introduced the reformulated source with an introduction to a *barayt'a.*[30]

The same applies to the *kelal uferaṭ ukelal* that is the center of our interest. Despite having all the characteristics of a post-*Tann'ayitic* Talmudic *kelal uferaṭ ukelal,* the *Talmud* introduces this interpretation as a *barayt'a.* This is because it reconstructs a true *barayt'a* that appears in the *Barayt'a* of R. Ishmael. That *Barayt'a* contains examples for each of the thirteen hermeneutics it lists, one of which is *peraṭ ukelal,* which is applied to a verse whose syntax presents an inclusive clause that follows a specifics clause. *Exodus* 22:9 is such a verse. Consequently, the *midrašic* interpreter explains what conclusion one can reach by applying this hermeneutic:

(ח) מפרט וכלל כיצד כי יתן איש אל רעהו חמור או שור או שה פרט וכל בהמה לשמור כלל פרט וכלל נעשה כלל מוסף על הפרט (ספרא ברייתא דרבי ישמעאל פרשה א)

> How does one interpret using the *peraṭ ukelal* hermeneutic? "If a man gives his fellow an ass, or an ox, or a sheep" (*Exodus* 22:9) – this is a specifics clause (*peraṭ*); "or any animal to guard" (ibid.) – this is an inclusive clause (*kelal*). If we have a verse in which an inclusive clause follows a specifics clause, the inclusive clause adds to the specifics.

In this case what the inclusive clause adds to the specifics clause are all kinds of animals besides asses, oxen, or sheep.[31]

The creator of our *kelal uferaṭ ukelal* in *Bab'a Meẓi'a'* 57b appears to have been aware of *Sifra*'s *peraṭ ukelal* or an approximation of it and used it as the foundation for his *kelal uferaṭ ukelal* interpretation. It is due to his use of *peraṭ ukelal* as a building block in his *kelal uferaṭ uelal* that it fails if we apply the actual rules governing of *kelal uferaṭ ukelal* to it. As noted above, his interpretation would not determine that the law applies to movable property with monetary value rather than to animals. Nevertheless, "rebuilding" a *kelal uferaṭ ukelal* out of a true *Tann'ayitic peraṭ ukelal* allows the Talmud to introduce the new interpretation with תנו רבנן, "our Rabbis taught," which signifies that the cited source is a *barayt'a.*

7. Conclusions

In the *Tann'ayitic* period there are two forms of *kelal uferaṭ ukelal,* one that requires the second inclusive clause to be wider in scope than the first. The logic of this form of *kelal uferaṭ ukelal* appears to be that the greater scope of the second clause prevents the inclusive clauses from being construed as being the same. If that were so, the result would require that the interpreter apply the *kelal uferaṭ* hermeneutic which would produce a different *halakhic* outcome than the *kelal uferaṭ kelal* hermeneutic. Interpretations using the *kelal uferaṭ* hermeneutic result in the application of the law only to the specifics listed after the inclusive clause.

A second form of *Tann'ay*itic *kelal uferaṭ ukelal* contains two equivalent inclusive clauses. The logic of this sort of *kelal uferaṭ ukelal* is that if the two inclusive clauses in the interpretation are the same, then one can be sure that the two clauses are addressing a single subject. When there is a difference between the first and second clause one might imagine that the two clauses are not related, which of course would prevent the formation of a *kelal uferaṭ ukelal* interpretation altogether. This form of *kelal uferaṭ ukelal* appears only twice in the *Talmudim*, but not in the mainstream *Tann'ay*itic *halakhic midrašim.* Those who created these two *Tann'ay*itic Talmudic *kelal uferaṭ ukelal* interpretations may represent a different interpretive school from that represented in the *Tann'ay*itic *halakhic midrašim.* It is possible, however, that there was only one interpretive school that made use of *kelal uferaṭ ukelal.* That school, when confronted by a verse whose syntax provided a basis for using *kelal uferaṭ ukelal* but whose content featured two equivalent inclusive clauses, chose to give weight to syntax and to defend that decision by finding a logical basis for accepting the equivalent inclusive clauses as legitimate. Given the rabbinic notion that not one word or sequence of words in the Torah is the result of haphazard writing since God is the Torah's author, this was a logical choice. That is, if a verse's syntax contained an inclusive clause followed by a specifics clause followed by an inclusive clause, then it was obvious that this verse was meant to be interpreted using *kelal uferaṭ ukelal.* If the verse contained two inclusive clauses, then God meant those inclusive clauses to be equally reasonable for use in a *kelal uferaṭ ukelal* as inclusive clauses that differed in scope.

A new form of *kelal uferaṭ ukelal* emerged in the *'Amor'a*ic period. The first instance of this new form appears in the Palestinian Talmud as a creation of third-fourth generation Palestinian *'Amor'ayim.* The creator of this form of *kelal uferaṭ ukelal* made use of verbs as inclusive clauses. Obviously, a verb only implies action or a state of being, but by its nature it does not imply inclusion of specific items. In order for verbs to function as inclusive clauses the reader must imagine that "any" or "anything" is part of the verb. Thus, a reader is expected to understand the Hebrew phrase that means "you shall not do" as an inclusive clause by adding the implied word "anything," rendering the verb's meaning "you shall not do anything." Further, the verb may imply some area of *halakah* that the Sages have attached to certain verbs. Thus, "do" in the framework of the rites of animal sacrifice includes four actions: slaughter, receiving the sacrifice's blood, bringing the blood to the altar, and sprinkling it on it. In the Palestinian *kelal uferaṭ ukelal* of this kind the specifics clause still contains only nouns. The outcome of these *kelal uferaṭ ukelal* interpretations is the same as that of all the others we have seen: the shared characteristics of the specifics clause determine the cases to which the law applies. In this singular Palestinian *'Amor'a*ic *kelal uferaṭ ukelal* the inclusive clauses are different from one another, but it is hard to tell whether that is a conscious act on the interpreter's part since the actual inclusive term is implied but not actually articulated.

The post-*Tann'ay*itic Babylonian Talmudic *kelal uferaṭ ukelal* appears to have its origins in the Palestinian *'Amor'a*ic form of *kelal uferaṭ ukelal.* The first instance of this form of *kelal uferaṭ ukelal* we can date makes its appearance in the sixth and seventh Babylonian *'Amor'a*ic generations (c. 371 – 460). Here, too, verbs function as inclusive clauses. Again, we are forced to add "any" or "anything" in order to make the verbs have an inclusive sense. The verbs forming the inclusive clauses are generally not equivalent. As in the Palestinian *'Amor'a*ic *kelal uferaṭ ukelal* the specifics clause always contains nouns, which from the point of view of logic makes sense: A noun indicates a specific item; a verb does not.

We find that named sixth and seventh generation Babylonian *'Amor'ayim* object to the application of the *kelal uferaṭ ukelal* hermeneutic when they see some disparity between the first and last inclusive clauses. The disparity is never related to the similar words the interpreter uses in his *kelal uferaṭ ukelal.* Rather, the objection is to the differing subject matter of the two inclusive clauses. For example, if one inclusive clause deals with a biblical prohibition carrying at most the punishment of stripes, and the other one deals with a prohibition punished by the more serious punishment of excision, an *'Amor'a* is likely to object that "the first (or second) inclusive clause is not the same as the last (or first)." The logic seems to be that if the two inclusive clauses are not discussing the same subject then they cannot join with each other to form the necessary elements for a *kelal uferaṭ ukelal* interpretation. The response to this is that the representatives of the School of R. Ishmael created interpretations of this sort. This appeal to classical *Tann'ay*itic authority was always sufficient to thwart the objection wherever it arose in the *Talmud.*

At the end of the development of *kelal uferaṭ ukelal* the use of verbs as inclusive clauses becomes a non-issue. The objection that two inclusive clauses do not deal with the same subject also disappears. In one instance of a post-*Tann'ay*itic Babylonian Talmudic *kelal uferaṭ ukelal* the shared characteristics of the specifics clause should include only animals. Yet the interpreter uses them to prove that the law applies only to cases that involve movable property with monetary value. This outcome runs completely counter to the rules of *kelal uferaṭ ukelal.* Therefore, it appears that the creators of this kind of *kelal uferaṭ ukelal* used them to connect existent rabbinic law to the Torah in order to give those laws heightened authority. In essence they used this hermeneutic to read an *halaḵah* into the Torah's text. This is the opposite of how the *Tann'ayim* applied the *kelal uferaṭ ukelal* hermeneutic to the Torah. Their use of this interpretive tool helped them to extract *halaḵah* from the text.

Finally, we found that sometimes a creator of a late *'Amor'a*ic or post-*'Amor'a*ic *kelal uferaṭ ukelal* uses part of a *Tann'ay*itic *barayt'a* for use in his interpretation. When this happens, the resultant *kelal uferaṭ ukelal* is edited to serve the needs of its new context. Since part of the *kelal uferaṭ ukelal* contains *barayt'a* material the Talmud introduces it with the typical introductory terms appropriate to a *barayt'a*.

References

1. Botterweck, G. J., and H. Ringgren (eds.). *Theological Dictionary of the Old Testament*, trans. by J. T. Willis, (Grand Rapids: William B. Eerdemans Publishing Company, 1975, revised edition 1977), vol. 2, s.v. בית.

2. Chernick, M. *The Development of Kelal u-Ferat u-Kelal Hermeneutics*, *Tarbiz* (Hebrew), v. LII, (Jerusalem: Magnes Press, 1982).

3. Chernick, M. *לחקר מידות כלל ופר וכלל וריבוי* (Eng., *Hermeneutical Studies*), Lod: Haberman Institute, 1984.

4. *Bar Ilan Digitalized Responsa Project, version 24+, Enzyklopedia Talmudic section*, s.v. לא תחמוד (Jerusalem and Tel Aviv: Bar Ilan University and R. Yitzhak Herzog Institute, 2015).

5. Harris, J. M. *How Do We Know This?: Midraš and the Fragmentation of Modern Judaism*, Albany: SUNY Press, 1995).

6. Stahlberg, L. C. *Sustaining Fictions*, New York: T & T Clark Library of Biblical Studies, 2008.

Notes

1. "Regarding all charges of misappropriation – pertaining to an ox, an ass, a sheep, a garment, or any other loss, whereof one party alleges, 'This is it…'" (*Exodus* 22:8). The penalty for a bailee's misappropriation of the bailor's property is payment of double the worth of the stolen item.
2. According to Jewish law only real estate is subject to lien.
3. Speak to the Israelite people, and say to them: When any of you presents an offering of cattle to the Lord, he shall choose his offering from the herd or from the flock (*Leviticus* 1:2 TNK).
4. You shall not covet your neighbor's house: you shall not covet your neighbor's wife, or his male or female slave, or his ox or his ass, or anything that is your neighbor's (*Exodus* 20:14 TNK).
5.

מכילתא דרבי ישמעאל יתרו - מסכתא דבחדש פרשה ח
מה הפרט מפורש בדבר שהוא קונה ומקנה, אף כלל בדבר שהוא קונה ומקנה; אי מה הפרט מפורש בנכסים המטלטלין שאין להם אחריות, אף אין לי אלא נכסים המטלטלין שאין להם אחריות, וכשהוא אומר במשנה תורה שדהו, על כרחך מה הפרט מפורש בדבר שהוא קונה ומקנה, אף אין לי אלא בדבר שהוא קונה ומקנה; אי מה הפרט מפורש בדבר שאינו בא ברשותך אלא ברצון בעלים, אף אין לי אלא דבר שאי אפשר לבא ברשותך אלא ברצון בעלים.

6. *Babylonian Talmud*, *Qiddushin* 2b; *Šulḥan 'Aruk̲*, *'Even ha 'Ezer* 42:1.
7. "And it shall be that on the seventh day (the leper) shall shave **all his hair** – his head, his beard, and his eyebrows – **all of his hair** shall he shave."
8. The *Palestinian Talmud* has the following parallel to the *Babylonian Talmud* passage:

תלמוד ירושלמי קידושין א, ב (נט ע"ד)
תני רבי ישמעאל והיה ביום השביעי יגלח את כל שערו כלל את ראשו ואת זקנו ואת גבות עיניו פרט וכשהוא אומר ואת כל שערו יגלח חזר וכלל כלל ופרט וכלל אין אתה דן אלא כעין הפרט לומ' לך מה הפרט מפורש שהוא מקו' כינוס שיער ובנראה אף אין לי אלא מקום כינוס שיער ובנראה והלכה אמר' יגלחנו כדלעת

"And it shall be that on the seventh day he shall shave all his hair" – this is an inclusive clause; "his head, his beard, and his eyebrows" – this is a specifics clause; "and when it says, "and all his hair he shall shave" – the Torah repeats an inclusive clause. This is a *kelal uferaṭ ukelal*, and we apply it by using the shared characteristics of the specifics. Which is to say: Just as the specifics are all areas with an abundance of hair that is visible, so (the recovered leper) must shave wherever hair is abundant and visible. But the law is that he must be shaved smooth as a pumpkin (i.e., totally) (*Palestinian Talmud*, *Qiddušin* 1:2 [59d]).
9. **"You shall apply the money to anything you desire** – cattle, sheep, wine, or other intoxicant – **or to anything you desire…."**
10. This *kelal uferaṭ ukelal* appears twice more in the *Babylonian Talmud* in *Nazir* 35b; *Bab'a Qam'a* 54b; and ibid. 63a. A parallel appears in the *Palestinian Talmud*, *Ma'aser Šeni* 1:3 (53a) and *'Eruvin* 3:1 (20c). See below, note 18 for the *Palestinian Talmud*'s version of this *kelal uferaṭ ukelal*.
11. Rashi, the eleventh century master commentator, defines "fruits that come from fruits" as not only grown animals but calves or lambs as well. Similarly, one's purchases are not restricted just to wine but one may also purchase grapes that come from their seeds. "Things that grow from the earth" he defines as produce that has its sustenance from the earth.
12. The *Palestinian Talmud*, *Ma'aser Šeni* 1:3 (52d-53a) introduces our *kelal uferaṭ ukelal* with ר' ישמעאל דרש ("R. Ishmael interpreted") suggesting that the interpretation was an actual quote of R. Ishmael's words. R. Ishmael is a third generation *Tann'ay*itic sage. In the *Palestinian Talmud*, *'Eruvin* 3:1 (20c) the interpretation appears preceded by תני ר' ישמעאל ("R Ishmael taught"). תני in the *Palestinian Talmud* often indicates a *Tann'ay*itic source, especially when it is attached to the name of a *Tann'ay*itic sage. The formulation of the *kelal uferaṭ ukelal* in the *Palestinian Talmud* is:

ונתת הכסף בכל אשר תאוה נפשך כלל בבקר ובצאן ביין ובשכר פרט ובכל אשר תאוה נפשך הרי כלל אחר כלל ופרט וכלל אי אתה דן אלא כעין הפרט לומר לך מה הפרט מפורש דבר שהוא וולד וולדות הארץ אף אין לי אלא דבר שהוא וולד וולדות הארץ.

This *kelal uferaṭ uekelal* is parallel to the one in the *Babylonian Talmud* and its meaning is essentially the same.

13. "Do not do thus to the Lord your God" (*Deuteronomy* 12:4). The reference is to the destruction of places of idolatry. Israel is warned not to do the same to the places where God is worshipped.

14. "One who sacrifices unto other gods, save only unto the Lord, shall be destroyed" (*Exodus* 22:19).

15. See *Mekilt'a d'R. Išma'el, Pisḥa'* 18, ed. Horovitz-Rabin, p. 72 and *Sifre Numbers. Qoraḥ* 118, ed. Horovitz, p.139 . The *kelal uferaṭ ukelal* uses *Exodus* 13:13 and *Numbers* 18:16.

16. *Numbers* 6:17: "He shall offer the ram as a *šelamim*-sacrifice to the Lord, together with the basket of unleavened cakes; the priest shall also offer the meal offerings and the libations". This is a description of one of the offerings that a nazirite must bring when he completes the period of his vow. A nazirite is someone who takes a vow that prohibits him from cutting his hair, drinking or eating any grape products, or becoming ritually impure by contact with the dead. See *Numbers* 6 for a full description of the laws concerning the nazirite. A *šelamim*-sacrifice is one that has part of it placed on the altar and the rest given as food to the donor and priests.

17. That *kelal uferaṭ* stated יעשה – כלל, זבח – פרט, "he shall offer" – this is an inclusive clause; "a slaughtered sacrifice" – this is a specifics clause." Ravina adds another inclusive clause to form a *kelal uferaṭ ukelal.*

18. "And if his *šelamim*-sacrifice to the Lord is from the flock, whether a male or a female, he shall offer one without blemish."

19. The word used as the first inclusive clause is זבח, that is, a slaughtered sacrifice. Offerings of birds, namely pigeons or doves, do not require slaughter. Rather, their heads are pinched off by hand. Meal-offerings by their nature are not subject to slaughter.

20. R. Sherira ben Hanina, head of the major Babylonian in Pumbeditha (906 – 1006 C.E.), speaks of post-*'Amor'a*ic contributors to the Talmud called *Sabor'ayim.* In his famous Epistle he also enumerates passages that he identifies as theirs. All these passages appear without attribution. Some medieval commentators also identified various Talmudic passages as *Sabor'a*ic, which also turn out to be anonymous. In the twentieth century academic Talmudists like Abraham Weiss, David Weiss Halivni, Yaakove Sussman, Shamma Friedman, and Y. E. Efrati posited that the post-*'Amor'a*ic anonymous stratum of the Talmud is far more extensive than earlier scholars thought and that it accounts for the larger part of the Babylonian Talmud. In the twenty-first century this view continues to inform the work of Richard Kalmin, David Kraemer, and Jeffrey Rubenstein among others. More recently Robert Brody of Hebrew University has challenged this hypothesis.

21. *Deuteronomy* 15:16-17: But should he (the Hebrew slave) say to you, "I do not want to leave you" – for he loves you and your household and is happy with you. Then you shall take an awl and put it through his ear into the door, and he shall

become your slave in perpetuity. Do the same with your female slave. This rule also appears in *Exodus* 21:5-6. The *kelal uferaṭ ukelal,* however, is based on the verse in the *Deuteronomy* which according to the interpreter has better syntactical qualities for this kind of interpretation.

22. Two later commentators, Samuel Shtrashun (Vilna, 1794 – 1872) and Ze'ev Wolf Lipkin (1788 – 1858), in their notes to the Vilna edition of the *Babylonian Talmud* emended the final inclusive clause of this *kelal uferaṭ ukelal* to match ms. *Vatican* 111 and the Spanish imprint. They did so on the basis of logic, not on the basis of a text they possessed. See *Hagahot v'Ḥiddušei ha-RaŠaŠ, Babylonian Talmud, Qiddušin* 21b, s.v. מרצע פרט and *Hagahot Ben Aryeh, Qiddušin* 21b, s.v. באזנו ובדלת.

23. Compare the Talmudic derivation of R. Yosi and Rabbi's rulings with that in *Sifre Deuteronomy* 122, ed. Finkelstein, p 180.

24. The formula for this interpretation as it appears in *Qiddušin* 21b is
ר' יוסי דריש ריבויי ומיעוטי; ולקחת - ריבה, מרצע - מיעט, באזנו ובדלת - חזר וריבה, ריבה ומיעט
וריבה - ריבה הכל, מאי רבי? רבי כל מילי, מאי מיעט? סם.
"R. Yosi interprets using 'extension-limitation-extension.' "You shall take" – this is an extension; "an awl" – this is a limitation; "in his ear and in the door" – this is another extension. An 'extension-limitation-extension' interpretation includes everything. What exactly does it include? Literally everything (that is a sharp object that pierces). What does it exclude? A chemical (that could pierce the slave's ear). The format of this interpretation forces the creator of the *kelal uferaṭ ukelal* to decline the use of the *kelal uferaṭ* hermeneutic.

25. The full verse is
ועשית מנרת זהב טהור מקשה תיעשה המנורה ירכה וקנה גביעיה כפתריה ופרחיה ממנה יהיו
"And thou shalt make a lampstand *of* pure gold: *of* beaten work shall the lampstand be made: its shaft, and its branches, its bowls, its knobs, and its flowers, shall be of the same" (*Exodus* 25:31).

26. "If a man deliver unto his neighbor an ass, or an ox, or a sheep, or any beast, to keep, and it die, or be hurt, or driven away, no man seeing it;..."

27. A salaried bailee need not pay for land which is stolen because it is not movable property and therefore does not fit the requirements of the *kelal uferaṭ ukelal*'s results. Land is not mentioned because it is not movable. Regarding what the Rabbis call Canaanite slaves, i.e., non-Hebrew slaves, the Torah says: והתנחלתם אתם לבניכם אחריכם לרשת אחזה, "And you may make them an inheritance for your children after you, to hold for a possession...." The Hebrew root נ-ח-ל sometimes connected to the term אחוזה refers to a land inheritance. See for example *Numbers* 2:1-7 and *Joshua* 15:20-62.

28. *Tosafot, Bab'a Meẓi'a'* 57b, s.v. כי יתן איש אל רעהו כלל points out that the result of the *kelal uferaṭ ukelal* in *Bab'a Meẓi'a'* 57b is derived using *perat ukelal uferaṭ* in *Nazir* 35a and by using *kelal uferaṭ* in the *Barayt'a* of R. Ishmael at the beginning of *Sifr'a*. *Tosafot*'s conclusion is that these *halakhic midraš*ic interpretations cannot all be the law's source. Rather, they form supportive prooftexts for it. In short, the law comes first and the interpretation follows suit. Maimonides in his *Mišnah Commentary* does not find it necessary to support the exemption of some of the various bailees from payment, each according to the contractual conditions appropriate to him, on the basis of *kelal uferaṭ ukelal.* Rather, he gathers all the various forms of deposits mentioned in each of the Torah's sections on bailees and

finds that what is common to them all is that they are movable property that has intrinsic monetary worth. In one way or another land, slaves, and promissory notes do not fit this definition. As to sanctified items, he derives them in the same way as the Talmud does. For that derivation, see our citation of *Bab'a Meẓi'a'* 57b. This suggests that he may have rejected the *kelal uferaṭ ukelal* interpretations in this Talmudic passage in favor of a more logical approach.

29. *Mek̲ilt'a*, *Neziqin* 15, ed. Horovitz, pp. 300-1.

30. I would not accuse the anonymous creator of this "*barayt'a*" of being a forger. It is quite likely that the original *barayt'a* was vaguely remembered and was "reconstituted" by the anonymous creator of the *kelal uferaṭ ukelal*. This is what David Weiss Halvni would call a מסורה, "a reconstituted tradition," that has replaced a מקור, "an original source."

31. See *Mek̲ilt'a*, *Neziqin* 16. *Mek̲ilt'a of R. Šimon bar Yoḥay*.

Medieval Judaic Logic and the Scholastic One in the 14th – 15th Centuries Provence and Italy: a Comparison of the Logical Works by Rav Hezekiah bar Halafta (First Half of the 14th Century) and Rav Judah Messer Leon (Second Half of the 15th Century)

Mauro Zonta

University of Rome,
Italy
maurozonta@libero.it

1. Introduction[1]

Hezekiah bar Halafta was a 14th century Provençal Jewish philosopher. From the short references to him, most of which are found in the *colophon* of the only three manuscripts where his works are now preserved, we know the name by which he was called among non-Jews: '*maestre Bonenfant de Millau.*' He was from Millau, now in the French department of Aveyron (near the Languedoc), and lived in the first half of the 14th century, probably in the Provençal city of Rodez. He seems to have been a physician, since he wrote at least one book of medicine, bearing the title *Book of Gabriel* (in Hebrew, *Sefer Gavri'el*). However, he was also interested into various philosophical matters, since he wrote a short book on theology and Jewish religion, *The Doors of Justice* (in Hebrew, *Ša'arey ẓedeq*).

He wrote in 1320 what was probably the first text on Peter of Spain's *Summulae Logicales* in Hebrew, in form of a 'gloss-commentary' – that is to say, a 'supercommentary' on a previous Latin commentary on the *Summulae* – and having the title *mavo'*, "introduction." This text, preserved in a unique manuscript and still unpublished, has been examined in its structure and sources in 2010. The structure was compared with that of Peter's work, while the many Latin, Greek, Judaeo-Arabic and Arab-Islamic sources are listed in detail.

Judah ben Jehiel, in Italian Giuda Messer Leon, was a Jewish writer, teacher, rhetorician, and philosopher of 15th-century North-East Italy. He was born in Montecchio Maggiore around 1420 – 1425, then he lived in Padua, where he apparently attended courses at the local university. Around 1450 or little later, he created his own Jewish academy (*yešivah*): this itinerant academy followed Judah ben Jehiel in his various workplaces, like Ancona, Bologna, Mantua. Later on, from 1480 onwards, he stayed in Naples; he fled from that place after 1495, and probably died some years later, around 1498.

In youth, probably in the years 1454 – 1455, he wrote and diffused three works, which may be included into a sort of Hebrew *trivium*, i.e. the lower division of the seven liberal arts in Medieval Latin schools, consisting of grammar, logic, and rhetoric. This seems to show Judah ben Jehiel was a real 'Hebrew Schoolman,' as can be found in many other works of his, particularly in the philosophical ones: he apparently employed concepts and methods he found in a number of works of classical Latin literature and Latin Scholasticism, for understanding aspects and characteristics of Aristotelian philosophy, and of the Bible as well. The three above mentioned linguistic works are: *The Pavement of the Sapphire* (*Livnat ha-Sappir*), about Hebrew grammar; *The Perfection of Beauty* (*Miklal Yofi*), about Latin Scholastic logic; *The Honeycomb's Flow* (*Nofet ṣufim*), about Latin rhetoric. The first and second of these works are still unpublished.

I will try to make a historical comparison between these two authors, Hezekiah bar Halafta and Judah Messer Leon, in order to find the birth and the end of the "Hebrew Scholastic logic", that is, the variable approach to Latin logicians among Jewish scholars from 1300 to 1450 circa, and the employment of that Scholastical logical methods by Medieval Judaic thinkers in Western Europe.

2. Comparison Between the Two Texts

2.1. Texts

We will consider the contents of the MS Oxford, Bodleian Library, Mich. 314, and of the MS Firenze, Biblioteca mediceo-laurenziana, Pluteus 88, n. 52, copied at Ancona in 1456, folios 1-129; very probably it is the archetype of the work – i.e., that from which the whole other manuscripts were copied. Generally speaking, the work is divided into two 'parts,' *ḥeleq* (including five sections and three ones respectively), 'sections,' *ša'ar* (about each treatise of the work), and 'chapters,' *pereq*. See also the general introduction to the book on folios 5r, l. 1 – 6v, l. 19.

In the following table, I draw a comparison of the general survey of Hezekiah's text and Judah Messer Leon's one, as it results from the chapters of the whole text of the former, and the three out of eight sections of the latter, where the themes seem to be pertaining to each other.

Table no. 1

Hezekiah bar Halafta, *Introduction (to the logic)*	Judah Messer Leon, *The Perfection of Beauty*
Introduction	Introduction
	Part 1, section 1, divided into nine chapters:
Chapter 1 (on dialectic and voice)	Chapter 1, on the meaning of logic and its causes
Chapter 2 (on sound and voice)	Chapter 2, on the meaning of definition (*gevul*) and its parts
Chapter 3 (on noun)	Chapter 3, on the meaning of noun and verb
Chapter 4 (on verb)	
Chapter 5 (on speech)	Chapter 4, on the meaning of subjectivity and the meanings of subject and object
Chapter 6 (on sentence)	
Chapter 7 (on categorical sentences)	
Chapter 8 (on sentences which agree upon both of them [i.e. terms] in one thing)	
Chapter 9 (on the three species of sentences)	

Chapter 10 (on negation and its being contrary)	
Chapter 11 (on the species of hypothetical sentences…)	
Chapter 12 (…and on their agreement)	
Chapter 13 (on modal sentences)	
Chapter 14 (on the five universals)	
Chapter 15 (on 'difference' [as such])	
Chapter 16 (on 'genus of genera')	Chapter 5, on the genus and the species
Chapter 17 (on 'property')	Chapter 6, on the difference, the property, and the accident
Chapter 18 (on 'accident')	
Chapter 19 (on the agreement of universals)	
Chapter 20 (on the many meanings of a universal thing)	Chapter 7, on the capacity of the objects and the meaning of the true and untrue subjectivity, as substantially and accidentally one, as well as the superior definition and the inferior one
	Chapter 8, on the meaning of the definition, the description (*rošem*), the definite thing, and the descripted one
Chapter 21 (on substance)	Chapter 9, on the meaning of the category (*ma'amar*) and its parts, i.e., the ten categories
Chapter 22 (on quantity)	
Chapter 23 (on relatives)	
Chapter 24 (on quality)	
Chapter 25 (on action and passion)	
Chapter 26 (on opposites)	
Chapter 27 (on prior and posterior)	
Chapter 28 (on what is together)	
Chapter 29 (on movement)	
Chapter 30 (on the previous categories)	
Chapter 31 (on a Scholastic	

question, namely: 'whether it is possible to determine the predicated subject as far as it is a subject, or not')	
Chapter 32 (on another Scholastic question, namely: 'whether the name [or: noun] of the adjective can be a subject in a sentence, (or not)'	
	Part 1, section 2, divided into 10 chapters:
Chapter 33 (on sentence and syllogism)	An introduction of the section, about the clear division of it into chapters
Chapter 34 (on the figures of syllogism)	Chapter 1, on the meaning of the speech and its introduction and its parts
Chapter 35 (on *loci*)	Chapter 2, on the meaning of that way (*ṣad*), and the introductions having those ways, and the order of the introductions into three (syllogistic) figures (*temunot*) and its general orders according to truth and untruth
Chapter 36 (a so-called 'introduction to the student' [not found in Peter of Spain's work])	Chapter 3, on the meaning of equality, together with some doubts (about it)
Chapter 37 (on sophistic disputations, and on fallacies)	Chapter 4, on opposite and its parts
Chapter 38 (on common noun)	Chapter 5, on the meaning of the complex introduction and its parts, and the meaning of the rhythmical (*tenahit*) introduction
Chapter 39 (on accidents)	Chapter 6, on the association (*qušeret*)
Chapter 40 (on various references of passages of treatise n. 7 of Peter of Spain's work)	Chapter 7, on the division
Chapter 41 (on various subjects in different passages of the work)	Chapter 8, on the causality (*sabatiyyit*)
Chapter 42 (on time)	Chapter 9, on the temporarily (*zemaniyyit*)

Chapter 43 ('the universals, not the individuals, have definitions': this passage might be an erroneous interpretation of treatise 12, chapter 1: 'Distribution is a multiplication of a common term, made by an universal sign')	Chapter 10, on the locality (*meqomiyyit*)
Final note (a defence of logic)	Part 1, section 3, divided into 8 chapters:
	An introduction to the section, according to the clear division of it into 8 chapters
	Chapter 1, on the meaning of the propaedeutics (*haẓa'ah*) and its parts
	Chapter 2, on the hypotheses (*ha-šorešim ha-munaḥim*) in a propaedeutic thing
	Chapter 3, on the meaning of the particular propaedeutic thing and the general one, in a limitation (*hagvalah*) and its specific generalities
	Chapter 4, on the meaning of the proposal no-limitation, which is not limited only, or not limited at all, and in a general way, with a permutation (literally, 'translation', *ha'taqah*), and its specific generalities
	Chapter 5, on the meaning of the proposal no-limitation, which is not limited only, or not limited at all, and in a general enthymeme (literally, 'semen', *simin*), without a permutation, and its specific generalities
	Chapter 6, on the meaning of true proposal
	Chapter 7, on the meaning of metaphor (literally, 'expantion', *harḥavah*)

	Chapter 8, on the meaning of exclamation (*qeri 'ah*)

From the above comparison we can suggest that Hezekiah's text and Judah Messer Leon's one have, at the beginning, the same purpose, i.e. that to be a sort of introduction to logic; but further on, they differ from each other in a more pronounced contrast.

2.2. Comparison

Now let us consider three passages from Hezekiah's work, which can be useful to notice the peculiarities of his text compared with Judah Messer Leon's one in his own introduction (MS Oxford, Bodleian Library, Mich. 314, folios 43r, ll. 13-19, 43v, ll. 1-6 and 9 sg., and 44r, l. 20 – 44v, l. 1):

> Upon them (i.e. the Latin philosophers), I have seen a commentary on the introduction (*mavo'*) which enclosed the generalities of logic in the most possible short space (…) and, in their language, it is called *Tractatus.* (…); (after) having looked for it for a long time, I have found it and I have read it (…) and I have translated it from their language into ours (i.e. from Latin into Hebrew). Since, in some passages, this commentary expatiated on (some points) for no reason, I have abbreviated it, and I have taken from it only the passages which aroused no doubts. I have not translated this work for somebody who is equal to Aristotle or Averroes, but for somebody who is equal to myself (…).
>
> We would better to gain the gifts of the commentator's mouth from the Prince of philosophers, Aristotle. He said, at the beginning of the *Physics*, that what is general is more clear to us than what is particular by nature. There is evidence of this that the perception of a general thing temporarily precedes the perception of a particular thing in the children. As a matter of fact, at first the child sees his father in every man and his mother in every woman; then, when his intelligence becomes stronger, he distinguishes his father among many men and his mother among many women (…).
>
> Now, logical texts are long and difficult for us, although they were not so difficult for their contemporaries (…) therefore a summary (of logic) was needed and (…) the scholar called Master Peter of Spain wrote this very useful summary that gives us many precepts about interesting subjects.
>
> Now, since everything should have four causes, i.e. material, agent, formal and final, let us be interested in this summary. We say that the material cause is the syllogism and its parts; the agent cause is the author (i.e. Peter of Spain); the formal cause is the division of text in two *summulae* and of *summulae* in parts. (…)

In every (logical) disputation three conditions should be: somebody who asks, somebody who replies, somebody who judges between the two. If so, this is a question among three people (point one). A four thing is needed, i.e. the argument of the disputation; therefore this is a question among four people (point two).
General answer to the two objections: one and the same person should ask and reply at the same time (…) and there is no need of a judge; moreover, the subject of the disputation would be included in the question too.
Reply: Without a question and an answer, a man by himself cannot dispute, that is to say, there should be two conditions in him, the answer and the question; therefore, you should say that the art of logic is a 'question among two people (…).'

There is difference between 'logic' 'proper' and 'dialectic' 'proper', since 'logic' denotes a mere term, whereas 'dialectic' denotes a question among two people, as we said above.

Let now consider some passages of the introduction to Judah Messer Leon's *The Perfection of Beauty*. I will paraphrase and comment on MS Florence, Biblioteca Mediceo-Laurenziana, Pluteus 88, n. 52, folios 5r, l. 4 – 6v, l. 19:

The great Rabbi… the Sage… Rabbi Judah, known as Messer Leon, said: 'As I saw some men of our Torah who devoted themselves to pose as philosophers (*mitfalsefim*)'. Here, as in other points of the text, the author wants to underline his full orthodoxy, for example, as to the creation of the world. He says again and again he is using the language of the Law (*lešon ha-dat*) but, at the same time, he uses full Latin Scholastic philosophical terms and concepts, translating them into Hebrew. It seems that Messer Leon is not explicitly translating word by word, but writing a personal work, in which there are no interpolations or influences by other authors. Often, in his introduction, he repeats the phrase 'I said' (*amarti*).

He expatiates upon the word *yofi*, 'beauty,' that he uses to underline the value of the work he is writing (see for example folio 5v, ll. 23 and 28).

On folio 6r, ll. 8 sg., he declares that: 'My intention to denote this text is in the form of an introduction and preface (*petihah we-mav'o*).' *Mavo'* is the typical term that Hezekiah bar Halafta uses as a title for his work, so we could suppose that Messer Leon know it – as a matter of fact, we have only one unique MS of the text of Hezekiah, made in Italy in 1469 in Nardò (South Italy).

At the end of folio 6r, Messer Leon explicitly quotes Book 2 of Aristotles' *Metaphysics* (*ka'ašer hitba'er ba-ma'amar ha-šeni mi-Sefer Ma'aḥer*): 'Here we read the name of this work as 'Perfection of Beauty', because there are in it, among the generalities, a great number of particularities… and 'Beauty' has correction as its aim… and it is my intention to carry the disciples from simpler thing to more complex ones, and from the general things to the particular ones.'

From folio 6v onwards he begins to explain the meaning of his work, part by part. Generally speaking, he affirms (on folio 6v, ll. 1-7) that his book is divided in general into two main parts: the first part would speak about the roots of his work (*šoršey ha-mela'kah*) and its generalities and its meanings in form of an introduction (*mav'o*) and the 'expansion of the centres' for understanding them in their depths and in their praises, in the translated books inside it. The second part would cause the destruction of the dialectical arguments and the ways of the sophistic elenchus, so that the man would be preserved from what is evidently not correct, deceitful and untruth, and on the contrary he would be sure about the beginning of the thought, without any studying and question (about it), be it beautiful or ugly. More in particular, the first five sections of the work, according to Judah Messer Leon himself, are about simply things, introductions, propaedeutics, syllogistic figures and a study of the introductions and some of their definitions.

See now how the same previous passage is given differently by both authors, Hezekiah and Messer Leon, about 'noun,' as follows (MS Oxford, Bodleian Library, Mich. 314, folio 50v, ll. 2-7):

> 'Chapter three. The definition of noun is: 'a signifying voice' etc.'
> Contrary to this one it is such. And 'Ptolemy' is a noun of a branch (*'anaf*) which this is not existent, and what is not existent does not teach anything. If so, the 'noun' of 'Ptolemy' is not signifying and, as they say, the noun is signifying.
> The response to it is as follows. Everything signifying noun is a certain thing, and, if the noun 'Ptolemy' is not signifying 'Ptolemy,' since it is not existent, this is signifying what it is, and how it is (for example) its expression in the living beings is also possible to be understood and interpreted, like a wall (*kotel*), and we said that this is the form of 'Ptolemy'. As a matter of fact, this noun is signifying to be a thing, and this is its form.'

On the contrary, in Judah Messer Leon (MS Florence, Biblioteca Mediceo-Laurenziana, Pluteus 88, n. 52, folios 8v, l. 17 – 9r, l. 9) it is written as follows:

Table n. 2

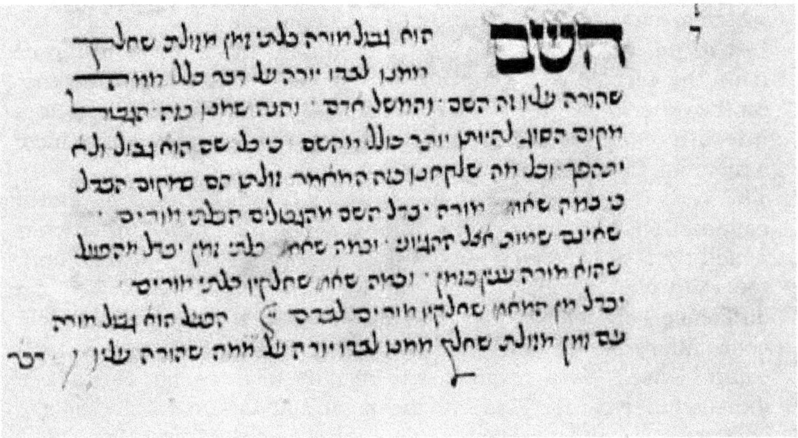
השם

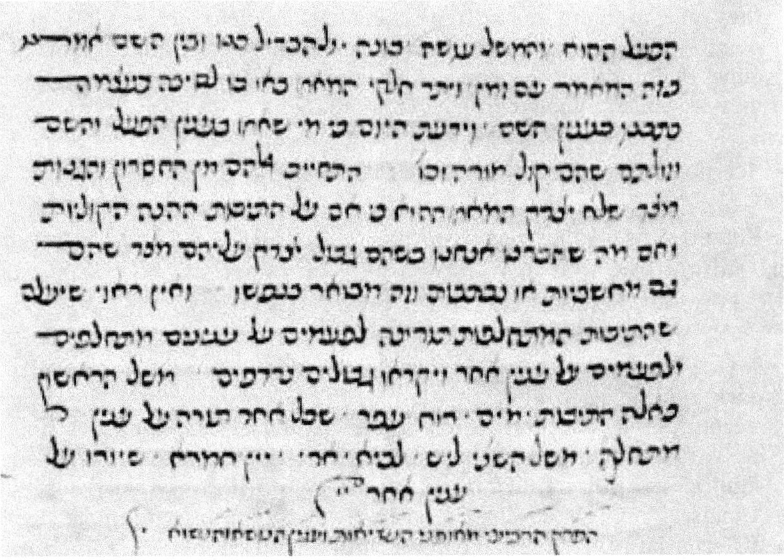

'Chapter three. The definition of noun and verb:

The noun is a definition which denotes something without giving it a temporal connotation, without a part of it signifying, in a general sense, **what this noun means, for example 'man.' Now they include in that definition a place of the genus**, because it is more general than the noun; **in fact, every noun is a definition, but not**

conversely. Moreover, what we have assumed in this speech outside it are in a different position, **since in what they say it means the noun is different in meaning from the definitions without a meaning, which are not nouns according to the logic. For what concerns the fact of not having a temporal connotation, the noun is different from the verb since it signifies (i.e. the verb) a concept with time; on the other hand, for what concerns its parts without a meaning, it is different from the speech, according to its species which have a meaning in themselves.**
The verb is a definition that signifies a 'thing' with a temporal connotation, and no part of it, alone, is significant, meaning from which derives from it. This is the speech related to the verb and, for example, 'speaks.' Intention: we have already explained the difference between the verb and the noun as regards the temporal connotation, and the other parts of the speech which are on them for a cause in itself, we said all that in relation to the noun. Nowadays, those who study the issue of the noun and the verb, and, on the contrary, are not interested in the 'voice' that signifies etc. – it is necessary that, since the misfortune and calamity, **this speech is not perfect**, if not on the basis of these words, i.e. the 'voices,' and if we have associated them as they are definitions, **the speech is perfect as they are thought or written** – and this is clear *per se*. It is not possible to determine whether the different words are significant either due to different meanings, or due to a different other thing, and they are called 'synonym *(nirdafim)* definitions'.'

See now a series of examples of these things (folio 9a, ll. 9-12).

Let now see some passages of Paulus Venetus, *Logica Parva*, first critical edition from the manuscripts with introduction and commentary by Alan R. Perreiah, Leiden, Brill, 2002, pp. 3-4, as follows:

9. [...] **Nomen est terminus significativus sine tempore cuius nulla pars aliquid significat ut 'homo.' In ista definitione ponitur 'terminus' loco generis quia omne nomen est terminus et non converso. Secundus dicitur 'significativus' quia termini 'non significativi non sunt nomina apud logicum** licet grammaticum ut 'omnis,' 'nullus' et similia. **Tertio dicitur 'sine tempore' ad differentiam verbi et participii qui significant cum tempore. Quarto dicitur 'cuius nulla pars aliquid significat' ad differentiam orationis cuius partes significant.**
[10] **Verbum est terminus temporaliter significativus et extremorum unitivus cuius nulla pars aliquid significat ut 'currit' vel 'disputat**.' Dicitur primo 'temporaliter significativus' ad differentiam nominis quod significat sine tempore [...] Ceterae autem partes ponuntur sicut in definitione nominis.

[11] Oratio est terminus significativus cuius aliqua pars aliquid significat [...] **Orationum alia perfecta alia imperfecta. Oratio perfecta est illa qua perfectum sensum generat in animo auditoris [...] Oratio imperfecta est illa qua imperfectum sensum generat in animo auditoris [...] etc.**

See also the translation by Alan R. Perreiah, Munchen – Wien, Philosophica Verlag, 1984, pp. 122-123, as follows:

Section 2 – Noun. [...] A noun is a term significative without time. No part of a noun signifies something separate: for example, 'man.' This definition places it in the genus of a term; because every noun is a term; but not every term is a noun. Secondly, it says 'significative' because those terms which are not significative are not nouns according to the logician; but they are nouns according to the grammarian; for example, 'every,' 'no' and the like. Thirdly, it says 'without time' in order to differentiate it from verbs and participles which signify with time. Fourthly, it says 'no part of which signifies something separate' *per se* in order to differentiate it from a statement (*oratio*) whose parts signify objects separate [from it].
Section 3 – Verb. A verb is a term significative temporally and unitive of extremes. No part of a verb signifies something separate; for example, 'runs' and 'disputes.' It says 'significative temporally' first to differentiate it from a noun which signifies without time [..] The remaining parts of the definition then are just like those in the definition of a noun.
Section 4 – Statement. A statement (*oratio*) is a term some of whose parts signify something separate [...] Statements (*orationum*) are perfect or imperfect. A perfect statement is what generates a perfect sense in the mind of a hearer [...] An imperfect statement is that which generates an imperfect sense in the mind of a hearer [...] etc.

As a matter of fact, the text of Paulus Venetus' *Logica parva*, if not the only one, is surely one of the main sources of these texts. It has to inform the context and the spirit of the *Perfection of Beauty,* as found in the above mentioned passages.

3. Conclusion

To sum up, a tentative comparative comparison of both works, Hezekiah bar Halafta's and Judah Messer Leon's ones, show that they were the first and the last ones of a general history, typically of the so-called 'Hebrew Scholasticism' as it arose from 13th-century Latin Scholasticism and developed in 14th-century Provence, in a simpler form (where the Arab-Islamic and Judeo-Arabic works were prevalent, as I have wrote in many articles), and concluded in 15th-century Italy. As a matter of fact, Judah

Messer Leon tried to follow the most magnificent aspects of Italian and especially Venetian Latin Scholasticism at the Paduan School, in particular following its previous master, Paolo Nicoletti Veneto (d. 1429), and (implicitly!) its contemporary master and scholar, Gaetano da Thiene (d. 1465) – and I would like to examine this one in the next future.

Notes

1. See Mauro Zonta, "Structure and Sources of the Hebrew Commentary on Petrus Hispanus's *Summulae Logicales* by Hezekiah bar Halafta, *alias* Bonenfant de Millau," in Andrew Schumann (ed.), *Judaic Logic*, 'Judaism in Context' 8, Gorgias Press, Piscataway N.J. 2010, pp. 77-116; see also Charles H. Manekin, "Scholastic Logic and the Jews," in *Bulletin de philosophie médiévale* 41 (1999), pp. 123-147, on pp. 145-146 (list of chapters of the *Perfection of Beauty*).

Suspending New Testament: Do the Two Talmuds Belong to Hermeneutics of Texts?

Sergey Dolgopolski

University at Buffalo, SUNY,
the United States of America
sergey@buffalo.edu

1. Introduction[1]

New Testament (NT) suspends Old Testament (OT), a (Christian) theologeme[2] teaches us. Can thinking about Rabbinic literatures through a comparative lens with theology help, once again, to understand rabbinic texts better? This time, that means to revisit the ways the characters in the two *Talmuds* approach the *Mišnah* and the apocrypha (*barayt'a*, in Medieval Talmudic parlance) they ascribe to *Mišnah*ic sages? Guided by this question, I retrieve a parallel (Rabbinic) theologeme. In this theologeme, any attempt at any new testament, i.e. at any new testimony or witness presenting the (divine) law in the form of a rule becomes programmatically suspended, in a variety of ways in which such suspension works.

By a necessity to which the argument below attends, navigating the two general theologemes of suspension – the suspension of OT in NT and the suspension of (any) new testament – leads to rethinking the role of, and to repositioning, the two *Talmuds* in relationship to the tradition of hermeneutics of texts. Additionally, that program of research leads to the task of reevaluation of the position of formal logic in relation to hermeneutics of texts; even if, in this essay, I would only be able to gesture towards this last element of equation.

At the same time and by the same token, the task of situating the two *Talmuds* vis-à-vis hermeneutics of texts involves yet another task: to situate the tradition of hermeneutics of texts vis-à-vis what I will introduce first as a theology of suspension, and secondly, and as I will claim, more fundamentally, as a philology of suspension.

The suspension in question articulates itself first of all in political theology[3] as a way of thinking, which invariably and by its very definition draws on the suspension of the OT in the NT. But this suspension articulates itself once again in rabbinic literature, and this time rather differently: it emerges as a suspension of any new testament (in general, i.e.) – and by extension as the suspension of any testament and/or witness to the divine or any other version of law. Crucially for my argument below, suspension of any new testament articulates in two different ways in the two corpora of rabbinic literature, dubbed as these corpora were from the middle ages and on, the *Palestinian* and *Babylonian Talmudim.*

My main claim in articulating that more general suspension of any testimony/witness/testament to a law in the form of a rule is that in suspending any (new) testament to the law, at work is a political philology or, as I will soon explain in more details, an analysis applying the powers of philology (Gumbrecht) to understand the political relationships between parties. Political philology sees the relationships expressed in philological forms as never transparent to the parties these forms involve, create, or presume. For a quick example of a political philology, for a devotee of NT, NT is coming from and is cancelling/suspending OT; however, despite on what that devotee can accept, the idea that there is OT is an effect, a result, and an outcome of an idea that there is NT. There can be no OT without NT having already emerged. NT thus both follows from and precedes OT. Political philology explores this inversion of cause and effect,[4] as well as other inversions in the texts and thought processes philology is a study of. As I will explain below, political philology also enables a way of looking at the two *Talmuds*, which precedes, grounds, embraces, and escapes political theology as a hitherto predominant way of thinking suspension in Christian theology and beyond – the suspension of OT by NT.

Of course, the characters in the *Talmuds* suspend a different (new) testament, the *Mišnah*, the apocryphal testaments of the rules of the law (the *Toseft'a* and the *Barayt'a,*) or perhaps even the Scripture and/or prophesy; and they do so in a different way as compared to Christian theologeme of suspension. That means not in the way of allegory or, and in particular, of prefiguration; but rather in a variety of other ways, which I can describe – preliminary and generally, but perhaps still usefully as a starting point – as refutations. That general description allows, at the very least, to begin laying out the complex claim, which will be of primary concern in this essay. It is the claim that political philology precedes grounds, embraces, and escape political theology as a way to think the suspension.

Justifying the necessity of, and evaluating, such complex claim will involve several steps; and these steps must be taken from necessary different starting points. I will thus proceed step by step, and starting point by starting point.

2. Starting Point One: Is *Talmud* Literature? A Philological Question

We live, Erich Auerbach teaches us,[5] in the world – or in the 'reality,' in his terms – which is 'represented' in literature. Speaking in his terms again, that means European literature both images and shapes that 'reality' or that world. In light of Auerbach's analysis of that representation of reality in Western literature, it however also means an almost impossible combination of a facade of the present, famously exemplified in Auerbach by Homer, with the faceless depth of the past, exemplified for him by Mosaic Scripture. Of the faceless depth of the past, the Mosaic scriptures registers only what is significant for the future of the reader. In contrast, of the facade of the present, Homers lets nothing escape. To rephrase Auerbach's argument in terms of style, the Mosaic Scripture never styles the faceless past as *praesens historicum.* That for Auerbach is a strong contrariety to the Homeric facade of the present, the on-going front-stage of action, in which nothing hides in background. The Homeric verse never goes beyond – neither behind nor before the facade; the Mosaic Scripture never puts the reader face-to-face with the past the Scripture accounts for. That contrariety between the face or facade of the present and the faceless depth of the past is radical, for Auerbach; and if taken in separation from one another, neither Mosaic Scripture nor Homer's poems are pieces of literature yet, for him. However, when Scriptures and Homer are combined and read as and through *figurae*, i.e. as descriptions and shapes that deviate from the typified, standard, normalized, or predictable facade of the things, European literature begins.[6] It then occupies, and indeed erects, the stage – the 'reality' and the world. What that means however is that we, for Auerbach, are always already the children of that difficult marriage between the facade of the potentially insignificant but always entertaining present on the one hand and the outmost significance of the depth of faceless past, on the other hand. That also means *figurae* are ways of doing impossible, of employing Homer's style to face the faceless but all-significant past from which Scripture comes.

Rabbinic literature is an example of such a difficult marriage. In rabbinic *exegesis* of Scripture (in *midrašey haggadah,*[7] in contemporary Talmudic parlance) an implied reader is provided with competing interpretations of Mosaic Scripture to complement the latter with *praesens historicum* they do not contain. It thus creates a facade, *praesens historicum*, in the places in Scripture where a reader is initially finding nothing but an account of the significance of the past. In such exegesis, the reader thus ascends to a facade from behind, from the faceless depth, which becomes a 'background' event, as the exegesis re-styles the past as *praesens historicum,* as fictive as it may be.

In an exactly opposite, and thus similar way, in rabbinic *isogesis* of Scripture (in *midrašey halaḵah*, in contemporary parlance) a reader faces the depths of the faceless past of the Scripture by approaching the latter with his or her own question. The reader is to approach a scripture with her present concern, point of view, or opinion, all formulated as almost rhetorical questions, to which the verses of Scripture provide answers to become 'obvious' from now on. In *isogesis*, the scripture, then, is mobilized to correct or even refute an answer the reader initially anticipates.

Both modes suspend the faceless depth of the past in the Scripture by converting into a *praesens historicum* and by gesturing to the limits of such conversion. In both *exegesis* and *isogesis*, the reader moves between the facade and the faceless past, ascending from behind the facade, as she is in the *exegesis;* or descending beyond the facade, as she is in the *isogesis* of Scripture. In either way, the reader moves along the path of suspension.

In this discussion, I left aside the question of comparison between this and the principles of allegory and pre-figuration, which Auerbach addresses explicitly in his analysis of the 'scenes from the drama of European literature'[8] where Christian theology of prefiguration and emergence of 'Western literature' go hand to hand (in a way, similarly to how politics and theology go hand to hand in Carl Schmitt and related authors) and where one finds no mention of rabbinic literatures or modes of thought.

Instead, as heuristically inspired by Auerbach as the analysis in this essay remains, at the center there still stays the role of Mosaic style as one of the two *conditio sine qua non* for the 'European literature' to emerge and develop. In that light, the question of the two *Talmuds* and of the tradition of hermeneutics assumes the following form: how, and indeed whether, the two *Talmuds* can find a place in the perspective Auerbach's work is drawing? Where do the two corpora of text and thought – dubbed, as they have been from Middle ages and on, the *Yerušalmi* and *Bavli* or *Palestinian* and *Babylonian Talmuds* respectively – belong on the scope of the emergence and development of 'Western literature' and to the hermeneutics of texts as a part thereof?

I have paused briefly for the dubbings because they have their power of framing. That power translates in presuming that each of the two *Talmuds* is an internally coherent body of thought. That presumption is yet to be justified or denied in each case, and the outcomes of such justification or denial are to be taken seriously. Yet the presumption was heavily at work beginning from the Medieval view of the *Bavli* as internally coherent tractate of tractates. It continued to work in Luzatto's view of the *Bavli* as the arch-paradigm of European Enlightened reason. Furthermore, projecting that assumed literary-intellectual integrity of the *Bavli* back onto the *Yerušalmi* informed how the *Yerušalmi* was both learned traditionally and studied academically. This perception of integrity is important for this essay in one respect only: in how such a perception of the *Bavli* informs both traditional and scholarly approaches to the *Yerušalmi*. The two *Talmuds* become shadows of each other. One approaches the *Yerušalmi* with the set of habits and expectations formed in one's reading the *Bavli* as a starting point, resulted in finding many contrasts between the two *Talmuds*. Alternatively, one considers the *Yerušalmi* the beginning, and the *Bavli* a logical continuation of the same work or of the same way of thinking, as *Mišnah*-centric as both of the *Talmuds* are assumed to be on that approach. For the purposes of and within the limits of this essay, I can only say that one has to keep this power of framing of corpora of rabbinic literature as two largely coherent '*Talmuds*' in a constant check.

I now come back to the main line of inquiry. I address the question of the placement of the two *Talmuds* vis-à-vis the traditions of hermeneutics of texts both in light and despite Auerbach's perspective.

I do so through a case study. That case study involves both a slow reading of two parallel texts from the two *Talmuds* and a very broad and therefore very preliminary mapping of these two texts vis-a-vis two competing paradigms in hermeneutics of texts. That would mean, in particular, that both 'hermeneutics' and 'texts' would need to be accessed in terms of whether they belong to 'European literature' in Auerbach's sense.

The first of the two paradigms of hermeneutics refers back to Aristotle's *Peri Hermeneias;* the second, to use his name as a synecdoche, to Schleiermacher's approach to interpreting both Homer and Bible in a hunt for the original intent of the assumed authors of these ancient compositions.

In broadest terms, Aristotle associates hermeneutics with prudence, or a reasonable action in view of the future that cannot be known. He locates the task of hermeneutics in the realm of what is possible as opposed to what is necessary or impossible, thus linking hermeneutics to rhetoric. He therefore associates that realm of the possible with the future, for the past for him has already taken place, can be known, is already determined, and thus, at least in principle, leaves no truly open possibilities. The future, however, is prone of possibilities, and therefore – unlike past – cannot be known. The task of the hermeneutics is the future. The question hermeneutics addresses is how to act prudently at a point of time based on as many possible futures, and thus on as many indeterminacies, as the fact of having many possibilities might involve. Hermeneutics is first of all about the possible, and about prudent action vis-a-vis the unknown play of possibilities in the future.

In contrast, in an equally broad if not in an even broader scope, Schleiermacher's hermeneutics of both Homer and Bible is directed towards the past, which Schleiermacher, like Aristotle, interprets as always determined, even if, unlike Aristotle, neither initially understood, nor unproblematic if one wants to attain its understanding. The task of interpretation for Schleiermacher is to understand that past, and in particular the 'historical' author's intention residing there. That presumes this task to be hard but doable, of course if proper philological, linguistic and cultural methods of interpretation are applied.

Despite an obvious contrast between hermeneutics of Aristotle and Schleiermacher, there is a common denominator. For both, the past is, arguably, a *fait accompli.* To come back to Auerbach's facade of the present and the faceless depth of past, both Schleiermacher and Aristotle remain on and only on Homer's side of equation, and thus outside of the full scope of 'Western literature.'

Hermeneutics is not quite literature, as it follows therefrom. What that means, however, is that both rabbinic *exegesis/isogesis* and – at least hypothetically – the two *Talmuds* do not belong to the tradition of hermeneutics of text, either. In the pages below I will test that hypothesis through first presenting results and then performing a slow reading of two parallel texts from the two *Talmuds*.

Allow me yet another pause here in order to explain another necessity of engaging with the question of the role of the tradition of hermeneutics of texts in relation to literature. This time it is an internal necessity that arises from the perspective of the discipline of Rabbinics, the academic study on rabbinic corpora. At this point, the question is: Why problematize hermeneutics of texts when approaching the *Talmuds*? An answer is two-fold.

Firstly, the academic study on the *Talmuds* has so far relied on empirical philology (i.e. 'curatorship of texts,' Gumbrecht[9]) at the expense of taking for granted what these texts are as a body of thought. This is where the above observation about dubbing the corpora as two *Talmuds* becomes relevant. It exemplifies how 'taking for granted' that the two *Talmuds* is a framing notion, informs how these – in fact much more multiple – bodies of text and thought have been approached. Such a framing approach to a corpus of texts and thought as if they were two *Talmuds* strongly informed academic scholarship on the *Talmuds* in the long 20th century. On that approach, one is not permitted to access any 'logic' and/or 'hermeneutics' of the 'thought' *in* the *Talmuds* without first committing text criticism. The argument goes along the lines of a pseudo-rhetorical question 'What kind of conclusions about the 'logic' or 'hermeneutics' at work in the texts of the *Talmuds* can one derived if these texts are not established reliably enough on empirical philological grounds of text criticism?' That implied hermeneutical distinction between 'text' and 'thought,' let alone the framing of the 'two *Talmuds*' in which it comes, already suffices to explain the internal urgency of the question of the relationships between hermeneutics of text and the study of the two *Talmuds*.

Secondly, and thinking further with and about this approach, text-criticism's deferral of analyzing 'thought' until such time when the 'text' is established is not problem-free in hermeneutical terms either. It is both heavily and tacitly based on a certain version of hermeneutics, which even if not found '*in* the text' as it were, still informs the approach of a text-critical scholar '*to* the text.' The very separation of the two bodies, the body of text and the body of thought is a hermeneutical principle, an inheritance of Schleiermacher's hermeneutics of classical texts, where thought was located in the outside of the text, in the past mistakenly controllable, – and by the same token effaced by the facade of the *present historicum.* More specifically, as already explained, that effacement of the faceless depth of the past took place in and by the authorial intent, which Schleiermacher's interpretation was seeking to restore behind the 'text' or its 'language.'

A problem is that together with this separation of 'text' and 'thought' came an automatically – and thus uncritically – accepted view on the very way in which texts can mean, as non-literary as, in Auerbach's terms, that mode of meaning can get. What is more, this hermeneutical, i.e. non-literary, view has been accepted even before, and as a foundation of how, any particular meaning of a given Talmudic text was approached via procedures of text criticism, as hermeneutical as they therefore were.

With this in mind, the case study can help questioning that very hermeneutical – rather than literary – assumption about how texts mean. Part of that assumption was that texts mean Platonically and/or Socratically; that is to say non-literary in Auerbach's terms; rather than, for example, along the lines of Mosaic approaches to meaning as being both definitive of the future and inexpressible as a present.

Without jumping ahead of myself, I can only say about the case study of slow reading below that in the framework of comparison between the traditions of the two *Talmuds*, of 'literature,' in Auerbach's sense, and of hermeneutics in Schleiermacher's sense, the temporality in the two *Talmuds* contrasts both Homeric and Mosaic one. That temporality entails, at the very least, a very unusual sort of 'literature' i.e. of combination of Homer and Moses, in Auerbach terms.

That 'literature' of the two *Talmuds* reverses Aristotle's prudence to think about the past that can never be fully known. Instead the past is only partially available through the record of its tradition, and getting to its significance requires not only a prudent reading, now directed to the past, but much more. That reversal also applies to intention, the main concern of modern hermeneutics. Even if intention remains of a concern, it also belongs to the past that can never be fully known, not because it is of multiple possibilities, but because it is fundamentally faceless. This is why prudence, even directed to the past, proves insufficient. That means, intention can no longer control the powers of philology.

Even more specifically, it means, as the case-study will help to exemplify, that the location of prudent action towards the past changes. The task is no longer to 'interpret' (in Aristotelian sense, i.e. almost to divinate in order to act prudently in view of future that can never be fully known). Instead, the task is to probe the record of tradition without necessarily committing to any *praesens historicum*, that tradition might be misconstrued to entail.[10]

In terms of the case-study below, and also more generally, that difference in where the prudent actions locates – in the past or in the future – has implication for the role of understanding. In modern hermeneutics, understanding of the past is reachable in the same way in which the knowledge of the future was for Aristotle. Understanding the past can be attained with prudence applied in reverse direction – the modern hermeneutics contents – if one advances to the past not right away but through initial step or steps of a carefully cultivated non-understanding. In contrast to that, the *Talmud*'s treatment of the traditional records of the past insists on a temporality of refutation, which draws on the necessity of ultimate failure or 'self-refutation' found in the argument of another person. Finding such a failure becomes the only authentic way to approach faceless past.

A parallel to that in modern hermeneutics would be non-understanding as the end of hermeneutical process. Yet this parallel is not full on at least two accounts: refutation is to fail the other interpretation (without insisting on the correctness or even on existence of any 'successful' one); and, as a result, a 'hermeneutical' process in the *Talmud* is never lonely: there is no one subject who interprets – neither an individual nor collective subject (for a nation, for example, can be as lonely as an individual subject, and can too be an agent of hermeneutical process). In that, to speak in advance one last time, refutation of the other and indeed of a tradition becomes a way to encounter the faceless past to which Schleiermacher's hermeneutics might not have any access.

In what follows I explore no more but also no less than one particular way of that encounter with the faceless depth of past, the way of suspending the traditions deemed to have come from that past and to have captured the law in a set of rules.

To highlight yet another important implication of this attempt: It has a bearing for the question of the role formal logic plays as a way to think of the hermeneutics of texts. That has to do with how different Auerbach's 'literature' is – not only from hermeneutics but also from logic. If one follows Auerbach in granting literature the two irreconcilable elements, the faceless depth of the past and the facade of the present brought forth in an explicitly stated language of foreground, then any attempt at a formal logic, however much constrained by the theorem of non-fullness of any formalization, places logic and literature as not only mutually exclusive but also mutually necessary. It is only once the faceless depth of the past becomes unavoidable in reading a language that one can conceive a necessity to develop a different language, a language fully controllable by calculation. It is therefore only in response to such an encounter with the faceless past that formal logic takes shape. Logic thus becomes the most authentic alternative to the 'literature,' and thus logic can only come into view when 'literature,' and not merely Mosaic Scripture, is around. Homer alone, and even Plato and Aristotle are not yet literature, either. That is to say, they do not have the sense of faceless depth of the past. These thinkers and writers alone therefore do not suffice for bringing logic into view or to make it a worthy pursuit. Perhaps this is why Aristotle does not have logic as a separate discipline either.

In intermediary sum, literature, logic, and modern hermeneutics of texts are born from a marriage between Homer and Bible which Auerbach helped describe. Logic and literature became rivals and both attempted attracting modern hermeneutics of texts on their respective sides.

3. Starting Point Two: Temporalities of Suspension

Let me now no longer use theory to think literature, but instead read literature to think theory. Let me begin, this time not from a theory of literature as before, but from reading a piece of literature, which would help shedding light on the theory. Franz Kafka's short piece, 'Er' ('He') provides a literary articulation of the powers of time Auerbach's theory of literature is dealing with. I will use a short line from the piece as an opening for this section:

> He had two opponents. The first besieged him from behind, from the origin [while pushing] ahead. The second denied him any way forward. He fought the both.
> ['Er hat zwei Gegner: Der erste bedrängt ihn von hinten, vom Ursprung her. Der zweite verwehrt ihm den Weg nach vorn. Er kämpft mit beiden.']

Kafka's character, 'He' as well as the piece, 'He,' is without doubt 'literary' by Auerbach standards, for the text does contain both explicit and inexplicable parts. Gesturing towards the inexplicable, Vivian Liska[11] asks about the source, the ground, the room, or the power in which or by which 'He' can fight. 'He's' sense of time is remarkably different from both Hermann Cohen's and Martin Heidegger's sense of time – for, in the latter thinkers, time has only one power, the power of the open future, from which time is coming, and which therefore creates its secondary effects, such as past as a necessary virtual starting point and present as no more than a secondary product of that virtual past. For these philosophers, such temporality is of course complex, but quite clear. For Kafka, however, the power of 'He' to fight both the past and the future, and in that sense to suspend the both, remains unthinkable and in that sense unclear in origin.

Despite, and precisely because of this, 'He' provides a helpful starting point to think the suspension, namely to ask about the source of its power.

Walter Benjamin's notion of the power of citation further helps to begin to approximate an inexplicable, and thus 'literary' (Auerbach) part of the suspension at work. To render Benjamin's take on citation, to cite is to destroy. First of all, it means to destroy the past which has never been present by making it present, even if only in the past. In Benjamin, that means to create *Niegewesende,* or 'that which has never been;' that is to say to bring the past to a closure, following Arendt's interpretation. Even if conceived as fantastic, such cited past is still committing a closure; it still effaces, that is to say both gives face and erases the faceless depth of the past. 'He' thus draws 'He's' power to fight precisely from that destructive side of citation. Citing past He destroys the past's power, and thus becomes able to fight the pressures of the past. Ostensibly, He does the same to the future. At work is a destructive side of citation: it is not only a fulfillment – let alone a substitution of the past by a *praesens historicum*, and not only an anticipation of the future to come, but also a destruction of the faceless past, as well as a destruction of a predictable future. Temporality of such suspension captures that double movement in how NT is suspending OT.

But suspension of OT in NT works in yet other – perhaps less radical but no less crucial – ways:

a. *Aufhebung* (sublation) in Hegel. That notion both applies to and stems from the concept of NT.

b. *Ausnahmezustand* (Suspension/Exception from the Law in Schmitt. That notion applies to and again stems from how Paul is read in Church Fathers through the lens of NT).

c. 'Hesitation' in Moses and Paul. In that, I follow Taubes' Rabbinic and anti-Schmittean reading of Paul.

d. 'Subversion' (in Galit Hasan-Rokem's reading of the story of Meir as God and God as Meir in *Leviticus Rabbah,* of which the *Palestinian Talmud* has a parallel version to be read slowly in a section below.)

e. Suspension means a spaceless cesura (Agamben): a Catholic and – in Taubes' terms – teleological reading of Paul; the caesura leaves room neither to love (which otherwise could undo the teleology of both hope and faith, in Taubes) nor to any resistance to forces moving to a goal, *telos*, one sets in advance.

f. Suspension means making room for life, for the space of life (Arendt,) which, as already briefly indicated, a *philosophic,* rather than literary reading of Kafka.

g. Suspension means literature as existence inside and despite the two powers of time, in Vivian Liska's interpretation of Kafka's 'He.'

The staccato of such competing attempts to think the power of citation and thus the power of suspension of OT in and by NT helps to begin to understand both the complexity and the elusive nature of what is at work in suspension of a new testament in the *Talmuds*, and what can be its temporality and/or structure. That both intimates and makes necessary a new disciplinary framework in which to think the powers of literary citation and of theological suspension together, and through which to draw on these powers in the discipline of philology and its 'powers' (Gumbrecht, again.) That takes me to my third and last starting point.

4. Starting Point Three: Political Philology[12] Precedes Political Theology

I am almost ready to approach the case study at hand. There is one last starting point on the way there. Now it explicitly has everything to do with what I was either implicitly or all too briefly engaging from the very start, with the relationship between political philology and political theology. This is a starting point in a double sense. Here, well into the middle of my argument, I start from a point which takes me to where one should be starting. I start from the discipline of philology and arrive to a thesis that political philology precedes political-theology, including both the literary and philosophical versions of political theology of suspension listed in the staccato above.

It is not only that, as Gumbrecht helps see, philology or curatorship of texts is a political move. It of course is – if not empirically, and even if not conceptually, then foundationally. Philology executes its powers, the 'powers of philology.' Neither is it only that the audience, the on-stage characters, the off-stage characters, the writers – and all the multiple audiences the 'texts' articulate, imply, induce, excite, or create – form an aesthetical (and by extension we learn from Kant) ethical stage of action, which the 'powers of philology' are to help to discern. Rather, it is also that the powers and the stage of action of 'texts' belong to what different followers of Kant – from Arendt to Schmitt – described as 'the political' – a dimension of the 'curatorship of texts,' which still awaits the attention of scholars.

The political, as one of Kant's followers, Carl Schmitt together with his rabbinically minded radical enemy (that is to say, more than merely an adversary and/or rival) Jacob Taubes[13] collectively help establish, is all about the form. A form always, of course, comes with content, but a 'political form'[14] is such that it tolerates many changes in the content without losing the core of the form, its ability to represent power regardless of any – even mutually exclusive – content it takes. Importantly to what follows, Taubes and Schmitt radically differ in where an individual stands in the works of political form. Schmitt makes an individual insignificant. Taubes, instead, in his analysis of Paul and Moses, pays most close attention to the invisible structure of the inter-personality, even between God and Moses, and surely between Paul and Israel, (which I would not be in hurry to call inter-subjectivity,) an inter-personality that comes with the political as a form. In that, in the present argument, I take Taubes' side. The individuality and interpersonality on the stage the Talmudic pericopae induce are all-important, and are still awaiting discernment.[15]

That renders the task of political philology of the *Talmuds* as the task of paying a much closer attention to the formal structure of the action of the characters in the 'texts' than the 'text-curatorship' afforded so far. One way to arrive to that formal political aspect of philology is to slow down or to turn on the procedure of reading slowly, a procedure that is complimentary for, but not reducible to, either reading closely (Strauss[16], Wimsatt-Beardsley[17], Halivni[18]) or to reading distantly (Moretti[19], Septimus[20]).

More generally, reading slowly and finding ways, in which to reach a political philology of the two *Talmuds* also means moving backwards in time, as scholars always did but not always sufficiently accounted for.

The three starting points – literary, hermeneutical, and political – lock in and interlock the case study to follow.

5. A Case in Suspending the Testified Rules of a Law of 'Suspected Adulteress'

Political philology thus always precedes political theology. Political theology (exemplified by Schmitt and Taubes as two rival schools) already presumes a political philology. Both Schmitt and Taubes approached NT; they both formulated a political theology as an outcome and the core of how they read NT, for Schmitt, or NT and Mosaic Scripture, for Taubes, in philological terms. Importantly, it is from reading these texts along (Schmitt) or against the grid (Taubes) of suspension of OT in NT that the political theology of these thinkers emerged.

At stake in a political philology that underlies their political theology is the question of where does a rule (as a testimony/testament to the law of the past) stand in regard to that law. It is the problem of law and rule. Can a verbally formulated rule be the law coming from the faceless past and/or can such a rule be the divine law? This question will be also central in the case study below.

In thinking about that general problem of law and rule, my general preliminary thesis is that if the corpora of both the *Bavli* and the *Yerušalmi* are considered '*Talmuds*,' that is to say internally coherent tractates centered around either the *Mišnah* (the *Bavli*) or around other formulations of the law in the rules and/or acts (the *Yerušalmi*) then a discussion about either their break one from another or their continuity becomes possible, and has already come to fruition.[21] In contrast, if the *Bavli* and only the *Bavli* is axiomatically considered centered on a codified testimony of the divine law, on the code called 'Our *Mišnah*' (מתניתין,) i.e. on a given formulation of the law of the faceless past in the form of a code of rules witnessed in a testimony or testament; and if it is only *Bavli*'s practice to probe and refute but ultimately to defend and thereby remember these codified rules to confirm/establish their status as the second[22] divine law, the Oral Law of the *Mišnah*, then the texts of the *Yerušalmi* can be interrogated differently. That different approach would mean asking: do the compositions in the *Yerušalmi* either initially or finally approve any testified rules, or do they instead act to suspend any formulations of the law, if it comes in the form of a rule?

The suspension thus (in whichever way it is construed – and how exactly it is in each corpus is a question for future analysis of which I am only making first steps here) is heavily at work in any formulation of law in the form of rules. And this is precisely what is at stake: to suspend any formulation of the law as a rule.

Instructively, in light of this question, the *Yerušalmi* would display an approach different from either *exegesis* or *isogesis* of Mosaic Scripture in *midraš*. In terms of its political form, that approach is not *midraš*, because *midraš* (per Azzan Yadin analysis, for one[23]) does not need any second law. Scripture is already the law, but scripture, in the economy of *midraš* is anything but a formulation/citation of that law in a court.[24]

Instead, at least some places in the *Yerušalmi* display precisely this: the characters perform the suspension of any formulation of the law in a form of a rule or a set of rules. The tone seems to be (to borrow in advance a theme from the text-study below) 'these are the rules of *Soṭah*-ritual; let's suspend them' in the *Yerušalmi*, as opposed to 'there are rules the *Soṭah*-ritual, let's defend them and let's show their consistency across the corpus of all the rules in the code and the apocrypha we can get testified,' in the *Bavli*.

The question then becomes how does the suspension work in the *Yerušalmi* and what does it represent? Can we just borrow Christian theologeme of suspension of OT in NT to think about how the characters in the *Yerušalmi* suspend the testified citations of the law in the form of rules and/or acts? Can a Christian theologeme of suspension work for that purpose?

Reading Slowly: the Political Form in the Bavli: the Mišnah as a Testimony of the Law?

Looking at how a testimony is put to a test in the *Bavli* is a work of a slow reading. I first proceed with a reading of the following record in *Soṭah* 7a:

> היו מעלין אותה לבית דין הגדול שבירושלים ומאיימין עליה כדרך שהן מאיימין על עדי נפשות ואומ׳ לה בתי הרבה יין עושה הרבה שחוק עושה הרבה ילדות עושה הרבה שכנים הרעים עושים אל תעשי לשמו הגדול שנכתב בקדושה ימחה על המים etc.[25]

> [*Mišnah*:] They used to bring her up to the great court that was in Jerusalem and admonish her in like manner as they admonished witnesses in capital punishment cases, and they said to her, 'My daughter, much [sin] is wrought by wine, much by light conduct, much by childishness, and much by evil neighbors; do thou behave for the sake of his great Name, written in holiness, so that it be not effaced through the water.' (Danby translation, slightly modified.)

A *Tann'a*, a mechanical reciter, who is the only type of a witness to offer a testimony of the oral law in a rabbinic court or a rabbinic house of study, offers her testimony. In this case, the law is cited in the form of acts of a court at the time of Jerusalem Temple. The Rabbinic court now turns on, as well. The judges in that latter court, or if one prefers, the students and teachers in the house of study are to decide whether to accept the testimony or to dismiss the witness. Their decision is of course not based on *ad hominem* argument against the personality of the reciter or *Tann'a*. Just as, in Schmitt's political theology, a personality of a representative of Church or even of a political sovereign is irrelevant in the political form of representation which is all about the dignitary office, rather than about individuality of its bearer, so too is the personality of the reciter. Her personality, in other words, is tellingly irrelevant. The personality of the reciter-witness, as mechanical as her memory might or even is supposed to be, is out of consideration of the judges, who perhaps by the same logic of political representation are the most politically important but surely least embodied characters on the stage. They have no names, and even their number is not explicitly defined. By extrapolation from other Rabbinic texts, the judges can be three, or twenty-one, or even seventy. The judges probe the validity of the testimony by attempting to see if it is refutable and if its defendable against a valid refutation. A general principle of the judges' deliberation articulates more clearly only centuries later, and is therefore only an approximation. In that approximation, however, the principle is as follows. If totally refutable, the testimony becomes invalid and must be dismissed. If totally irrefutable, the testimony must be dismissed as well. The only acceptable testimony is the one that can be both refutable and defendable. That of course might, and *de facto* does, mean several rounds of probing.

Upon having heard such testimony/testament of the law, the judges, in *Soṭah* 7b deliberate on whether to accept that testimony in the court.

Round 1 A rhetorical question?

מנהני מילי א"ר חייה א"ר יוסי בר 'חנינא אתיא תורה תורה כתיב הכא ועשה לה הכהן את כל התורה וכתיב התם על פי התורה אשר יורוך ועל המפשט מה להלן בשבעים ואחד אף כאן בשבעים ואחד:[26]

Whence such words? Rabbi Ḥiy'a said Rabbi Yosi in the name of Rabbi Ḥanin'a said, there is an analogy between two chapters in the Scripture, each using the term 'torah.' Here [in describing the *Soṭah* ritual in *Leviticus* 5] it says, 'And the Priest will do to her all the *torah*...' And there, [in describing other matters judged by the Priests and Levites in *Numbers* 17] it says, 'according to the *torah* which they shell teach and according to the judgment.' Just as there it is done in the court of seventy, so too here in the court of seventy.

I will read it slowly. The first round of refuting and defending begins with what is an almost rhetorical question, 'Where these words are coming from? מנהני מילי.' This question would be fully rhetorical if the answer could have come from the judges themselves, i.e. from those on stage. Yet the judges are not entitled to answer for a witness. Instead, an invisible, bodiless, and completely silent agent on stage calls up for another witness, who provides yet another testimony to serve as an answer. According to that testimony, Rabbi Yosi Bar Ḥanin'a drew an exegetical analogy between two sections in Scripture, one about a priest administering the ritual of *Soṭah* (in *Numbers* 5, in particular 5:21) and another about a rebellious sage (in *Deuteronomy* 17:11, where Priests and Levites, in plural, are mentioned as instructing the judgment.)

אתיא תורה תורה...

A judgment by analogy can be derived from a similarity in wording between two verses in the Scripture...

Rabbi Yosi Bar Ḥanin'a draw an analogy from a thematically different place in *Numbers* to the thematically relevant place in *Leviticus*. The analogy is that just as the rebellious son matters require a full court of 70, so too, the other matters of the *Soṭah* are to be judged in the full court of 70.

(It is quite possible that this analogical judgment of *midraš* was formulated in a different context and for a different purpose; yet it is clearly cited here to assure the judges on the stage that the suspected adulteress shell be brought to the court in Jerusalem, just as the reciter proscribed.) At any rate, citing Rabbi Yosi Bar Ḥanin'a downplays the initial refutation – מילי מנהני ('Whence such words?') – by converting it into a merely rhetorical question with an obvious answer – obvious not for the judges yet, but as the readers are to believe, for Rabbi Yosi Bar Ḥanin'a, of course. That transforms the initial problem into a rhetorical question. In turn, that reduction of a refutation to a rhetorical question concludes the first round and allows the judges to move on to examine other parts of the testimony of the reciter. The best way to undermine an attack on the *Mišnah* is to convert the attack into a trivial, rhetorical question. The first part of the *Mišnah* becomes thereby re-approved.

The judges on the stage now move on to the second part of the testimony of the law in the *Mišnah*, '[the judges] admonish her the way they admonish the witnesses in capital punishment cases.'

Round 2 Testimonies Clash

> ורמינהו כשם שמאיימין עליה שלא תשתה כך מאיימ׳ עליה שתשתה אומ׳ לה בתי אם ברור לך שטהורה את עמדי על בורייך ושתי לפי שאין המים המאררים דומין]אלא [לסם יבש שמונח על בשר חי אם יש שם מכה מחלחל ויורד אין שם מכה אינו מועיל כלום לא קשיא כאן קודם שנמחקה המגילה כאן לאחר שנמחקה המגילה [27]:

> [The judges] called up another reciter. [She recited,] Just as they shell admonish her so that she would not drink [the cursed water] so too they shell admonish her so that she would drink it. They say to her, 'My daughter, if it is clear to you that you are pure, you should stand in front of your creator and drink [the cursed water] for these cursed waters are like a dry poison which is placed on a healthy flesh. If there is a wound, the poison is getting in and down, but if there is no wound the poison has no effect.'

The reader and the judges are to believe now that this was not a valid refutation of the initial testimony in the *Mišnah* because the *Mišnah* was referring to a point in the *Soṭah*-ritual before the Holy name is effaced by the water, and the testimony at hand to a point in the ritual after that.

That second attempt to refute the *Mišnah* was turned on by considering a possible refutation of it. If one objects by calling up another testimony, in which the suspected adulteress is not only *discouraged* to drink the cursing waters (as the *Mišnah* had it) but is also *encouraged* to drink them (as the *Mišnah* did not), the defense would proceed by claiming the applicability of the *Mišnah* to an earlier stage in the ritual only, while allowing the other testimony to apply to the ritual in all stages thereof, one by one. That move first of all created and second of all alleviated the contrast between the *Mišnah* and the other testimony. The judges called up an apocryphal text to counter the precision of the testimony of the reciter at hand. In the previous case, judges could not argue for the testimony and thus needed a citation to be brought in front of them by somebody else. Now, however, they argue against the content of the recited, and this was their procedural right to call up a testimony against a testimony. They thus call up another reciter, i.e. another testimony in order to attack the testimony at hand. That concludes 'Round 2.'

The two rounds already indicate that the discussion in the *Babylonian Talmud* is centered on the *Mišnah* as a testified code of the cited law; a conclusion, which is hardly contested in the scholarship on the *Bavli*. Even if some pericopae in it may not begin as immediate responses to the *Mišnah*, they nevertheless are centered on the *Mišnah*, and, more specifically on the validity of its testimony, at the end.

The centrality of the *Mišnah* as a codified testimony of the law in the form of rules and/or acts thus proves to be a formal principle coextensive with the principle of moving through refutations and counter-refutations in the *Bavli*'s discussion. Both are animated by an effort to decide on the acceptability of the *Mišnah* as a testimony in a version in which it arrives to the court. Despite seeming openness of such an approach, it means a formal-political attempt to validate the testimony of the *Mišnah*, rather than to dismiss it all together.[28] For convenience, I term this connection between formal principle of refutation and a no less formal political preference to remember the *Mišnah* better rather than to have it dismissed 'a principle of *Mišnah*-centrism.'

It is beyond the scope of this essay to explore further aspects of this *Mišnah*-centrism by reading the balance of the pericope in question slowly enough to show the dynamic of the relationships between the almost disembodied political characters of the judges on stage and the much more embodied but no less politically necessary number of the off-the-stage characters, such as R. Ḥiya and Rabbi Yosi Bar Ḥanin'a. Such reading would describe more specifically the formalism of the political action of the almost bodiless judges on stage, in their pure political form of accepting or dismissing the testimony of the law in its politically complex delivery as a cited law. I therefore stop here and move on to the parallel composition in the *Palestinian Talmud*.

6. From *Mišnah*-Centrism to Suspending New Law (The Political Form in the *Palestinian Talmud*)

I am now moving backwards from the *Bavli* to the parallel pericope found in the *Yerušalmi*. I had to say 'found in the *Yerušalmi*' because I am neither attempting to derive conclusions about the *Yerušalmi* as a whole, nor presume in advance that the *Yerušalmi* is a whole (such an assumption would be similar to how the authors of *Tosafot* construed the *Bavli* to be a tractate of tractates, as coherent within itself as it therefore, for them, had to be.) Instead, I read slowly, rather than either closely or distantly. In this case, it means reading even slower than the implied reader of the parallel pericopae in the *Yerušalmi* would. That implied reader had so far either read the *Yerušalmi* as 'just another *gemor'ah*' that is to say according to the habits and expectations such a traditional reader would have developed in reading the *Bavli*. In contrast, in reading slowly, I follow, and work against the grain, of the path of the scholarship on the *Yerušalmi* that moved from the *Yerušalmi* to the *Bavli*. In this venue, the scholars argued either that *Bavli* is radically different, or that what we find in the *Bavli* is only a further development of that which the *Yerušalmi* already had.[29] Yet, unlike this line of scholarship, the path of slow reading proceeds backwards, from a pericope in the *Bavli* to that in the *Yerušalmi*, now in order to highlight the formal political – and thus political-philological – difference in the role of not only the *Mišnah* but also of all *Tann'ay*itic material in general in the discussion that the almost disembodied on-stage characters in the pericope are performing.

Reading A Palestinian Stage, Slowing Down

What can a reader say about the nearly disembodied characters on the stage when the flesh and blood characters, such as R. Ḥiya, or R. Yosi, or R. Chanina in the *Bavli* composition, are taken as they are, that is as characters off the stage? This path is easier and is already traveled to some extend in the *Bavli*, including my own exposition above. The *Yerušalmi* however presents new challenges to the task. This path is much harder to travel when it comes to the stage *Yerušalmi* presents.

The *Yerušalmi* arrives to us organized according to the order of the *Mišnah*, thereby creating an impression that it is also *Mišnah*-centric. Yet, leaving the question of the positioning of the record below in the larger corpus aside, the action in p. *Soṭah*, Folio 4, chapter 1, *halaḵah* 4 begins, as it does, without any direct invocation of the *Mišnah* material.

Rather, the on-stage action begins with an invisible, bodiless and speechless character(s) who summon a *Tann'a* to recite 'Just as [the priests and/ or judges] are admonishing/coercing/persuading/ her 'to withdraw her claims' of innocence in what her husband alleged her to have committed,[30] so too they are admonishing/coercing/persuading her not to withdraw such a claim of innocence.' A *Bavli*-oriented reader would assume this testimony would be a gloss or even an attack on the *Mišnah*, because the *Mišnah* describes and/or prescribes coercion in one direction only (see the analysis of the *Bavli* above.) However, there is nothing in the *Yerušalmi* action on stage to necessitate that assumption.

What is more, the performance on the stage is of a rather different nature – it is not to contrast or cohere between the two testaments of the rules of the same law of the *Soṭah*-ritual, but rather to suspend, although of course not to destroy, the citation of the rule of the priestly *Soṭah*-ritual all-together. As we will see, it is done on the stage by summoning another testimony, a testimony of an act, the one about what an off-stage character, Rabbi Meir committed.

The invisible, bodiless and voiceless characters on the stage now summon a report, a testimony about acts of a number of the off-stage characters – a story about Rabbi Meir, his female student, and her not-so-well-educated husband, as well as about Rabbi Meir's male students. It is a story of domestic jealousy, and of Rabbinic resistance to allegations made by that not-so-well-educated husband about his wife for having listened to Rabbi Meir's teachings.

The story, which I will immediately translate, is staged in the domain of the priests, in a synagogue, where, nevertheless, a rabbi, not a priest, expounds the scripture. The husband's impatience of and resistance to education in general, or at least to education of a woman, threatens to turn on the priestly ritual of the *Soṭah.*

The story continues to show that it is the noble role of the rabbi to go as far as to humiliate his own honor and/or office publicly in order to turn the ritual off, whatever the testimony of the details of that ritual might be. That, however, once again, does not deny the validity of the ritual, for this is not a concern. The story suggests that it is better to erase the name of a learned sage than to let the priest capitalize on the jealousy of an ignoramus, the husband. At least this is what the implied audience is able to see, that is to say if such an implied audience is not already immersed in the Babylonian concerns about defending the accuracy of the record of the *Mišnah*.

In terms of form, such staging of the pericopae – from a *Tann'ay*itic citation to a Rabbinic act – performs a suspension of the priestly ritual by a peculiar means of rabbinic self-restrain from executing authority. Again, as we will immediately see, Meir would rather erase his name, and outdo G-d[31] in that, then humiliate either the wife by the *Soṭah*-ritual or the husband with lashes for suspecting the rabbi of an undue relationships with the wife. This is along the same lines in which, in Taubes, Moses and Paul restrain themselves from assuming any position of direct political leadership.[32]

I arrive to these formulation and conclusions through the following verbal interpretation and analysis of pt. *Soṭah* Folio 4, chapter 1, *halakah* 4, Sussmann edition, pp. 908-909:

היו מעלין אותה לבית דין הגדול שבירושלים כול׳ כשם שמאיימין עליה שתחזור בה כך ממאיימין עליה שלא תחזור בה. ואומ׳ לה. בתי אם טהורה את. דבריא לך שאת טהורה. עמדי על בורייך. שאין המים האילו דומין אלא לסם יבש שהוא נתון על גבי בשר חי ואינו מזיקו. מצא שם מכה התחיל מחלחל ויורד.

ר׳ זבדה חתניה דר׳ לוי הוה משתעי הדין עובדה.

ר׳ מאיר הוה יליף דריש בכנישתא דחמתא כל לילי שובא. והוה תמה חדא איתתא יליפה שמעה קליה. חד זמן עני דריש. אזלת בעית מיעול לביתה. ואשכחת בוצינא מי טפי. אמ׳ לה בעלה הן הוייתה. אמרה ליה מישמעא קליה דדרושא. אמ׳ לה. מכך וכך דלית ההיא איתתא עללה להכא לבייתה עד זמן דהיא אזלה ורקקה גו אפוי דדרושא. צפה ר׳ מאיר ברוח הקודש ועבד גרמיה חשש בעייניה. אמ׳. כל איתתא דידעה מלחוש לעיינה תיתי ותלחוש. אמרין לה מגירתא. הא ענייתיך. תיעלין לביתיך עבדי גרמיך לחשה ליה ואת רקקה גו עייניה. אתא לגביה. אמ׳ לה. חכמא את מלחוש לעיינא. מאימתיה עליה אמר ליה לא. אמ׳ לה. ורוקקים בגויה שבא זימנין והוא טב ליה. מן דרקקה אמ׳ ליה אזלין אמרין לבעלך חד זמן אמרת לי. והיא רקקה שבע זימנין. אמרו לו תלמידיו. ר׳. כך מבזין את התורה. אילו אמרת ל!ו !לא הווית מייתי ליה ומלקין לה ספסליה ומרצייין. ומרצייה ליה לאיתתא.אמ׳ לון. ולא יהא כבוד מאיר ככבוד קונו. מה אם שם הקודש שנכתב בקדושה אמ׳ הכתוב שיימחה על המים בשביל להטיל שלום בין איש ואישתו. ובבוד מאיר לא כל שכן.

In Neusner's translation, heavily amended:

[I:1 A] Just as [the judges] admonish her to withdraw [her claim of innocence,] so they admonish
her not to withdraw [it]. And one says to her, ‘Now my daughter, if [it is perfectly clear to you that] you are clean, hold to that, and stand before your Creator [and drink.] For these waters are like a dry salve which is put on living [=healthy] flesh and does no harm, but if there is a wound, it penetrates and goes through.
[I:2 A] R. Zabedeh, son-in-law of R. Levi, would tell the following story.
[B] R. Meir would derive an expounding [from reading the Scripture] in the synagogue of Hammata every Sabbath night. There was a woman who would come regularly to derive from listening to his voice. One evening the expounder struggled with time [i.e. lasted longer than usual.]
[C] She went back home, wanted to enter but found that the flame had gone out. Her husband
said to her, ‘Where have you been?’
[D] She replied to him, ‘I was listening [in]to the voice of the expounder.’
[E] He said to her, ‘May it be such-and-so and even more, if this woman

enters my house before she goes and spits in the face of that expounder!'

[F] R. Meir perceived with the help of the Holy Spirit [what had happened] and he developed a boil in his eye.

[G] He said, 'Any woman who knows how to recite a charm over an eye — let her come and heal mine.'

[H] The woman's neighbors said to her, 'Look at your affliction. Go back home. Prepare the healing mixture, recite charms over it, and spit it in his [R. Meir's] eye.'

[I] She came to him. He said to her, 'Do you know how to heal a sore eye through making a charm?'

[J] She felt admonished and said to him, 'No.'

[K] He said to her, 'Do they not spit into [the mixture or into the eye?] seven times, and it is good for the eye?'

[L] After she had spit in there, he said to her, 'let them go and tell your husband, 'You told her to spit one time, and this woman did seven times!

[N] R. Meir's disciples said to him, 'Rabbi, in such a way do they disgracefully treat the Torah [which is yours]? If you had told us [about the Incident with the husband,] would we not have brought him and flogged her [sic!] at the stock [to bend his will,] until he was [willing to] reconcile with his wife?'

[O] He said to them, 'And should not be the honor of Meir as the honor of Meir's creator? Now if the Holy Name, which is written in a state of sanctification, the Scripture has said is to be effaced with water so as to bring peace between a man and his wife, should not it be even more obvious that the honor of Meir is to be dealt with in the same way!'

Notably, the disciples of Rabbi Meir resist not only the effacement of Rabbi Meir's title or name. They also, and perhaps more strongly, both resist and share his concern with the applicability of this citation, and by extension any other citations of *Soṭah*-ritual in any form of a testament and/or testimony. That resistance finds an expression in their making Rabbi Meir a clearly absurd proposal in [N] to have 'brought him [i.e. the husband – S.D.] and flogged *her*' in order to stop the husband suspecting her in improper relationship with the rabbi. Quite ostensibly the disciples accomplish that by making a parody of the cited *Soṭah*-ritual. The ritual proposed to humiliate the wife in order to deal with the husband's suspicions. To resist that, the disciples sarcastically propose to do even more, to flog her for the same purpose. Although clearly, in the story, Rabbi's Meir's strategy of suspending the ritual wins over his disciples' strategy to take the ritual to an even greater extreme, and thus show it was absurd in the first place. The story thus displays two lines of resistance to a citation of the rule of the law of the past here. One is Rabbi Meir's; another is his disciples'. He is ready to outdo (and protect) G-d by effacing Meir title and name in public. They are ready to show to him that taking the cited rule as seriously as he did leads to absurd. As the story ending makes clear, Rabbi Meir, and with him the strategy of suspending the citation rather than dismissing it as an absurd one wins over.

Comparing with the parallel place in the *Babylonian Talmud* above, the composition in the *Yerušalmi* shows no concern with contradictions to the *Mišnah* (a *Bavli* concern – in general and in the parallel place *Soṭah* 7 ab – 8a, as above.) But in the *Yerušalmi ad locum*, there is a concern with limiting the use of the law of the *Soṭah* as it comes in a testimony, either in the *Mišnah*ic one or, as is the case here, in the apocryphal testimony of the law. It is a concern about taking the cited/testified law for the authentic law of the past. This concern is expressed here twice. First of all, it is by offering to go to such a satiric extreme as offering Rabbi Meir to flog the wife to test the firmness of the husband's suspicions against her (that is to say reducing the cited law to absurdity); and second of all, by Rabbi Meir, who is rather taking the cited law seriously enough to suspend it by sacrificing the honor of his office in order to suspend, that is to say neither deny nor apply the cited version of the law of *Soṭah*-ritual.

The story makes the case for avoiding the *Soṭah*-ritual at all costs, even at the cost of the sage's stripping off from his title (Rabbi Meir becomes Meir) and even at the cost of losing his personal name and dignity (Meir is ready to outdo G-d, in sacrificing his personal name.) On the surface, the sage becomes ready to let his name and title be 'erased' or effaced by public humiliation just as G-d is ready to let His name erased or effaced by water. In both cases the effacement of the name is for the sake of making piece between husband and wife. Yet it also means a sage is willing to humiliate (lit. 'erase' or 'efface' his honor not to get G-d to the point of letting G-d's sacred name written in sanctity to be erased ('wiped out') by the *Soṭah*-ritual, either.

At the bottom, as the on-stage action suggests, the *Yerušalmi* here is against activating the cited *Soṭah*-ritual on (even in theory) as opposed to, and as a response to the *Mišnah* and the *Barayt'a* where this ritual becomes much crueler and much more humiliating as compared to how it is described in the Scripture. Even more importantly, the *Yerušalmi* here displays a response to presenting the law of such a ritual in the form of a cited rule delivered as a (by definition new) testament in the form of either the *Mišnah* or the apocrypha. The *Yerušalmi* thus tames or suspends the citation of the law of the past in the rule.

7. Conclusion

To conclude or rather to indicate whereto and how the argument is to continue, the Babylonian and the Palestinian versions of suspending new testament differ one from another. The Babylonian version of suspension is *Mišnah*-centric. The very efficacy and possibility of witnessing the law as a codified set of rules is accepted, and only the accuracy of these testimonies, however competing and contrasting they might be one against another, remains in question. The Palestinian suspension is much more radical: in the case analyzed it suspends all *Tann'ay*itic materials, apocryphal, and by extension, *Mišnah*ic ones. It thereby suspends any possibility to formulate the law which comes from the faceless depth of the past in a testimony in the form of a rule.

This radical suspension of any testimony of the law that comes from the faceless depth of the past entails a political philology which is suspending – that is both enacts and restrains – the powers of citation. Unlike Kafka's 'He' the power and the direction of that resistance to citing law is not in directing the citation against itself, but rather in suspending the applicability of any citation i.e. of any testament of the law of the past in the first place. The political philology of such a suspension precedes, grounds, exceeds, and escapes the political theology of suspension of one testament in or by another. This is a suspension neither Kafka nor Benjamin nor any other versions of suspending of OT in NT can account for. These thinkers are necessary but not sufficient. They account for the power of citation to foreclose the faceless depth of the past, but they do not account for the power to suspend that foreclosure, a power which the political philology of the *Palestinian Talmud* helps to discern.

The Rabbinic compositions I read, therefore, are 'literature' in Auerbach's sense, yet the marriage between faceless depth and the façade, between the law of the past and citing it as a present gives birth, in this case, to a different kind of suspension, the suspension of any new testament, that is to say of any testament whatsoever. To that, Auerbach did not – and perhaps programmatically could not – attend; for, his notion of literature follows the lines of a more familiar path of suspension, the suspension of OT by NT. Furthermore, and along the same lines, even if Auerbach had political philology and political theology, his political philology followed his political theology, not the other ways around.

Where, then, does it leave hermeneutics of text vis-a-vis the 'literature' in Auerbach's sense? Does that allow continuing reading the *Talmuds* under the rubric of hermeneutics of texts? And where can formal logic reside when applied to reading rabbinic texts, if, as oriented to the explication, to the facade, and to the face as it is, that logic claims to be able to read and interpret the facade of a (new) testament/testimony of the law, which however comes, as it does, from the depth of the faceless past?

Can one conceive hermeneutics of text that suspends any testament, rather than taking any testament, and thus any text at its face-value, or according to its formal value, or else as prefigured or otherwise fore-thought by a text that is coming from the imagined before? If logic has, as it conventionally does, anything to do with hermeneutics of texts, the questions become: Can logic either enter in or get out from the circuit of the traditional theologeme of suspending one testament by another? Can one conceive of hermeneutics of texts and/or of formal logic there, where the political philology of suspending any testament is to come first?

References

1. Auerbach, Erich. *Figura*. [New York]: [Meridian Books], 1959.
2. Auerbach, Erich. *Mimesis: the representation of reality in Western literature*. Princeton: Princeton University Press, 1953.
3. Boyarin, Daniel. *Socrates and the fat rabbis*. Chicago: The University of Chicago Press, 2009.
4. Gumbrecht, Hans Ulrich. *The powers of philology: dynamics of textual scholarship*. Urbana, Ill: University of Illinois Press, 2003.
5. Harnack, Adolf von, and John Richard Wilkinson. 1925. *New Testament studies. VI. The origin of the New Testament and the most important consequences of the new creation*. London: Williams & Norgate, 1925;
6. Hayes, Christine Elizabeth. *Between the Babylonian and Palestinian Talmuds accounting for halakhic difference in selected sugyot from Tractate Avodah zarah*. New York: Oxford University Press, 1997
7. Liska, Vivian. *Giorgio Agambens leerer Messianismus: Hannah Arendt, Walter Benjamin, Franz Kafka*. Wien: 'Schlebrügge.Editor,' 2008.
8. Schmitt, Carl. *Political theology: four chapters on the concept of sovereignty*. Cambridge, Mass: MIT Press, 1985.
9. Schmitt, Carl, and G. L. Ulmen. *Roman Catholicism and political form*. Westport, Conn: Greenwood Press, 1996.
10. Septimus, Zvi. *The Poetic Superstructure of the Babylonian Talmud and the Reader It Fashions*. UC Berkeley: Jewish Studies. [Ph.D. Dissertation], 2011.
11. Strauss, Leo 'How to Study Spinoza's 'Theologico-Political Treatise'. *Proceedings of the American Academy for Jewish Research*, Vol. 17. (1947 - 1948), pp. 69-131.
12. Taubes, Jacob, and Aleida Assmann. *The political theology of Paul*. Stanford, Calif: Stanford University Press, 2004.
13. Waite, Geoffrey 'A Short Political Philology of Visceral Reason (A Red Mouse's Long Tail),' *Parallax*, 2005, vol. 11, no. 3, 8–27.
14. Yadin, Azzan. *Scripture as Logos Rabbi Ishmael and the Origins of Midrash*. Philadelphia: University of Pennsylvania Press, Inc., 2011.

Notes

1. This essay was first conceived as a contribution for the University of Krakow October 2016 conference on Talmudic Hermeneutics. A part of a further developed version was presented at the Association of Jewish Studies in San-Diego in December 2016. I thank Andrew Schumann for the initial invitation and for organizing the conference in Krakow. I further thank Zvi Septimus, James Redfield, Galit Hasan-Rokem, and Bruce Rosenstock for conversations and discussions of the materials in this essay. I would also like to thank Vivian Liska for a series of conversations that Fall, which have mainly indirectly but no less powerfully informed my argument. Preparation of this paper for publication was made possible with the assistance of funds from The University at Buffalo Gordon and Gretchen Gross Endowed Professorship in Jewish Thought.

2. Similar to a phoneme or morpheme, which are elements contributing to, but not limited to, any particular linguistic expression, for example to a sentence, theologeme is an element contributing to, but not limited to, any particular theology. Thus, the theologeme of NT suspending OT informs a horizon of theologies about NT and OT. Both (1) supersessionism or a Christian view of OT and of Jews as atavism or an obstacle on the way to accepting NT, and (2) denial of supersessionism of OT as having been never abrogated and still true for the Jews, as mutually exclusive as these two positions are, still belong to the same horizon of Christian theological thinking. The following formulation of Harnack helps illustrate how the theologeme of suspension tacitly informs that horizon. In his outline of 'motives" leading to creating the New Testament as a document, Harnack writes, 'The third motive belongs … to Saint Paul and to those who learned from him. It finds expression in such words as these: 'Christ is the end of the Law," 'The Law is given by Moses, Grace and Truth came through Jesus Christ," and the like. Pauline Christians, and many that were not Pauline, were convinced that what Christ has brought with him, in spite of His connection with Old Testament, was something 'new" and formed a 'New Covenant." The conception of the 'New Covenant" necessarily suggested the need for something of *the nature of a document*; for what is covenant without its document?" (Harnack, Adolf von, and John Richard Wilkinson, 1925; p. 12-13.) The 'in spite" in Harnack's formulation is the key of suspension. To wit: To be 'convinced" 'in spite of His connection with Old Testament" i.e. with Scripture that Messiah's life and death in Gospels is a record of New Covenant of Grace and Truth is automatically and tacitly positing the canonical Scripture to have become 'old." That positing happens before and predetermines 'the motive," which Harnack outlines. The motive is always already a fulfillment of that tacit positing. This is why Harnack's explanation of the motive is both necessary and insufficient. Missing is the recognition that the new creates the old, a recognition of the theologeme of suspension at work here. The formal theologeme of the 'new" creating the 'old" came before 'the motive." The latter was only a concretization of that theologeme in a concept, or rather in several, even mutually exclusive ones. Supersessionism or the idea that NT makes OT atavism is one such concretization. Denial of supersessionism is another. Yet they both stem from one and the same non-linear theologeme of suspension, and both attempt to concretize that theologeme in a linear way.

3. Cf., for one: Schmitt 1985.
4. See Waite, 2005.
5. See: Auerbach, 1953.
6. Cf.: Auerbach, 1959.
7. I follow the volume's standard of Hebrew characters transliteration, except for common terms, such as *midraš* and *Yerušalmi*, which are already coined in their English spellingю
8. Idem.
9. Gumbrecht, 2003.
10. By way of a contrasting clarification in passing, according to Auerbach that would be not only and not simply about the past that has never been present, but even about that past that has no face.
11. See an analysis of these lines by Kafka in: Liska, 2008. I am also citing Kafka from this edition.
12. I am following and, to say the least, extending the notion of political philology articulated by Geoffrey Waite, 2005: vol. 11, no. 3, 8–27. pp.
13. Cf.: Taubes, Jacob, and Aleida Assmann. 2004.
14. The term comes from Schmitt, 1996.
15. I have begun working in this direction in my forthcoming *The Political in the Talmud* (Fordham U. Press, 2017) where I addressed Carl Schmitt, but not Jacob Taubes.
16. Leo Strauss 1947-48; pp. 69-131.
17. W.K. Wimsatt, Jr., and Monroe C. Beardsley. 1954.
18. Halivni, Daẓid. 2012.
19. Moretti, Franco. 2015.
20. Septimus, Zvi. 2011.
21. I refere here to scholarship on comparative study of the two Talmuds beginning from Saul Lieberman and continuing to its implementation in Christine Hayes, where *Yerušalmi* is considered to be foreshadowing *Bavli*. See the analysis and bibliography in Hayes, 1997.
22. The question of the *Mišnah* as 'second law" becomes even more interesting and more important, if thought of in view of Greek dismissal of any articulated law as inferior to any divine law. The latter is immediately given to humans, the former takes human articulation either in writing (Scripture) or in speech (Recitation of the *Mišnah* by heart). Both would be secondary to the Greeks, an approach Antigone, who insisted on preferring diving unspoken and unwritten law to the man-made edict of Creon, can clearly illustrate. In this perspective both Scripture and the *Mišnah* are secondary, even if such an approach misses the style of Mosaic Scripture, in Auerbach's term, i.e. misses the faceless depth of the past, by thinking face can mean law immediately, before one writes, reads, and/or memorizes.
23. Yadin, Azzan. 2011.
24. In that way, *midraš* as an approach to Scripture, can escape any 'Greek" dismissal of Scripture as a formulation of law in a rule.
25. Kaufman A 50.
26. Vatican Ebr. 110-111.
27. Ibid.
28. See: Boyarin, Daniel. 2009.
29. Hayes, Christine Elizabeth. 1997.

30. You will note the difference with the *Bavli* version, where it is about to admonish her ‘not to drink” and then ‘to drink.”
31. See the analysis of the narrative by Galit Hasan-Rokem at: Hasan-Rokem, Galit. 2003.
32. Notably, but also beyond the immediate scope of this essay, Jacob Taubes reads both Paul and Moses, relying as he is, upon rabbinic *midraš* in order to highlight Moses suspending God’s wrath against Israel.

The Genesis of Arabic Logical Activities: From Syriac Rhetoric and Jewish Hermeneutics to āl-Šāfi‘y’s Logical Techniques

Hany Azazy

Faculty of Arts,
Ain Shams University,
Arab Republic of Egypt
hany.moubarez@art.asu.edu.eg

1. Introduction

He who tries to write a history of the earlier informal Arabic logic has to do two things: (1) reconstruct the historical facts concerning its development, and (2) reformulate it formally[1] according to that reconstruction. Thus, (1) is a necessary step for (2). In this paper I shall concentrate only on (1) letting (2) for further research. The reason for (1) is due to that most of the accounts we have about it were not intended to be a definite history of the Arabic informal logic but as a complementary history to other branches of study such as history of Islamic law (for example: [82, ch.9] [35] [45, ch.3] [98, ch. 2]).[2] Furthermore, these accounts disagree with each other[3] as a result to the paucity of the resources or its fabrications. Thus, the historian of informal logic is compelled to reconstruct history on his own, introducing to this process some hypotheses and theories about the real history and the mental activities such as the translation movement and how texts transform as we shall see in due course.

However, the history of informal Arabic logic could be written through four disciplines: (1) Islamic law and exegesis (of the Scripture), (2) Arabic rhetoric, (3) Arabic and Islamic theology, and (4) Islamic peripatetic, especially its commentaries on Aristotle’s *Topics* and *On Rhetoric*. In this paper, I shall trace its development only through Arabic and Islamic law, exegesis and rhetoric. That is because these disciplines were the first ones to formulate laws and rules of the informal logic in Arabic. This happened in the Arabic translation of Aristotle's *On Rhetoric* (which was made by Syriacs) on the one hand and in āl-Šāfi'y's *Risāla* on the other.

2. A preliminary Outline of the Development of the Logical Activities of the Semitic Peoples

Up to the middle of the seventh century C.E., and at the eve of the prophet Muḥammad's death (d.632), the Semitic peoples had been having three logical traditions: (i) the Hebrew informal logic[4] which founded in the first millennium by Hillel the Elder and developed into two traditions, one in Palestine ('Aqiva's tradition) thriving in its *yešhivah*s, and the other in Mesopotamia (Yišm'a'el's tradition) growing in Pumbedton and Sura *yešhivah*s,[5] in addition to Yemen.[6] The later tradition adopted strongly Hillel's seven rules for interpreting the Bible; i.e. '(1) an argument *a fortiori* (*qal wa-ḥomer*), (2) an argument by analogy (*gezerah šawah*), (3) a generalization (*binyan av*) based on one instance, [a generalization based on] two instances, (4) universal and particular terms, (5) particular and universal terms, (6) analogy drawn from another passage, and (7) the conclusion drawn from the context' [91, *San*. 7.11]. The first six of these are (informal) logical rules. Yišm'a'el, however, extended them to be thirteen rules. For the purpose of lucidity, these rules shall be called the Rabbinic sequence and shall be abbreviated as RS from now on, (ii) The second logical informal tradition arose at about the middle of the second century C.E. due to the Syriac polemical theology initiated by the writings of Tatian (d.172)[7] and Ephrem of Edessa (d.373),[8] and (iii) The Syriac formal logic tradition which started off in the sixth century C.E. with translations of Porphyry's *Eisagoge* and Aristotle's *Organon* [32, pp. 42; 115 – 116; 122].

The Arabs, up to this period, did not have a logical tradition. This only developed about two centuries later when they had an articulated informal logic thanks to āl-Šāfi'y (d.820). How can this be explained? Answering this question means providing a history of the development of that tradition. However, we have three theories: (1) The first theory stipulates that the rules of the informal logic of āl-Šāfi'y are a result of independent evolution of the methodological practices of earlier ancestors' jurists without any foreign influence. Thus, 'having had so many developments that it became mature to a great extent, the method [informal logic] was handed down to āl-Šāfi'y... who analyzed and presented it in an organized way' [11, p.83]. (2) The second theory considers that āl-Šāfi'y borrowed his informal techniques from the Rabbinic traditions via earlier jurists. This theory which was first articulated by Margoliouth [68, pp.73 – 97] and then defended by Schacht [83, p. 13], and followed by many others (for example: [97], who claims that the influence is direct and without mediation, p. 67), is based either on (a) the existing similarity between the two used terms for analogy, i.e. *qiyās* in Arabic and *heqqeš* in Hebrew [67, p. 320] [82, p. 99] [83, p. 14], both of them mean literally measurement, or (b) on 'striking parallels with the Talmudic method' [97, p. 60] i.e. the fact that there is the same succession in RS and āl-Šāfi'y's rules. (3) The third theory argues that āl-Šāfi'y borrowed his rules either from (a) the Iraqis who borrowed them from the Babylonian Rabbis [93, pp. 17-20; 23-25], and either (b) Aristotle's *prior analytics* to the extent that *qiyās* (definitely analogy not the *a fortiori*) is a form of Aristotelian syllogism [*ibid*., pp. 14 – 16] or (c) from Aristotle's *Topics* [1].

The first theory cannot be adhered to, because the cultural diversity of the Islamic civilization compelled us to assume the fact of foreign influences on Arabic and Islamic disciplines. Although the second theory seems to be reasonable, there is no strong evidence for it. Concerning its (a), the linguistic and philological analysis alone is not enough for proving the borrowing, especially as the *Palestinian Talmud* employed the term *heqqeš* in a way different from how the Babylonians employed it, i.e. the *heqqeš* in the *Palestinian Talmud* was an attempt to search for the common element,[9] while *heqqeš* for the Babylonians (Yišm'a'el's School) was analogy of the judgement as a result to 'the proximity of two terms within a verse' [27, p. 82]. Given that most of Muslim jurists in the earlier period were living in the Arabian Peninsula or Mesopotamia, and that 'In applying *qiyās* the Kufians seek the element which is common to both the original and the assimilated case' [23, p. 209], this theory needs more scrutiny. Concerning part (b) of this theory, we do not find any sequence in āl-Šāfi'y's *Risāla* like the RS one. In *Risāla* K: 122 – 125,[10] āl-Šāfi'y speaks about *qiyās* mentioning only analogy without any hint to the *a fortiori* argument. In *Risāla* K: 179 ff., he talks about the general and the particular after mentioning the importance of the Arabic language in understanding the *Qur'ān* but not as a term in a sequence. In *Risāla* K:1482 ff., when he mentions the *a fortiori* followed by analogy, there is no mention after this to the rest of RS. The same criticism of (2-a) can be applied to part (a) of the third theory. Its part (b) is either unacceptable or unreasonable. It is unacceptable because if Triyanta meant[11] Ibn āl-Muqaffa''s translation of an incomplete epitome of prior analytics [36, pp. 63 – 93] [87, p. 530], we find a great difference in the terminology, Ibn āl-Muqaffa' does not use the term *qiyās* at all; instead he uses the term '*ṣan'a*' for syllogism [36, p. 64] given that Ibn āl-Muqaffa' himself uses the term *qiyās* for another mode of inference different from syllogism, i.e. analogy.[12] And it is unreasonable because if Triyanta meant the later translation of *Prior Analytics* by a certain Theodore, then it should be noted that this translation appeared in the ninth century only [88, p. 533], probably after āl-Šāfi'y's death (in 820). If Triyanta tried to reduce āl-Šāfi'y's analogy to *Prior Analytics*' syllogisms, Abdel-Rahman tried to reduce āl-Šāfi'y's the *a fortiori* to Aristotle's *Topics*. Thus, the (c) of the third theory seems probable especially that Timothy's (d.823) translation of *Topics* was current (about 782; [42, p. 61]) even in the time before āl-Šāfi'y's arrival to Baghdad (about 795; [34, p.182]). But the difference in the number of the *a fortiori* rules in *Topics* – Aristotle defines seven rules for the *a fortiori* in his *Topics*, ii, ch.X, 114b 37 – 115a 2 while in āl-Šāfi'y's *Risāla* there are only three [(*Risāla* K: 1483 – 1485] – makes this part of the theory also improbable.

In order to explain the rise of the informal logical tradition in āl-Šāfi'y oeuvre we need: (1) to reconstruct the Islamic legal and exegetical activities after Muḥammad's death on the one hand, and (2) to reconstruct also the earlier history of the translation movement in the Islamic civilization on the other hand. Both of these reconstructions will allow us to discuss the rise and development of the informal logical tradition in āl-Šāfi'y's *Risāla* and how he was influenced by RS and the Arabic translation of Aristotle's *On Rhetoric*.

3. The Islamic Legal and Exegetical Activities After Muḥammad's Death and the Earlier History of the Translation Movement in the Islamic Civilization

After Muḥammed's death and the extension the Arabic empire through many territories, the caliphs faced the problem of judicature between the members of the conquering tribes. In Muḥammad's days, believers used to obey his injunctions, but now faced new situation because they had new facts without Muḥammad being there. However, these first caliphs appointed many officers and judges who were judging, in addition to the *Qur'ān*ic injunctions, according to customs and previous traditions and they were using their own opinions in some cases [47, p. 55]. 'Umar I (d.644) himself supported their using of their opinion (*ra'y)* by using analogy in a famous letter[13] to Ābw Mwsā āl-Āš'ary: '(1) Know the likes and the similes (2) then measure things /اعرف الأشباه والأمثال، ثم قس الأمور عند ذلك' [7 *ii*, p.49]. The authenticity of This letter was apt to doubt by many scholars in the first half of the last century because it was contained 'the most weighty arguments of the defenders of *ra'y*, who endeavoured to fabricate for its validity an old tradition, and an authority going back to the earliest time of Islam' [41, pp. 8 – 9] as Goldziher claimed. But after then, other scholars such as Bravmann [31, p. 179 *ff.*] considered it trustworthy because of the identification of *rā'y*, *'ilm* and *'ijtihād* in earlier Islam. In fact, as we shall see, both of them are not right; the passage number (1) in which 'Umar I talks about the likes and similes is genuine, till here Bravmann is right, but the second part of the citation (2) where 'Umar I talks about *qiyās* is not genuine. This can be deduced from the continuation of the letter where we find 'Umar I saying ‘and adopt the judgment which is most pleasing to God and most in conformity with justice so far as you can see / ثم اعمد إلى أحبها إلى الله، وأشبهها بالحق فيما ترى’ [7 *ii*, p. 49] [67, p. 312]. this passage is in nearly coincidence with Ibn āl-Muqaffa‘’s criterion for choosing amongst analogies:

> *qiyās* is a tool for inferring good things, if it led to what is good and known it should be taken, but if it leads to what is bad and denied it should be abandoned; that is because he who uses *qiyās* is not pursuing only *qiyās* but the good and known things and what is assigned as justice by its people.
>
> وإنما القياس دليل يستدل به على المحاسن، فإذا كان ما يقود إليه حسناً معروفاً أخذ به، وإذا قاد إلى القبيح المستنكر ترك لأن المبتغى ليس غير القياس يبغى ولكن محاسن الأمور ومعروفها وما ألحق الحق بأهله
> [53, p.317].

Thus, ‘the defenders of ‘*ra*ʾ*y*’’, as Goldziher said, fabricated the second part of the cited passage (2) to enforce their position.

However, this letter is a keystone for discovering the evolution of the Arabic intellectual movement (translation movement) and the transmission of the Rabbinic logical tradition into the Arabs and Islamic legal system as we shall show.

3.1. ‘Umar I and the Translation Movement

‘Umar I was not illiterate, ‘he was reading the books’ [61 *iii*, p. 248] [cf. Also, 20 *iv*, p. 201]. Moreover, he had always been interesting in the Bible or the ancient religious books[14] and Jewish narratives,[15] he was even copying the Bible,[16] he also permitted to Tamym āl-Dāry (d.660) to tell religious stories[17] in the mosque, and let the Jewish Rabbi Ka‘b āl-Āḥbār[18] (d.653) and the scholar most influenced by Jewish traditions, i.e. Ibn ‘Abbās (d. 688),[19] have been the most prominent members of his circle. These facts make us infer that ‘Umar I was a man of culture,[20] especially that he was alleged to have had important role in collecting the *Qur*ʾ*ān* [61 *ii*, p. 307] [50 *i*, p. 166].[21] Although Muḥammad’s objection to his reading and copying books,[22] when he became a caliph he made the translation of the Bible more disciplined than it was at Muḥammad’s time.[23] Thus, we can infer that he established the first translation movement in the Arabic and Islamic civilization from the other Semitic languages into Arabic[24] as a result to his previous interest in the scripture on the one hand and the need to understanding the *Qur’ān*ic hints to the Semitic stories on other hand. The two figures who mainly carried the burden of this movement were the Yemenites Tamym āl-Dāry and Ka‘b āl-Āḥbār. As the early Muslim society was as yet unfamiliar with organized institutions, story-telling was the first way of translating; hence the translation was oral not written. Thus, ‘Umar I gave permission for āl-Dāry to narrate in the mosque, he did so also with Ka‘b,[25] and the secretary of this movement was Ibn ‘Abbās,[26] and it is not surprise that Ibn ‘Abbās’ family had the legal guardianship on Ka‘b[27] (he was their *mawlā*).

But which books were being translated by Ka‘b and the others? By answering this question we can at least partly solve the problem of how āl-Šāfi‘y was influenced by the Rabbinic logical tradition. The answer also will let us get rid from what I would call it *the ḵaldwnian hypothesis*, i.e., that the first Muslims were influenced only by Jewish oral recounts and superstitions,[28] anecdotes [2, p. 1] or at best some isolated sayings of the Rabbis (from the *Talmud*) [40, pp. 40; 44].

There are two books candidates to have been translated orally by ‘Umar’s translation movement, i.e. *Avot de Rabby Natan* or *The Fathers according to Rabbi Nathan* version A (henceforth referred to as *ARNA*) and the *Toseft’a*. In this paper I shall concentrate only on *ARNA* sayings and themes from which many passages were frequently cited by and from ‘Umar’s secretary of the translation movement (Ibn ‘Abbās) and his circle and the adherents of this heritage. If we are able to prove this, it will be easy to prove in addition the transition of the Rabbinic hermeneutical sequence through this book to the early Arabic and Islamic legal traditions, and then to āl-Šāfi‘y, because *ARNA* contains that sequence.

To wit: What I shall do would run as the following: Firstly, I shall prove that ‘Umar’s translators transmitted this book into Arabic through embedding it in some of the prophet’s traditions on the one hand, and through its influence on Ibn ‘Abbās and his circle on the other. Then, I shall show the influence of the Hebrew logical tradition on Ibn ‘Abbās and his circle. Secondly, I shall show how most of ‘Umar’s translators were Yemenites which implies the spread of this book and the Rabbinic logical tradition in Yemen. Thirdly, I shall trace āl-Šāfi‘y’s biography to show how he was indirectly influenced by the Jewish logical tradition and how he amended it and why.

3.2. The Fathers in Arabic and Islamic Traditions

We have two versions of *The Fathers according to Rabbi Nathan*: A and B. Though *ARN* has a Palestinian origin, both of its versions were known to the Babylonians [80, pp. 16 – 18]. Some scholars even think that version A may have been written in Babylonia [*ibid*., n. 44]. Because of this, Version A then is our target, and it is thought to have probably been compiled sometime between the seventh and ninth centuries [39, p. xxi]. This would be sufficient for it to be known for Ka‘b and the Jews of Yemen. We know that Ka‘b āl-Āḥbār had books other than the *Torah*,[29] and he possibly belonged to a Rabbinic tradition,[30] therefore it is probable that *ARNA* was one of these books. What supports this is the following sentence of a certain exilarch to the Muslims about Ka'b: 'what Ka'b told you about what shall happen is from Israel's prophets and their companions as you tell from your prophet and his companions / ما حدثكم كعب بما يكون، فإنما هو من أنبياء بنى إسرائيل وأصحابهم كما تحدثون أنتم عن نبيكم وأصحابه'[55 *l*, p. 171].[31] These sayings of 'the companions of the prophets' could not be anything other than the books of the Rabbis, and *ARNA* is one of these books. Moreover, I shall prove now the influence of *ARNA* in the fabricated prophets' traditions and in Ibn 'Abbās and his circle opinions.

However, such influence happened on three axes, literal translation, translating the meaning and transmitting themes of *ARNA*.

But first of all, I have to refer briefly to a methodological problem about the traditions which we are going to depend on (and also to the ones we have quoted so far). Some of these traditions are relating to the sayings of the prophet (*Ḥadyṯ*), and others are relating to the exegetical and legal traditions, especially of Ibn 'Abbās' traditions. On the whole, there are three positions concerning the authenticity of these traditions weather in respect of their content (*matn*) or ascription (*'isnād*).[32] The first position is extremely skeptical about them. Thus, Schacht thought that 'legal traditions from the Prophet began to appear, approximately, in the second quarter of the second century A.H.' [81, p. 145], and 'traditions from Companions, too, were put into circulation during the whole of the literary period, including the time after Shāfiʿī' [82, p. 150]. Wansbrough [96] extended this skepticism to all types of Islamic literature before the third century A.H. [96, pp. 52, 78, 88, 92, 97, 98, 101],[33] including Ibn 'Abbās' traditions [*ibid*., p. 158]. Thus, A. Rippin [78] claimed that we cannot know anything about what happened in the first two centuries of Islam [78, p. 157].[34] The second position accepts most traditions after applying philological methods on them[35] [29, pp. 21 – 23; 72] [71, pp. 35 – 36]. Thus, F. Sezgin believes in the authenticity of the books which were attributed to Ibn 'Abbās [2, p. 17]. However, we cannot accept this second position, the quasi full trust in the traditions is not acceptable, Rippin's analysis of the alleged Ibn 'Abbās books according to methodological and philological considerations seems to be correct.[36] But on the other hand the skepticism of Wansbrough is not acceptable either; we cannot imagine a sudden appearance of the written Islamic literature at the beginnings of the third century A.H. without there being a background for that emergence. This brings us to the third position. This position, on the whole, claims that if we denied the authenticity of the traditions, we could accept that the ideas which lie behind them go back to the earlier Islam. Thus, U. Rubin expresses this position concerning the prophet's sayings as follows: 'But the fact that traditions cannot be dated earlier than 100 A.H. [719 C.E.] does not mean that the *ideas* reflected in them were not circulated prior to 100 A.H. The lack of documentation does not mean non existence. In other words, the dates of traditions and the dates of exegetical ideas must be considered separately' [79, p. 149]. Schoeler and his school believed also in the possibility to reach to the ideas of the first century A.H. by *isnād* cum *matn* analysis.[37] Thus, the sayings of the prophet or of Ibn 'Abbās express on traditions, in the technical meaning of this term,[38] therefore it will not come as a surprise to find that even some of the words of Ibn 'Abbās' sayings were kept sometimes literally in the minds of their transmitters as I shall show. This position seems plausible and it is our position in this paper, and our reconstruction will prove it. It is the time now to show how *ARNA* influenced Ibn 'Abbās and his circle.

3.2.1. The Literal Translation

I shall display in this subsection only two traditions, the first one is attributed to Ibn 'Abbās and the other to the prophet:

> 'قال ابن عباس: العلماء يتغايرون / Ibn 'Abbās said student of the *Qur'ān* are jealous'[39]

In *ARNA* we find the same wording: 'היו עושין מקנאין זה לזה/they [students of the *Torah*] acted jeaously toward each other.'[40]

The following second tradition I divided it into two divisions, the first division does not interest us here, though I shall discuss it in the next subsection of translating by meaning.

'...عن أنس مرفوعاً: '(a) العلماء أمناء الرسل على العباد (b) ما لم يخالطوا السلطان/ ... from Ānas tracing in back to the prophet '(a) Students of the *Qur'ān* are secretaries of the messengers for the worshipers, (b) unless they make intimacy with ruling powers'.'[41] In *ARNA*, we find: 'ואל תתודע לרשות / Do not make intimacy with the ruling powers' (my translation).[42]

However, it should be noted here the following:

1. Both the verbs תתודע and تخالطوا are verbs in the increased conjunctional form, and both of them are close semantically, i.e. acquaintance, affinity, knowledge, intimacy and communion.
2. The meaning of the Arabic word *āl-sulṭān* does not signify a king, this was a later development,[43] but it signifies power, authority or sovereign,[44] and this is the same meaning of רשות, hence I translated it in both of the texts as ruling powers. (Nuesner, J. [77], was translating it sometimes as authority, pp. 84-5, and sometimes as sovereign, p. 84)
3. *ARNA* continues 'for once his name comes to the attention of the ruling powers,' (Goldin's [39] trans. P.62). This sentence has close

relationship to the concept of intimacy or *āl-mukālaṭa*[45] in the Arabic tradition.

4. Again, *ARNA* continues 'they cast their eye upon him and slay him,' (*ibid.*). This we shall find in another tradition transmitted by Abw-Hurayra, but the translation will be by meaning.[46]

3.2.2. Translating the Meaning

The following traditions are translations from *ARNA* by meaning; I shall first provide the Arabic tradition then its equivalent(s) in *ARNA*:

1.
ابن عباس مرفوعاً يا إخوانى تناصحوا فى العلم ولا يكتم بعضكم بعضاً...
[16 *i*, p. 207].

Ibn 'Abbās tracing in back to the prophet 'O my brethren, do advice each other in learning and do not conceal it from each other'.

רבי מאיר אומר אם למדת מרב אחד אל תאמר דיי אלא לך אצל חכם ואחר ולמוד
תורה [26, p. 16]

Rabbi Meir says, If you have studied the *Torah* with one master, do not say, 'That is enough,' but go to another sage and study the *Torah* (Nuesner's [77] trans., p. 33).

והוי מתאבק בעפר רגליהם כיצד בזמן שתלמיד חכם נכנס לעיר אל תאמר איני
צריך לו אלא לך אצלו ואל תשב [26, p. 27]

AND SIT IN THE VERY DUST AT THEIR FEET: how so? When a scholar comes to the city, say not 'I have no need of him.' On the contrary, go and sit with him (Goldin's [39] trans. With my modification.).

2.
... عن أبى هريرة، قال: قال رسول الله:'من ولى القضاء، أو جعل قاضياً بين الناس، فقد ذبح
بغير سكين
[17 *iii*, 1325].

...Abw Hurayra said: The messenger said: 'Whoever become a judge or is appointed as a judge for the people, has been slain without a knife'.

כיון שיצא לו שם ברשות סוף גותגין בו עיניהם והורגים אותו
[26, p. 46]

For once his name comes to the attention of the ruling powers, they cast their eye upon him and slay him (Goldin's [39] trans., p.62).

3.

... عن أبى عمران الجونى، عن عبد الله بن الصامت، عن أبى ذر. قال: قال لى النبى ' لا
تحقرن من المعروف شيئاً، ولو أن تلقى أخاك بوجه طلق'

[74 *i*, 2626)

... From Abw ʿimrān āl-Jawny, from ʿAbdallāh b. āl-Ṣāmit, from Abw Ḏarr. He said: The prophet told me '(a) Do not disdain anything of the good, (b) even if you were to receive your brother with a cheerful face'.

In *ARNA* we find:

והוי מקבל את כל האדם בסבר מקבל יפות כיצד מלמד שאם נתן אדם לחברו כל
מתנות טובות שבעולם ופניו כבושים בארץ מעלה עליו הכתוב כאלו לא נתן לו
כלום אבל המקבל א ת חבירו בסבר ס נים יפות אסילו לא נתן לו כלום מעלה עליו
הכתוב כאלו נתן לו כל מתנות טובות שבעולם

[26, p. 57]

AND RECEIVE ALL MEN WITH A CHEERFUL FACE: what is that? This teaches that if one gives his fellow all the good gifts in the world with a downcast face, Scripture accounts it to him as though he had given him naught. But if he receives his fellow with a cheerful face, even though he gives him naught, Scripture accounts it to him as though he had given him all the good gifts in the world. (Goldin's [39] translation, p.73. with my qualifications).

We should note the following points of the last tradition and its equivalent in *ARNA*:

a) The Arabic tradition can be divided into two units; (a) and (b). Also the *ARNA* divides into two units; (a) the text of the Talmudic father's tractate, (b) explanation.
b) The Arabic tradition kept *ARNA* text; but it brings the explanation first, then the main text of the Talmudic tractate.
c) The second unit of the Arabic tradition is nearly the same of *ARNA*'s first unit, it has even the same words, i.e. تلقى = **מקבל = receive. طلق = סבר = cheerful.**
d) Abw ʿImrān āl-Jawny is one of the transmitters on the authority of Abw āl-Jalad, who was influenced by the Jewish traditions and belonged to Ibn ʿAbbās' tradition.[47]

4.

... عن سلمة بن كهيل، عن هزيل بن شرحبيل قال: قال عمر بن الخطاب:'لو وزن إيمان أبى بكر بإيمان أهل الأرض لرجح بهم'
[3 *i*, Ḥ35].

... From Salāma b. Kuhayl, from Huzayl b. šuraḥbyl, from ʿUmar b. āl-Ḵaṭṭāb: 'If Abw-Bakr's faith was weight against the faith of the people of the world, his would outweigh them all.

הוא היה אומר אם יהיו כל חכמי ישראל בכף מאזנים ורבי אליעזר בן הורקנוס בכף שנייה מכריע את כלם [26, p. 58]

He used to say: if all the sages of Israel were in one scale of the balance and Rabbi Eliezer ben Hyrcanus were in the other scale, he would outweigh them all (Goldin's [39] trans., p. 75).

We should notice here the name of Salāma b. Kuhayl, who transmitted many traditions from Ibn 'Abbās circle,[48] in the Isnād chain. This is an indicator that that tradition was current in the Jewish circle of Ibn 'Abbās.

5.
...عن ثابت، عن أنس، قال: مات ابن لأبى طلحة من أم سليم، فقالت لأهلها: لا تحدثوا أبا طلحة بموت ابنه حتى أكون أنا احدثه ... قالت: يا أبا طلحة، لو أن أهل بيت أعاروا عاريتهم أهل بيت آخرين، فطلبوا عاريتهم أترى لهم أن يمنعوهم؟ قال لا؟
[3 *xii*, Ḥ9283].

From Ṯābit that Ānas said: 'A son of Abw Ṭalḥa by Umm Salym died, then she said to her family: 'Nobody should tell Abw Ṭalḥa about his son's death except me'...she said to him: 'O Abw Ṭalḥa, if some people lent others something, and then asked it back, do you think they will be allowed to refuse them?' He said No.'

In *ARNA*, we have the following advice from the mouth of Rabbi Eleazar to Rabban Johanan after the later had lost his son:

נכנס וישב לפניו ואמר לו אמשול לך משל למה הדבר דומה לאדם שהפקיד אצלו המלך פקמן . בכל יום ויום היה בוכה וצועק ואומר אוי לי אימתי אצא מן המקדון הזה בשלום .אף אתה רבי היה לך בן קרא תורה כקרא נביאים וכתובים משנה הלכות ואגדות ונסטר מן העולם בלא הטא ויש לקבל עליך תנחוכין כשהחזרת סקדונך שלם .[26, p. 59]

Rabbi Eleazar entered, sat down before him, and said to him:
'I shall tell thee a parable: to what may this be likened? To a man with whom the king deposited some object. Every single day the man would weep and cry out, saying: 'Woe unto me! when shall I be quit of this trust in peace?' Thou too, master, thou hadst a son: he studied the *Torah*, the *Prophets*, the *Holy Writings*, he studied *Mišnah*, *Halaḵah*, *'Aggadah*, and he departed from the world without sin. And

thou shouldst be comforted when thou hast returned thy trust unimpaired' (Goldin's [39] trans., p. 77).

We should note in the last tradition the name of Ṯābit āl-Bunany (d.123/741) in the chain of the 'Isnād. He has Yemenite roots [10 iv, p. 342], and Yemen was the principal supply for this early translation movement; he is also reported to have been a storyteller (*qāṣṣ*) [*ibid*., pp. 346-47].

6.
عن عبد الله بن عمرو، قال: قال رسول الله: ما من مسلم يموت يوم الجمعة أو ليلة الجمعة إلا وقاه الله فتنة القبر
[17 *ii*, Ḥ1074].

From 'Abdallā b. 'Amr that the messenger said: If a Muslim dies on Friday or the night of Friday, God will protect him from the grave's suffering.

מת בערב שבת סימן יפה לו.

If one dies on the Sabbath eve, it is a good sign for him (Goldin's [39] trans., p. 107)

We should notice in this tradition the following:

a) The parallelism between the Sabbath eve בערב שבת and the night of Friday ليلة الجمعة.
b) The Arabic tradition is attributed to the prophet on the authority of ʿAbdallāh b. 'Amr (d.683), who was known for his reading of the *Torah* books,[49] his acquaintance with Ka'b,[50] his relationship to Ibn 'Abbās' circle[51] (i.e. the translation movement) and the distinction between the written and oral (*Mišnah*) *Torah*.[52]

3.2.3. Transmitting Themes and the Rabbinic Sequence

The two most important themes of *The Fathers according to Rabbi Nathan* are the number seven and the hermeneutical theme as we shall see, but before displaying them I shall display another one as more evidence to translating *ARNA* and its influence on the Arabic intellectuals.

In *ARNA*, there is a theme in the chapters 1 to 14 about the transition of the *Torah* from Moses to Joshua to the elders to the Judges to the prophets to the men of great assembly to students of the *Torah*,[53] and after chapter 14 we read mainly the sayings of these students. This theme Ka'b transmitted to his colleague Abw āl-Dardā'[54] and the later put it on the tongue of the prophet as '…Scholars are heirs of the prophets / إن العلماء لهم ورثة الأنبياء' [8 *i*,

p. 105]. A second variant of this tradition is the first clause of Ānas' marfw' report: 'العلماء أمناء الرسل / Scholars are secretaries of the messengers' [16 *i*, p. 219], which we referred to before. However, it should be noted here that in the chain of the transmitters of the first *ḥadyṯ* there was one of the members of Ibn 'Abbās' Jewish tradition, i.e. 'Aṭā' Ibn Aby Muslim āl- Ḵurāsāny (d.752) [*ibid.*].[55] It should be noted also that Ka'b was interested[56] in the Qur'ānic verse which talked about bequeathing the book to the worshipers,[57] and his interest is mentioned in the context of his replying to the Rabbis who blamed him for his conversion to Islam. Thus, he was establishing a new generation of scholars by his contribution in 'Umar's translation movement, following *ARNA* steps.

In *ARNA* there is a complete chapter (Goldin's [39] trans. Ch. 37, pp. 152 – 157) about number 7, this I shall call the seven theme. This theme talks about how many things are arranged in seven levels. Thus, 'there are seven created things;' 'seven types of Pharisee;' seven things God created the world with; 'seven heavens;' seven characteristics for the righteous man, clod and wise men… etc…, we find this theme also with Ibn 'Abbās and his circle. Our claim here is in opposite to Goldfeld's opinion that the seven theme (especially in exegesis) only founded at the beginning of the second century A.H. [38, p. 20] by Ibn 'Abbās' disciples via introducing it on the mouth of Ibn Mas'wd [*ibid.*, p. 21]. But as I have referred before, we can assume that many of Ibn 'Abbās' traditions, not necessarily literally, probably go back to him, and Goldfeld believes in this too [*ibid.*, p. 8]. In addition, we have a tradition (see below) that goes back to Ibn 'Abbās himself concerning the number seven, therefore why would Ibn 'Abbās' disciples fabricate a tradition on the authority of Ibn Mas'wd while they have already at their disposal a tradition that goes back to their own master? Moreover, we find also the seven theme in 'Abdallāh b. 'Amr's traditions, which means it was so spread in early Islam that we can be sure that it were current due to 'Umar's translation movement. However, the tradition which transmits clearly the seven theme is running as follows: On the authority of Sa'yd b. Jubayr, 'Umar asked Ibn 'Abbās, while they were being amongst the immigrants, about determining the time of *laylat āl-Qadr*, then Ibn 'Abbās replied:

> God is an odd number and loves odd numbers, among his creation he has created seven heavens…, and he has created the earth in seven parts, and he has created the days to be seven in number, he has ordered the circling around the Ka'ba to be seven, throwing the stones to be seven, going and coming to Ṣafā and Marwā to be seven, he has created the human being from seven and, he has made his daily sustenance from seven.

الله وتر يحب الوتر، خلق من خلقه سبع سماوات... وخلق الارض سبعا، وخلق عدة الأيام سبعا وجعل طوافاً بالبيت سبعا، ورمى الجمار سبعا، وبين الصفا والمروة سبعا، وخلق الإنسان من سبع، وجعل رزقه من سبع,' [61 *vi*, p. 328].

After this, Ibn 'Abbās is going to interpret some *Qur'ān*ic verses according to that [*ibid*., p. 329]. In the *Musnad* of 'Abdallāh b. 'Amr as transmitted in āl-Ṭabarāny's *Mu'jam* we find much more application for that theme (for example: [18 *xiii*, Ḥ14172; Ḥ14173; Ḥ14195; Ḥ14248; Ḥ14260; Ḥ14299; Ḥ14358]). In some of these traditions, we have to notice the names of Ibn 'Abbās' disciples in the chain of Isnād, such as Ḥ14173; Ḥ14282; Ḥ14299 (Mujāhid), Ḥ14260 ('Aṭā'), Or the name of the Yemenite Wahb b. Munabbih Ḥ14358354. Other traditions do not contain Ibn 'Abbās disciples' names such as Ḥ14264, this fact confirms the authenticity of all these traditions as an expression of 'Abdallāh b. 'Amr and Ibn 'Abbās' opinion which both of them learnt from *ARNA* against their fabrications by Ibn 'Abbās' disciples as Goldfeld would have claimed.

The third thesis relates to the interpretation and understanding of scripture. However, *ARNA* 'is entirely devoted to the *'Aggadah*' (Goldin's [39] introduction, p. xviii), it is a book in and about interpretation.[58] By Ka'b's translation of *ARNA*, he also transmitted the importance of interpreting the *Qur'ān*. Therefore, it is not strange to find Ibn 'Abbās' concentration to have been in exegesis, and to have had a great reputation as interpreter to the *Qur'ān* (cf. [29, pp. 129 – 131]). Thus, Muqātil Ibn Sulaymān reports on the authority of Ibn Jubayr that Ibn 'Abbās said 'Learn interpretation (*tā'wyl*) before some people come and interpret it falsely / تعلموا التأويل قبل أن يجئ أقوام يتأولونه على غير تأويله,' [73 *i*, p. 26]. This exegetical attitude was surely a result of the influence of *ARNA* on Ibn 'Abbās because he saw that 'God did not send down a book without his wanting that its interpretation should be known / ما أنزل الله كتاباً إلا أحب أن يعلم تأويله' [*ibid*.]. This saying is in harmony with *ARNA* which is an invitation to interpretation. Also we have a fabricated *ḥadyṯ* on the authority of 'Ikrima that the prophet said 'O God, give Ibn 'Abbās wisdom and teach him interpretation' [61 *vi*, p. 322].[59] Thus, Ibn 'Abbās interprets Q3:79 'Be Rabbis,' as be 'wise and jurists,' [19 *vi*, 7313], and his disciples kept the same interpretation [*ibid*., 7306 – 7312] as a continuation for the master's tradition. Ibn 'Abbās also was known as 'the Rabbi of this community / رباني هذه الأمة' [61 *vi*, p. 347]. This identification of interpretation, wisdom and jurisprudence on the one hand, and the interpreter, Rabbi, jurist and scholar on the other hand is a sign of extending the Rabbinic tradition in the Arabic environment by the translation movement and evidence of an oral translation of *ARNA* which bears all these features. This supports my claim that the transition of informal logic to the Arabs was through *ARNA*, especially if we recognized that *ARNA* puts down the rules of interpretation of Scripture in ch. 37, and connects them with the number seven which also was adopted by Ibn ‘Abbās.

If we have a look at Ibn ‘Abbās’ method of interpretation we find it in harmony with these rules. In a recent study on the early interpretation of the *Qur’ān*, its author defines the method of Ibn ‘Abbās (and others) and his school in interpretation as follows: ‘Semantic similarity, that is, synonymy (*āl-’āšbāh*): In this technique, the exegete makes a semantic analogy between two *ayahs* through synonymy that exists between them either at the word level or at the thematic level.’ [2, p. 157]. This corresponds to RS: 2, 3, 6. The Method of Ibn ‘Abbās contains also ‘Explaining the generic by the specific,’ [*ibid*., p. 158].This corresponds to RS: 4 – 5. But what about RS:1? Here, we have to return to the history of early Islamic law. Ibn ‘Abbās was not only interested in the *Qur’ān*ic narrative's, but also in legal matters in it [38, pp. 15 – 16] [71, p. 287]. Thus, ‘lbn ‘Abbās, encouraged his students, such as Mujāhid and ‘Ikrima, to critically debate *Qur’ān*ic matters and provide their exegetical personal opinions, that is, to practise *’ijtihād* and *’istinbāṭ* in *Qur’ān*ic exegesis’ [2, p. 148]. This *’ijtihād* (independent reasoning) is nothing other than *Rā’y* (opinion) which prevailed in early Islamic Law [31, pp. 177 – 178]. However, this *Rā’y* contains many kinds of reasoning [*ibid*., p. 193] including of course the *a fortiori* or RS:1. And according to Bravmann [*ibid*., pp. 178 – 185] ‘Umar I himself was practicing *Rā’y*. This brings us back again to ‘Umar’s letter where he talks about the likes and similes as mental tools to the judge. Thus, ‘Umar I himself (and the earlier judges alongside with him) the sponsor of the translation movement seems to have been influenced by RS.[60]

Accordingly, the Hebrew informal logical tradition was transmitted to the Arabs within their legal activity and hermeneutics or exegesis of the *Qur’ān* through *ARNA* thanks to ‘Umar’s translation movement. And the informal logical rules of that tradition continued especially with Ibn ‘Abbās’ school and his disciples[61] until they were delivered to āl-Šāfi‘y who articulated them by the instruments of Aristotle’s *On Rhetoric*. In the next section I shall show how this happened.

4. The Influence of the Rabbinic Sequence and of Aristotle’s *On Rhetoric* on āl-Šāfi‘y

Ibn ‘Abbās’ tradition (in law and exegesis) was prominent in two centers, Mecca and Yemen. It concentrated on exegesis, law and translation. In Mecca there were ‘Atā' Ibn Abw Rabāḥ (d. 733), Mujāhid (d. 722), ‘Ikrima (d. 723) and Ibn Abw Mulayka (d. 735) [71, p. 287] and others. In Yemen there were Ṭawws (d.724), Salam āl-Ṣan‘āny (d.770) who were telling on the authority of Ṭāwws [61 *viii*, 2592] and Yuswf Ibn Ya‘qwb, [*ibid*., 2595], Hishām Ibn Yuswf[62] (d. 197) [*ibid*., 2600] ‘Abd āl-Razzāq (d.826) and his father [*ibid.*, 2601]. Also, there were who followed up Ka'b's translations or rather 'Umar's translation movement such as Munabbih's family (Wahb [d. 728],[63] Hammām (d. 132),[64] Ma'qil, and 'Umar) [*ibid.*, pp. 103 – 107] and Wahb āl-Zzimāry who 'read the books' [*ibid.*, 2579].

The first center was the place where āl-Šāfi'y studied [34, p. 182] and the other where he worked as an officer (including judgment) [4 *i*, p. 106] [34, p. 182]. Being in these two centers, which kept the Hebraic informal logic tradition, increases the probability of his being influenced by RS. However, in Mecca Ibn 'Abbās' tradition continued up to Sufyān Ibn 'Uyayna [71, p. 289], āl-Šāfi'y's teacher [37, p. 43] [34, p. 182]. Ibn 'Uyaynah kept 'Umar's tradition in informal logic, he was one of the chain of the transmitters of 'Umar's letter to Abw Mwsā āl-Ash'ary about how an officer should judge [8 *i*, 535], which has in it RS: 2, 3, 6. Also, he is reported to have said on the authority of 'Ubaydallāh Ibn Abw Yazyd 'whenever Ibn 'Abbās was being asked about something, then if it was in the *Qur'ān* he told it and if it was not but reported from the messenger of God then he told it, and if it was not in the *Qur'ān* and was not reported from the messenger of God *he formulated his own judgment based on his own opinion* / كان ابن عباس إذا سئل عن الأمر فإن كان فى القرآن أخبر به وإن لم يكن فى القرآن وكان عن رسول الله أخبر به، وإن لم يكن فى القرآن ولا عن رسول الله اجتهد رأيه' [61 *vi*, pp.33-34]. The last clause in this tradition '*he formulated his own judgment based on his own opinion /ijtahada rā'yuhu*' is nothing but RS: 1-3; 6. Of course Ibn 'Uyayna transmitted also to āl-Šāfi'y the RS: 4-5. But we notice here two things: (a) that āl-Šāfi'y uses the two terms 'general and particular' (*'āmm wa ḵāṣṣ*) for the RS 4-5 which did not happen in Ibn 'Abbās' tradition and Ka'b's translations, (B) Also he uses the term *qiyās* for RS 1-3; 6. This can be explained as follows:

RS:4-5, was already articulated with Muqātil by giving them their names: 'in the *Qur'ān* there are particular and general / فى القرآن خاص وعام' [73 *i*, p. 27]. And we know that āl-Šāfi'y said 'People are dependent on Muqātil in interpretation' [24 *iv*, p. 173]. This is an indicator about his borrowing Ibn Muqātil's terminology for general and particular.

āl-Šāfi'y studied also at Medina[65] which had a linguistic school influenced by Iraqi schools [89, p. 228] where the term *qiyās* was being used for analogy [95, p. 35].[66] And we know how āl-Šāfi'y was interested in the linguistic analysis of the *Qur'ān* [*Risāla* K 133-178], and his estimation of āl-Kisā'y (d. 799), one of the champions of grammatical *qiyās*,[67] is well known.[68] Thus, āl-Šāfi'y joint this term for RS: 1-3; 6.

But after his confrontation with Iraqis Jurists,[69] who we do not have any exact formulae for their methods, he felt that he needed to articulate his informal logical techniques (RS: 1-3; 6) which he inherited from Ibn 'Abbās' tradition. It seems that he found he could supersede the Iraqis by doing this, thus he says: 'who has no instrument at his disposal, has no permission to say anything in scholarship / 'فأما من لا آلة فيه فلا يحل له أن يقول فى العلم شيئاً' [15 *ix*, p. 17]. Somehow, when he was in Iraq[70] he had Aristotle's *On Rhetoric*, which was already translated from Syriac into Arabic, at his disposal.[71] This is what I shall prove now by analyzing his logical passages in his *Risāla* and their counterparts in Aristotle's *On Rhetoric*. And for the convenience, I shall abbreviate the Arabic translation of Aristotle's *On Rhetoric* as *TAR*, and when I quote from Badawi's 1979 edition [28] for this translation I shall abbreviate it as *TAR* B, while quoting from Lyons' 1982a [65] edition for the same translation will be abbreviated as *TAR* L. Also, I shall abbreviate the translated Aristotle as TA.

Along his writings, āl-Šāfi'y had only five explicit informal logical rules, three of them for the *a fortiori* argument, and the remaining two for analogy.[72]

4.1. āl-Šāfi'y's Three Rules of the a Fortiori

As we have said above, āl-Šāfi'y had three rules for the *a fortiori*, these rules are the same as in *TAR*. āl-Šāfi'y even cites them in the same order as in *TAR*, though he breaks Aristotle's first rule into two parts (Aristotle has only two rules for the *a fortiori* in his *On Rhetoric*: [24, 1397b12-25]. However, I shall prove that by citing first *TAR*'s rule then citing its counterpart in āl-Šāfi'y's *Risāla* showing how the later articulated his rules through *TAR*.

TAR's first rule = The first and second of āl-Šāfi'y's rules (the *argumentum a minore ad maius*).

***TAR*1.** 'فإما أن يثبت أنه إن كان الذى هو أقل، كان الذى هو أكثر / [E]ither to demonstrate that if it was the less then it would be the more' [*TAR* B, p. 155; *TAR* L, p. 149].

āl-Šāfi'y's first two rules are as follows:

> **Sh1.** فأقوى القياس أن يحرم الله فى كتابه أو يحرم رسول الله القليل من الشىء، فيعلم أن قليله إذا حرم كان كثيره مثل قليله فى التحريم أو أكثر، *بفضل الكثرة على القلة* / The strongest kind of *qiyās* is when God, in his book, or God's messenger, forbids a little of something, It is understood that since a little of it is forbidden, then a lot of it would be like a little of it in respect of its being forbidden, or even more so, *because of a great quantity is better than a lesser one* [*Risāla* K: 1483; Lowry's [64] trans., p. 153, except the underlined clause].

Sh2. 'وكذلك إذا حُمد على يسير من الطاعة، كان ما هو أكثر منها أولى أن يحمد عليه / Similarly, if it were praiseworthy to be obedient in a small way, then to do so in a greater *way* would be even more appropriately praise' [*Risāla* K: 1484; Lowry's [64] trans. p. 153].

We should here notice the following remarks:

1. āl-Šāfi'y has retained some of the very words in *TAR*'s text in his wording, i.e. *āqall* and *ākthar* in *TAR* and *kaṯyr*, *ākṯar*, *āl-kaṯra*, *qalyl* and *āl-qilla* in āl-Šāfi'y's wording.
2. āl-Šāfi'y's second rule (*iḏā ḥumida 'alā yasyr…*) is not valid,[73] It is valid only for prohibition. But āl-Šāfi'y as a faithful follower to *TAR* (as I shall show below) introduced it for both prohibition and permission.
3. In āl-Šāfi'y's formulation, there is no mention to subjects and predicates. This is because *TAR* has none of these terms. That means that āl-Šāfi'y's source was Aristotle's *On Rhetoric* not *Topics* as Abdel-Rahman [1] has thought. That also explains why āl-Šāfi'y did not adopt the subject-predicate scheme.
4. That the mentioned principle of *bi faḍl āl-kaṯra 'alā āl-qilla* is an Aristotelian principle; we have two places in which TA speaks about that principle. In [*TAR* B, p. 32; *TAR* L, p. 35] he says: ' إن السعة أفضل من القلة / large amount is better than little one.' Again, in [*TAR* B, p. 28; *TAR* L, p. 29] he says: 'لأن الأفضل أعظم من الأخس / because the best is greater than the least.' The synonymy of *āl-āfḍal*, *āl-si'a* and *āl-kaṯra* on the one hand, and the synonymy of *qilla* and *āl-āḵaṣṣ* on the other hand can be deduced from a later passage of *TAR* [*TAR* B, p. 137; *TAR* L, p. 133]:

   فأما الكبر والصغر فى الأمور ومعنى الأكبر والأقل وما هو خسيس ألبتة، أو كبير أو صغير ألبتة، فمعلوم مما تقدم من قولنا. فقد بينا فى ذكر المشورات عن عظم الخيرات، وعن الأفضل والأخس / Concerning the greatness and smallness in things, the meaning of the greatest and the less, and the least, the very great or the very small, all of these are known from what we said before. When we talked about deliberative advice we explained what is the greatness of the good things, the best and the least.

This is why I evaded Lowry's translation of *bi faḍl āl-kaṯra 'alā āl-qilla* as 'because of the [implied inferential] relationship of the greater to the lesser amount' [64, p.153]. The expression 'the implied inferential relationship' in Lowry's translation is not in āl-Šāfi'y's text. It is formal while āl-Šāfi'y's principle is rhetorical, religious, ethical and informal as in *TAR* (we should note here how the Syriac translator translated 'the least' as *āl-āḵas* which can mean also the vilest. Thus, there is an ethical connotation in the principle.).[74]

5. However, we find alongside every formulation of this (ethical) principle in *TAR* a justification for using it from the lesser (good) to

the greater (good), thus the full sentence of *TAR*'s first sentence is as follows:

أن السعة أفضل من القلة، لأن منفعتها أعظم، فإن التى تكون كثيراً أعظم من التى قليلاً ما تكون / large amount is better than little one because its benefit is much more, i.e. the more is the better [*TAR* B, p.32; *TAR* L, p. 35].

The full second sentence is as follows:

يستفيد مكان الخيرالقليل فائدة[75]فمن الاضطرار أن تكون استفادة الخيرات خيراً...فأن [وان] كثيرة [كبيرة]... لأن الأفضل أعظم من الأخس / It necessarily follows that acquisition of the goods is good...and the necessity of acquisition of much good instead of a little one... because the best is greater than the least [*TAR* B, pp. 27-28; *TAR* L, p.29].

Thus, each citing of the very principle is supplemented or preceded with justification which could be understood as a a justification for using the *argumentum a minore ad maius* in case of permission, and this is what āl-Šāfi'y did as a result of his reading of *TAR*; he put his invalid second rule of his informal logic immediately after his citing the principle.

6. It is clear now that āl-Šāfi'y understood that principle literally, which gave him justification to extend the *argumentum a minore ad maius* to apply on permissions cases too, and in this way he divided *TAR.1's* rule into two. Of course, if he had read *Topics* he would not have done this. That means more evidence that āl-Šāfi'y's source was *TAR*.

The third rule is the *argumentum a majori ad minus*, and we find it also at the same page in which TA speaks about the more and the less topic. Thus, TA says:

TAR.2 'وهذا الموضع هو أنه إن لم يكن ذلك الأمر للذى هو أحرى أن يكون، فواضح أنه ليس للذى هو أقل أو أنقص / This topic is if it was not the case for what is more likely to be, then it is obvious that it cannot be the case for what is less or from what something is missing' [*TAR* B, p. 155; *TAR* L, p. 149].

Somewhat later, we read:

فإما أن يُثبِت أنه إن كان الذى هو أقل، كان الذى هو أكثر؛ وإما أن يثبت أنه إن لم يكن كذا فلا كذا، فإنما يثبت واحدة من اثنتين: إما أنه، وإما أن ليس كما يقال من أجل أنه لم يكن الذى هو بزيادة، فلم الذى هو أقل / either to demonstrate that if it was the less then it would be the more or to demonstrate that if it was not this then it would not be that, by doing so he is demonstrating one of two: either it is, or it is not because whenever what is more was not the case then it would not be what is less.

āl-Šāfi'y reformulates this rule in a positive formulation. In fact, he gives us a valid converse for the *argumentum a majori ad minus* as follows:

Sh.3 'وكذلك إذا أباح كثير شيء كان الأقل منه أولى أن يكون مباحاً /Also, if He permitted a large amount of something, then a lesser amount of it would be even more appropriately permissible' [*Risāla* K: 1485; Lowry's [64] trans. P. 153].

As noted above, āl-Šāfi'y's converse formulation is valid. And he seems to have preferred the positive mood of the rule for his purposes.

4.2. āl-Šāfi'y's Two Rules of Analogy

First of all, Aristotle and TA have two definitions for Analogy or παράδειγμα [*TAR* B, pp.11; 14-15; *TAR*L, pp. 10, 14]. āl-Šāfi'y also has two definitions for analogy, thus he says: 'وموافقته [القياس] تكون من وجهين / its conformity [i.e. *qiyās*/analogy] is to be based on two aspects' [*Risāla* K: 123].[76] And he says in another passage: 'والقياس من وجهين / *qiyās* [analogy] has two aspects' [*Risāla* K: 1334]. Also, we can easily recognize that the content of *TAR*'s two definitions is the same as āl-Šāfi'y's two definitions.

TAR introduces the first definition of παράδειγμα as following:

> ***TAR*.3**
> أما البرهان... فإنه... كالجزء إلى الجزء والشبيه إلى الشبيه إذا كانا جميعاً <u>يمكنان</u> تحت ذلك الجنس بعينه
> ولم يكن واحداً [واحد] منهما يدل على أنه برهان للآخر
> / concerning paradeigma… it is … like part to part, like similar to similar, on the condition that both of them <u>could be fallen</u> under the very same genus and that not one of them is an example for the other [*TAR* B, pp. 14-15; *TAR* L, p. 14].

We should notice here that the word '*yumkinnān*' can be read as 'could be' or 'to fall under,' i.e '*yakmunnān*'. I put both readings in the translation until the text to be understandable. I think that āl-Šāfi'y also read both readings as it is clear from his wording of this rule below. However, the meaning of *TAR*'s rule is:

1. παράδειγμα is reasoning from part to part, and from like to like.
2. This happens when (a) The similar things *could be* fallen under the same genus or meaning, and (b) there is obscurity about their similarity.

Accordingly; we have āl-Šāfi'y's definition of analogy which is dependent on the *TAR* as follows:

Sh.4

وموافقته [القياس] تكون من وجهين: أحدهما: أن يكون الله أو رسوله حرم الشيء منصوصاً أو أحله لمعنى فإذا وجدنا ما فى مثل ذلك المعنى فيم لم ينص فيه بعينه كتاب ولا سنة، أحللناه أو حرمناه، لأنه فى معنى الحلال أو الحرام / its conformity [i.e. *qiyās*] is to be based on two aspects: the first of them is that God or His messenger have either forbidden a certain thing by a text or permitted it by a meaning. If we find such a meaning in something neither the book nor a *sunna* has a text about it itself, then we shall permit or prohibit it, because it is in such a meaning of permission or prohibition [*Risāla* K: 123-24].

Khadurri [62, p. 79] and Lowry [64, pp. 149-50] translated the word *ma'nā* as reason. But this misses the point. Firstly, the exact English equivalent of the word *ma'nā* is meaning not reason. Secondly, āl-Šāfi'y's intention is to search for a meaning not a reason, this is clear from the adjective 'such' in 'if we find such.' Thirdly, if we agreed that he was indirectly influenced by *RS*, it would naturally be that he intended a meaning not a reason. That is because *RS*:3 is related to searching for genus, a common meaning, or *binyan av* (establishing a principle) which is equivalent to the Arabic *binā' aṣl*. āl-Šāfi'y himself used the word 'أصل / principle or element' in another wording for his rule: ' والقياس من وجهين: أحدهما أن يكون الشيء فى معنى الأصل / *Qiyās* has two aspects; the first one of them is that the thing has the same meaning of the original thing' [*Risāla* K: 1334].[77]

W. Hallaq [45] considered this rule as *ratio legis*, i.e. 'If the new case has the same *ratio legis* (*ma'nā*, lit. meaning) as that given to the parallel textual case, the ruling in the text must be transferred to the new case' [*ibid.*, p.23]. Therefore, a jurist has to search for 'the 'purpose of a statute' [99, p. 310] according to the *ratio legis*. But āl-Šāfi'y did not mean that,[78] what he meant is that searching for a meaning covers both the known and the unknown cases. What confirms this is the example which āl-Šāfi'y gives for his **Sh.4**.:

> since the child is [an issue] of the father, he [the father] is under an obligation to provide for the child's support while [the child] is unable to do that for himself. So I hold by analogical deduction when the father becomes *incapable of providing for himself* by his earnings-or from what he owns-then it is an obligation on his children to support him by paying for his expenses and clothing. Since the child is from the father, he [the child] should not cause him from whom he comes to lose anything, just as the child should not lose anything belonging to his children, because the child is from the father. So the forefathers, even if they are distant, and the children, even if they are remote descendants, *fall into this category* [*Risāla* M, p. 310. My italics].

Here what āl-Shafi'i calls '*fall into this category*' is nothing but the meaning, not the purpose, of '*incapability of providing for himself*' which both the father and the child *fall under it*. Thus, āl-Šāfi'y is building a principle or genus or *binyan av*.

The other *TAR* definition of παράδειγμα is as follows:

TAR.4. 'فالنحو الذى يكون بإثبات أن هذا فى شيئين متشابهين... هو... برهان / The way of demonstrating that this is in two like things is paradeigma' [*TAR* B, p. 11; *TAR* L, p. 10].

With the helping of the auxiliary 'could' of the first definition (as a result of āl-Šāfi'y's reading of يمكنان), which means that a thing may have many likes, āl-Šāfi'y gives his other definition.

> **Sh. 5.** أو نجد الشيء يشبه الشيء منه والشيء من غيره، ولانجد شيئاً أقرب به شبهاً من أحدهما، فنلحقه بأولى الأشياء شبهاً به / or we find the thing to resemble one thing or another, and if we find nothing closer to it in resemblance than one of them, then we should relate it to the most closer to it in resemblance [*Risāla* K: 125].

We should note here that this definition contains the term *šabah*, which I translated as resemblance and its derivatives, so also *TAR* contains the term *mutashābih*, one of the derivatives of the term *šabah*.

This rule has another variant which connects it with the previous rule. āl-Šāfi'y says that the resemblance between two things is at the surface [*Risāla* K: 118; 119; 125], but in his variant rule he introduces the resemblance as if it is in meaning. Thus, he says about resolving contradictory analogies:

> بأن تنظر إلى النازلة، فإن كانت تشبه أحد الأصلين فى معنى والآخر فى اثنين، صرفت إلى الذى أشبهته فى الاثنين، دون الذى أشبهته فى واحد / you have to look at the case, if it resembles one of the two known cases in a meaning but resembles the other known in two meanings, then you should relate it to the one which resembles it in two meanings not the one which it resembles in one meaning [15 *ix*, p. 80].

Lowry considered this as a confusion between **Sh. 4** and **Sh.5** [64, p. 151, n. 134]. But it seems to be a result of the influence of *TAR* and *RS*:2-3 on āl-Šāfi'y.

Also, our previous critique of Hallaq's reading to **Sh.4** applies on his reading to **Sh.5** where he considers **Sh.5** as argument of *a similitude* [46, p. 23], but the *argumentum of a similitude* is 'concerning the purposes of the 'lawgiver'' [99, p. 313] while āl-Šāfi'y's intention is meaning.[79]

5. āl-Šāfi'y's Argumentative Rationality

Even if we accept the above reconstruction, there might still be doubts concerning the influence of *TAR* upon āl-Šāfi'y's logic. One might argue that the resemblance of words and the logical structure of the rules do not provide inclusive evidence. However, āl-Šāfi'y did not only articulate *RS* by *TAR* but he even borrowed from the later a theory of argumentative rationality. To prove this, I shall first reconstruct *TA*'s theory of argumentative rationality in *TAR*, and after this I shall reconstruct āl-Šāfi'y's theory.

5.1. The Theory of Argumentative Rationality in the Arabic Translation of Aristotle's On Rhetoric

According to TA humans have several modes of speech. These modes lead to truthfulness or *āl-taṣdīq*, or as TA says: ' فكل الناس...يستعملون الفحص وتقليد الكلام والاعتداد [الاعتذار] والشكاية فيصدقون / All humans are using investigation, speak according to habit, trust [apology], and complaint to consider truthful' [*TRA* B, p. 4; *TRA* L, p. 1]. Also, there are two kinds of art and therefore truthfulness or *āl-taṣdīq* [80] in respect of their aim; the aim of the first one is that 'إذا المتكلم تكلم[بغير العدل] أن ننقض عليه / if the speaker spoke [without justice], then we would refute him' [*TAR* B, p. 8; *TAR* L, p. 6]. The art which deals with this kind of truthfulness is dialectics or *āl-dyalīqṭqya* [*ibid.*]. Thus, this art has dialectical truthfulness. The other aim is ' أن تعرف المقنعات فى كل أمر من الأمور / to recognize the persuasive things in every matter' [*TAR* B, p. 8; *TAR* L, p. 6]. The art which deals with this kind of truthfulness is Rhetoric or *āl-rīiṭūrīa* [*ibid.*]. Thus, this art has rhetorical or persuasive truthfulness. This last kind of truthfulness is divided into two types: the first one is artificial and the other is non-artificial, ' فأما التصديقات فمنها بصناعة ومنها بغير صناعة / the truthful things are either artificial or non-artificial' [*TAR* B, p. 9; *TAR* L, p. 7]. The non-artificial truthful things are 'ليست تكون بحيلة منا / without our interference' [*TAR* B, p. 9; *TAR* L, p. 7]. *TA* defines five kinds of the non-artificial things; these are 'السنن، والشهود، والعقد، والعذاب، والأيمان / *Sunan* (customs or laws), testimony, contract, punishment and oaths' [*TAR* B, p. 71; *TAR* L, p. 73].

Artificial truthfulness may be reached by demonstration: ' والتصديق إنما يكون بالتثبيت / And truthfulness have to be by demonstration' [*TAR* B, p. 6; *TAR* L, p.4].[81] There are two kinds of demonstration in every Art, in dialects there are consideration or *'i'tibār*[82] and *saljasa*;[83] their counterparts in rhetoric are proof or *paradeigma* or *burhān*[84] and thinking or *tafkyr*[85] respectively.

In addition to the two kinds of demonstration there are also pseudo-consideration and pseudo *saljasa* in dialectics, pseudo-proof and pseudo-thinking in rhetoric.[86] Most rhetorical demonstrations are proofs, but the most powerful are thinkings or *tafkyrāt*.[87] The premises of thinking are either truths or signs,[88] and the latter is either mappings or signs.[89] We should note here the following: (1) the obscureness of *TA* about *Analytics*, (2) that Aristotle's Theory of argumentative rationality has been modified.

Concerning the first point, the (ancient) reader of *TAR* either believes (a) that there is nothing new in *Analytics*, or (b) he may understand that *On Rhetoric* contains *Analytics*.

Concerning (a); *TA* says after talking about the ways of demonstration in dialectics and rhetoric 'وهذا بيْن واضح فى كتاب أنولوطيقى / this is obvious and clear in the *Analytics*' [*TAR* B, p. 11; *TAR* L, p.10] without any more clarification. And he says after talking about the first kind of the rhetorical premises, i.e. 'the truths or the necessities,' ' فأما الاضطرارية فمن الاضطراريات، وهذا بين واضح فى كتاب أنولوطيقى / The necessary premise is from the necessities, and this obvious and clear in *Analytics*' [*TAR* B, p. 13; *TAR* L, p. 12] without any more clarification too. Again, after talking about the true, mapping (*rāsim*) and sign, he says 'أما كنه البيان وحقيقته ففى أنولوطيقى / but the essence of the account and its truth is in *Analytics*' [*TAR* B, p.14; *TAR* L, pp. 13 – 14]. This clause does not mean that there would be something different in *Analytics*, this is because before it directly *TA* said that he had showed the differences between them, thus he says: ' أما ما الصادق، وما الرواسم، وما الدلالة، وما الفرق بينهن، فقد بينا عنه ها هنا أيضاً / concerning What are the true, mapping (*rāsim*), and sign, and what is the difference between them, we have clarified this here too' [*TAR* B, p.14; *TAR* L, p.13]. Even after his saying 'but the essence… etc.,' he tells us about this essence, thus he continues

> وأخبرنا أن من هذه أيضاً ما هو لعلة من العلل، غير ذى سلوجسموس، ومنها ما هو مسلجس، وحددنا ذلك وبيناه / And we said that there are also, for a cause among many causes, amongst those; what is not syllogistic and what is syllogistic, and we defined that and made it clear [*TAR* B, p. 14; *TAR* L, p. 14].[90]

TA already spoke about non-syllogistic mappings (*rawīsim*).[91] Moreover, he talkes about the cause of the non-syllogistic when he talkes about false signs:

> ونحو آخر من قِبل العلامة، فإن هذا أيضاً بلا سلجسة... إن قال قائل إن ديانوسيوس< كان لصاً> لأنه شرير؛ فهذا غير س<لجسة لأنه ليس كل شرير بلص، وإن كان كل لص <شريراً/and there is another topic from sign; this is not syllogism either…if one said that Dionysus <was a thieve> because he was wicked, then this would not be s<yllogistim because not every wicked man is a thieve, while every thieve is a wicked man>.[92]

Moreover, the reader who is interested in *On Rhetoric*, like āl-Šāfi'y, will not be interested to go back to *Analytics*, because syllogism is specific to dialectics not rhetoric.

Concerning (b); *TA* says ' أعنى قولنا إن الريطورية مركبةمن العلم الأنالوطيقى ومن الفوليطية التى فى الأخلاق / I mean our saying that rhetoric is <u>composed *of* *analytics*</u> and politics which is a part of ethics' [*TAR* B, p. 19; *TAR* L, p. 19].

Concerning the second point, i.e. the modification of Aristotle's Theory of argumentative rationality, this happened as follows: first, in *TAR* there are only two kinds of syllogisms (or *saljasa*) not three,[93] i.e. dialectical and rhetorical. Over all *TAR* there is no mention of analytical syllogisms, only the dialectical and rhetorical ones. Moreover, *TA* was always connecting the two later ones so that he gives the impression that there is no a third one.[94] This is being entrenched in the (ancient) reader's mind by the obscurity of *TA*'s hints to *Analytics* already mentioned. Accordingly, there are only two types of argumentative rationality, i.e. dialectical and rhetorical (and the last one leads to truthfulness). Second, the concept of demonstration became very different from Aristotle's.[95] It is now aiming to persuasion[96] without qualification, i.e. 'والتصديق إنما يكون بالتثبيت / the truthfulness has to be by demonstration.' Thus, in *TAR* there is no room for scientific deduction, there is only demonstration aiming at truthfulness. If the aim of the truthfulness, on the one hand, is refutation then the demonstration will be dialectical, and if the aim, on the other hand, is persuasive then the demonstration will be rhetorical. Rhetorical demonstration is of two kinds: (1) analogy or proof, and (2) syllogism or *saljasa* or thinking or the *a fortiori*. Third, the structure and meaning of syllogism has changed. In *TAR* the only passage about the nature of syllogism is very obscure and does not explain its very essence:

> والنحو الذى يكون بأن يكون شىء موضوع يحدث من أجل شىء آخر سوى ذلك الموضوع بذلك الموضوع نفسه: إما بالكلية وإما بالأكثر فهو هناك سلوجسموس / and the way which being that something posited happens because of another thing other than that posited thing but by that very posited thing, either universally or all the more is syllogism there [*TAR* B, p. 11; *TAR* L, p.10].[97]

Thus, in *TAR* there is no mention of the major, middle and minor terms, therefore syllogism in *TAR* is just reasoning.

5.2. āl-Šāfi'y's Theory of Argumentative Rationality

I shall try now to reconstruct āl-Šāfi'y's theory of argumentative rationality showing how he followed *TA*.

5.2.1. The General Framework

First of all, āl-Šāfi‘y, like *TA*, recognizes two kinds of argumentation. The first kind, like *TAR*, is dialectics or *āl-jadal* or *āl-kalām* which he rejects (there is no dialectics in *TAR*) because ‘لو علم الناس ما فى الكلام فى الأهواء، لفروا منه / if people know what inclination is in *Kalām*, then they will escape from it’ [57, 203]. This underestimation stems from *TAR*’s description of dialectics goal as just attacking [*TAR* B, p.8; *TAR* L, p.6] and that in dialectics we are pronouncing what we wanted and are inclined to ‘بما شئنا وهوينا,’ [*TAR* L, p.11]. In this last clause we have the verb *hawā*, while in āl-Šāfi‘y’s we have its nominal plural *āhwā’*. On the other hand, there is rhetorical argumentation or what āl-Šāfi‘y calles *bayān* or perspicuous declaration as M. Khadduri translates it.[98] This *bayān*, in addition to its being God and his messenger’s way of argumentation,[99] is also the way of muftis and judges for knowing what shall be acted if God and his messenger did not say anything about some case,[100] and that is by reasoning or *’istidlāl* [*Risāla* K: 70]. This reasoning is nothing but rhetorical *qiyās* [*Risāla* K: 121], which even God uses it in his argumentation.[101] Thus, āl-Šāfi‘y borrowes *TAR*’s general framework for argumentation.

To āl-Šāfi‘y the first task for a *mujtahid* or a jurist is to judge; ‘ فاعلم أن للحاكم الاجتهاد، والمفتيين فى موضع الحكم / know that *’ijtihād* is to judge, and muftis in the position of judging’ [15 *viii*, p. 73]. This judgment is the equivalent of *TA*’s ‘truthfulness or *āl-taṣdyq*’. Also, like *TAR*, there is no truthfulness without demonstration or *taṯbyt*. Judges and muftis have to demonstrate their judgment. āl-Šāfi‘y is using here the same term and its derivatives in *TAR* for demonstration, i.e. *yuṯbit*, *’iṯbāt*, *taṯbyt* and *taṯabbut*. Thus, he says

> أمر رسول الله فى الحكم خاصة ألا يحكم الحاكم وهو غضبان؛ لأن الغضبان مخوف على أمرين: أحدهما قلة التثبت / the messenger of God commanded with respect to the judgment especially that no judge should give judgment while angry, because the angry man may fall in two faults; one of them is lack of demonstration... [15 *viii*, p. 211].[102]

āl-Šāfi‘y is even using that term (*taṯbyt)* for demonstrating the prophet’s sayings or *ḥadyṯ*. Thus, he says: ‘ تفرق أهل الكلام فى تثبيت الخبر عن رسول الله / *ahl āl-kalām* divided concerning how to demonstrate the messenger’s sayings’ [15 *ix*, p. 5].[103] And he is also using the same term for demonstrating the sayings of the companions or *Ṣaḥabā*:

> وذكر له رجل يوماً مسألة، فأجاب فيها، فقال له: ‘خالفت على بن أبى طالب‘، فقال له: ‘ثبت لى هذا عن على بن أبى طالب‘ / someone asked him someday a question, and he replied, then that man told him ‘you disagreed with ‘Aly Ibn Abw Ṭālib’, then he said to him ‘demonstrate this to me from ‘Aly Ibn Abw Ṭālib’... [54 *iii*, p. 38].

5.2.2. The Ways of Demonstration

Following *TA* in saying that there is artificial and non-artificial truthfulness, āl-Šāfi'y defines (a) the latter as only the book and *sunan* / سنن , while he defines (b) the former as only analogy or the *a fortiori* which (c) has reasoning by sign as a sub-category. This schema is matching with *TAR* as I shall show below.

5.2.2.1. 'Uswl/Elements (Sunan Theory)

TA divides customs or '*sunan*' into two kinds, i.e. general and particular.[104] The particular one is specific for one man, while the general is absolute.[105] Both of them are binding for people.[106] The general *sunna* cannot be modified or changed, because 'ليست تكون بحيلة منا لكن بأمور متقدمة / we are not interfere in it because it is a priori' [*TAR* B, p. 9; *TAR* L, p.7] as *TA* says about non-artificial truthfulness. If the particular *sunna* contradicts with the general one, people have to obey to the general one,[107] therefore the general *sunna* is working as duty, while the particular one is working like *derivative duty*. In addition, the one who writes down *sunan* has to be a wise man, thus *TA* says: ' وينبغى أن يكون فى السنة وأفعال السنة حكيماً ما هو أحداً، أعنى أنه قد يرذل من لم يكن حكيماً فى السنن المحمودة / it should be in *sunna* and its actions some wise man who is unique, I mean that he who is not wise in the praised *sunan*, may be getting bad.'[108]

Following *TA* āl-Šāfi'y calls both of *TA*'s *sunan* '*usūl* / elements'[109], because they are non-artificial according *TAR*. These *usūl* / elements, as *TA* did, āl-Šāfi'y divides into two: the *Qur'ān* (the general *sunna*), and the messenger's *sunna* (the particular *sunna*).[110] Thus, he says

> لم أعلم مخالفاً فى أن من مضى من سلفنا والقرون بعدهم إلى يوم كنا قد حكم حاكمهم وأفتى مفتيهم فى أمور ليس فيها نص كتاب ولا سنة / I did not know about anyone who objected that the people, who preceded us and their successors up to our day, had a judge who has judged and a mufti who has issued a fatwa in things had had not a book or a *sunna* [15 *ix*, p. 19].

This sentence proves that āl-Šāfi'y read Aristotle and how he read him.

Before leaving this subsection I must refer to two remarks: the first one is related to the concept of *sunna* in āl-Šāfi'y's works which matches with *TA*'s concept and attests my reconstruction. It is known that the concept of *sunna*, in its early developing phase 'as the traditional usage of the community' [82, p. 3; (cf. also, [23, p. 28]) up to āl-Šāfi'y's time when, with him, it became to signify mainly to 'the model behavior of the prophet' [82, p.2], was including the customs, practices, sayings…etc. of the messenger.[111]

But there is also another meaning of āl-Šāfi'y's usage; that is *sunna* as a law or a legal rule. Thus, he says explaining one of the meanings of *bayān*: ' ما سن رسول الله مما ليس لله فيه نص محكم / what the messenger of God legitimated / *sann* in what God has no a concise text' [Risāla *K*: 85; also 96; 292; 301 – 302]. Here, āl-Šāfi'y' is using the verb '*sann*' in the meaning of legitimating a law or a legal rule. This usage of '*sunna*' is matching *TA*'s meaning where the Syriac translator of Aristotle's *On Rhetroic* rendered νομός (law) as *sunna* (compare [64, p. 102]).

The second remark is related to āl-Šāfi'y's insistence on the wisdom or *ḥikma* of the prophet.[112] As Lowry noticed, 'Shāfi'ī offers several arguments in support of the authority of Muḥammad's *Sunna*, all of which depend on passages in the *Qur'ān*. ... The second concerns a number of passages in the *Qur'ān* in which the word *ḥikma*, 'wisdom,' is paired with the phrase 'God's Book' or an equivalent. In these passages, Shāfi'ī tells us, *Ḥikma* means '*Sunna*,' so that the passages may all be understood to refer to the complementary pair of the *Qur'ān* and the *Sunna* [64, p. 170]. But Lowry believed that this equivalence between *Sunna* and *Ḥikma* is a result to āl-Šāfi'y's inventiveness [*ibid*., p. 186], and his using to a primitive Basran concept of equivalence between *Sunna* and *Ḥikma* [*ibid*., pp. 184-85]. But if my reconstruction is right, it will be more reasonable to believe that āl-Šāfi'y paired *ḥikma* with *sunna* because *TAR* insists on the necessity of the giver of *sunna* being a wise man.

The real inventiveness of āl-Šāfi'y lies not in his usage of the primitive Basran concepts of *ḥikma*, but in (a) using this primitive equivalence for convincing scholars of his own time with his borrowed theory, and in (b) his considering that *sunna* is commanded in the *Qur'ān* itself [*Risāla* K: 244], thus he connected what *TA* left unconnected, and by doing so he (c) escaped from the possibility that there could be a contradiction between the general *sunna* and the particular one; between the *Qur'ān* and the messenger's *sunna*, in case of the validity of *sunna*.

Accordingly; we do not need to J. Wegner's hypothesis of the borrowing of the concept of *ḥikma* from the Rabbinic literature [97, pp. 52 – 53], especially as Lowry has shown that the opposite is correct, namely that the *Ge'on*ic literature borrowed this concept from Islamic literature [64, pp. 185 – 186].

5.2.2.2. The Artificial Demonstrating (qiyās)

As I have shown before, āl-Šāfi'y considered *qiyās* to consist of two main mental activities, i.e. analogy and the *a fortiori*. By doing so he is following TA's argumentative rationality concerning the types of argumentation in rhetoric. *TA* considered that all artificial demonstrating is either by paradeigma/proof (analogy) or enthymeme/thinking, thus he says: ' فقد يفعلون

/ التصديقات كلها بالتثبيت، وذلك إما بإحضار البرهان، وإما بالتفكير لا فى شىء آخر سوى هذين they can fulfill all truthfulness by demonstration, and this is either by bringing proof/paradeigma or by thinking/enthymeme, there is nothing more than these two' [*TAR* B, p. 11; *TAR* L, pp. 9 – 10].

Similarly, āl-Šāfi'y paired *'ijtihād* with *qiyās*, 'هما اسمان لمعنى واحد / they are two names but have the same meaning' [*Risāla* K: 1324]. *'Ijtihād* is a mental activity special to human beings, 'ومنه: ما فرض الله على خلقه الاجتهاد فى طلبه / another one of it [*bayān*] consists of what God commanded His creatures to seek through *'ijtihād* (personal reasoning)' [*Risāla* K: 59; *Risāla* M: 68]. This consideration of *'ijtihād* as mental activity goes back to *TA*'s saying that 'وأما اللاتى بالصناعة فما أمكن إعداده وتثبيته على ما ينبغى بالحيلة وأنفسنا / concerning those [truthful speech] which are artificial they are what can be prepared and demonstrated by trick and by ourselves as they should be' (*TAR*B, p. 9). Of course the term *''ijtihād'* had a history before āl-Šāfi'y,[113] but āl-Šāfi'y's inventiveness lies in his integration of that history with *TAR*'s theory of argumentative rationality especially as the translator of *TAR* rendered enthymeme as thinking/تفكير/فكر, and we know how the meaning of *fikr*, *'ijtihād* and *rā'y* are so interrelated to.

My reconstruction can answer some puzzling questions about āl-Šāfi'y's rationality. The first question is relating to āl-Šāfi'y's argumentative rationality: Why did āl-Šāfi'y consider the *a fortiori* to be stronger than analogy?[114] This question can be answered easily by citing some texts from *TAR* which confirm superiority of the *a fortiori* or thinking over analogy or proof. Thus, TA says: 'التثبيت الريطورى هو التفكير، لان هذا فى الجملة هو الأصل المتقدم للتصديقات / the rhetorical demonstration is thinking, because it is in the main the prior principle of truthfulness' [*TAR* B, pp. 6 – 7; *TAR* L, p. 4]. Also: 'التفكيرات التى هى عمود التصديق / *thinkings*/enthymemes (which) are the pillar of truthfulness' [*TAR* B, p.4; *TAR* L, p.1]. Also,

> فقد ينبغى أن نستعمل البرهانات فى التثبيت إذا لم يكن الكلام موضع تفكير[فى التثبت إذا لم يكن فى الكلام موضع تفكير]، فإنه بهذه يكون التصديق / we should use proofs/analogy in demonstration if the speech was not thinking/enthymeme[in demonstration if there were not thinking in speech], because truthfulness is by this (thinking) [*TAR* B, p.141; *TAR* L, p.136].

The second question is relating to the relationship between āl-Šāfi'y's argumentative rationality and *TA*'s: why did āl-Šāfi'y choose only the *a fortiori* argument from all the kinds of enthymemes topics which TA offered? This is for two reasons. Firstly, the Jewish or Hebrew rules of hermeneutics did not recognize any enthymemic rules except the *a fortiori*, and āl-Šāfi'y was a follower of the *RS* without following their contents as we have shown before. Secondly, the mistranslation of Aristotle's *On Rhetoric* or *TAR*. This mistranslation identified the *a fortiori* and the most part premises, and by doing so made the *a fortiori* the most important topic of enthymeme. This happened in two passages[115] Aristotle was talking in both of them about the most part premises but the translation rendered them as if Aristotle were talking about the *a fortiori* (and sign) as the most important enthymemic topic. I shall discuss here the first passage which was quoted before. In this passage [24, 1356b 15-16], Aristotle talks about how (dialectical) syllogism is the counterpart to enthymeme, but the translation identifies enthymeme and the *a fortiori* as follows:

> والنحو الذى يكون بأن يكون شىء موضوع يحدث من أجله شىء آخر سوى ذلك الموضوع بذلك الموضوع نفسه: إما بالكلية، وإما بالأكثر فهو هناك سلوجسموس، وهو هنا يسمى تفكيراً / and the way which being that something posited happens because of another thing other than that posited thing but by that very posited thing, either universally or all the more is syllogism there and called thinking here [*TAR* B, p.11; *TAR* L, p.10].

If you do not already know what Aristotle means by 'the most part,' and of course you do not know in case you read only *TAR*, you will identify it as 'all the more', and that is what āl-Šāfi'y did. Thus, the topic of the *a fortiori* (and its supplements as we shall see in the next subsection when we shall analyze āl-Šāfi'y's concept of sign) became thinking/enthymeme itself, therefore there were no need for the other topics of enthymeme.

5.2.2.3. The Premises of Demonstration and Inference by Sign

In fact, āl-Šāfi'y did not borrow only the 'more and the less' topic from *TAR*, but he also borrowed 'sign' topic.[116] This becomes because *TA*'s talking about the sign relates it to 'the more and less' topic. In the previous subsection I have analyzed two mistranslated passages which made Aristotle talks about 'the more' topic instead 'the premises of the most part'. In the Greek original text Aristotle says: 'it is evident that [the premises] from which enthymemes are spoken are sometimes necessarily true but mostly true [only] for the most part' [24, 1357a 31-33]. While *TA* says: ' فهو معلوم الآن أن من هذه التى تسمى تفكيرات ما هو اضطرارى، فإن كثيراً منها مما يوجد بالأكثر / it is known now that from these which called *thinkings* there is what is necessary, and many of them [i.e. *thinkings*] exist as all the more' [*TAR* B, pp.13-14; *TAR* L, p.12]. After that Aristotle talks immediately about the premises of enthymeme and how they should be either probabilities or signs, but the translator(s) of *On Rhetoric* changed the meaning and made the premises of enthymeme or *āl-tafkyrāt* being the true propositions or *āl-ṣadiqāt* and signs or *āl-dalā'il*. This is very interesting because making the premises of enthymeme/*āl-tafkīrāt* as the true propositions gave āl-Šāfi'y the justification for considering them as God's duties. On the other hand, TA's consideration signs/الدلائل as another category of enthymemes or *āl-tafkyrāt* was adopted by āl-Šāfi'y. He even borrowed the term *dalyl* (sign) for describing this kind of inference: ' ومعنى هذا الباب معنى القياس، لأنه يطلب فيه الدليل على صواب القبلة / the meaning of this subject is the same as the meaning of *qiyās*, because in it *a sign* is sought for the right direction in prayer' [*Risāla* K:121]. He also defines *qiyās* as sign (*dalāla*): 'القياس ما طلب بالدلائل / *qiyās* is what was sought by signs' [*Risāla* K: 122]. āl-Šāfi'y tries to justify *'ijtihād* and *qiyās* through finding a justification of inferring by sign from within the *Qur'ān*. Thus, after quoting *Q*:16-16 he says:

> فخلق لهم العلامات، ونصب لهم المسجد الحرام، وأمرهم أن يتوجهوا إليه، وإنما توجههم إليه بالعلامات التى خلق لهم، والعقول التى ركبها فيهم، التى استدلوا بها على معرفة العلامات / Thus [God] has created signs (*'alāmāt*) [for men to be guided by] and erected the sacred Mosque and ordered them to turn their faces towards it [in prayer]. Their turning in that direction [is determined] by the signs He created for them and by reason which He has implanted in them and by which they are guided to recognize the signs [*Risāla* K:114].

6. Conclusion

In this paper, I have tried to outline a history of the development of informal logic at the Arabic and Islamic culture as it appeared in the first definite formulations for its rules in āl-Šāfi'y's *Risāla*. I have followed this development in the fields of law, exegesis and rhetoric. Contrary to J. Schacht and others, I have argued that, there was no influence on the informal logic of the Arabs by the rhetorical Hellenistic schools of Mesopotamia, or by the Jews of Iraq.[117] The main influence was from the Rabbis of Yemen who translated *orally the Fathers to Rabbi Nathan* which contained Jewish or Hebrew informal logic rules. This could not have happened without a translation movement which I have called 'Umar's translation movement. This is contrary to D. Gutas' [42] hypothesis that the translations into Arabic before Abbasid times' were mainly administrative or for communicative purposes. There was indeed a disciplined translation movement before the Abbasid's. However, the Jewish or Hebrew informal logic spread amongst the scholars of exegesis and law especially in the school of Ibn 'Abbās (the secretary of the first disciplined movement translation) from which āl-Šāfi'y learnt these rules. āl-Šāfi'y also coined the term *qiyās,* which was current in Medina's linguistic school, to include the *a fortiori* and analogy. Having been confronted with Iraqi scholars, he articulated the Hebrew logic by Aristotle's *On Rhetoric* from which he borrowed his argumentative rationality. In doing so he returned to the founder of informal logic unlike the Rabbis who learnt informal logic from the Hellenistic rhetorical schools.[118] Accordingly, āl-Šāfi'y developed the Semitic informal logic even though he partly misunderstood Aristotle because of the mistranslation into Arabic of the latter's *On Rhetoric*. Thus, my paper brings us to further researches. Firstly, analyzing āl-Šāfi'y's informal logic formally and comparing it with its Hebraic counterpart syntactically and semantically. Secondly, tracing 'Umar's translation movement, especially that 'Uṯmān Ibn 'Affān (d. 35/656) the third caliph permitted Tamym āl-Dāry to continue story telling[119] (translation), and Ka'b established a new generation of translators, i.e. his sons.[120] And if we can trace this movement, then we may solve partly the methodological problem in Arabic and Islamic scholarship concerning the authenticity of *Hadyṯ* and the sayings of the companions and the successors. Thirdly, because of the influence of Aristotle on *'uswl āl-fiqh* as I have proved, there is a need to reexamination of the relationship between *fiqh* or rathar *'uswl āl-fiqh* and rhetoric and philosophy in the Arabic and Islamic systems of knowledge, especially as both Arabic and Islamic philosophy depended on the misunderstanding of Aristotle because of its Arabic translation.[121]

Acknowledgement

I would like to thank professor Dr. Regula Forster for her helpful notes and critical comments on this paper, and I do not need to say that any mistakes are only mine. Also, I would like to thank Erasmus Mundus foundation for its financial supporting writing this paper.

References

1. Abdel-Rahman, H. L'argument a maiori et l'argument par analogie dans la logique juridi-que musulmane, *Rivista Internazionale di Filosofia del Diritto*, 98, 1971, pp. 127-148.
2. Abdul-Raof, H. *Schools of Qur'anic Exegesis*, London and New York: Routledge, 2010.
3. āl-Bayhaqy, *āl-Jami' li Shu'ab āl-'ymān.* Maktabat āl-Rushd: āl-Riyaḍ, 2003.
4. āl-Bayhaqy, *Manāqib āl-Šāfi'y*. Dār āl-Turāṯ: Cairo, 1970.
5. āl-Bukāry, *āl-Jāmi' āl-Ṣaḥyḥ.* Dār Ṭawq āl-Najāḥ: āl-Madyna āl-Munawwara.
6. āl-Hayṯamy, *Kašf āl-Āstār 'an Zawā'īd āl-Bazzār*. Mw'asasat āl-Risāla: Beirut, 1979.
7. āl-Jaḥiẓ, *āl-Bayān wa āl-Tabyyn*. Maktabat āl-Ḵānjy: Cairo, seventh edition, 1998.
8. āl-Ḵaṭyb āl-Baġdādy, *Kitāb āl-Faqyh wa āl-Mutafaqqih*. Dār Ibn āl-Jawzy: āl-Riyaḍ, 1996.
9. āl-Ḵaṭyb āl-Baġdādy, Tāryḵ Baġdād. Dār āl-Ġarb āl-'Islāmy: Beirut, 2001.

10.āl-Mizzy, *Tahḏyb āl-Kamāl fy Āsmā' āl-Rijāl*.Mū'asasat āl-Risāla: Beirut, second edition, 1983.
11.Alnashar, A. S. *Manāhij āl-Baḥṯ 'ind Mufakkiry āl-'Islām*. Dār āl-Nahḍa āl-'Arabya: Cairo, 1984.
12.āl-Rāzy, *Kitāb āl-Jurḥ wa āl-Ta'dyl*. Dār āl-Kutub āl-'Ilmya: Beirut, 1953.
13.āl-Ṣan'āny, *āl-Tanwyr Šarḥ āl-Jami' āl-Ṣaḡyr*. Dār āl-Salām: āl-Riyaḍ, 2011.
14.āl-Šāfi'y, *Risāla*. Maktabat Muṣṭafā āl-Ḥalaby: Cairo, second edition, 1983.
15.āl-Šāfi'y, *Umm*. Dār āl-Wafā' lil Ṭibā'a wa āl-Našr: āl-Manswra, 2001.
16.āl-Suywṭy, *āl-Lā'ly' āl-Maṣnw'a fy āl-Āḥādyṯ āl-Mawḍw'a*. Dār āl-Ma'rifa: Beirut, 1975.
17.āl-Tirmiḏy, *āl-Jāmi' āl-Kabyr*. Dār āl-Ḡarb āl-'Islāmī: Beirut, 1996.
18.āl-Ṭabarāny, *āl-Mu'jam āl-Kabyr*. Maktabat Ibn Taymya: Cairo, 2015.
19.āl-Ṭabary, *Jāmi' āl-Bayān 'an Tā'wyl āl-Qur'ān*. Maktabat Ibn Taymya: Cairo, 1953.
20.āl-Ṭabary, *Taryḵ āl-Rusul wa āl-Mlwk*. Dār āl-Ma'ārif, second edition: Cairo, 1967.
21.āl-Ḏahaby, *Myzān āl-'I'tidāl fy Naqd āl-Rijāl*. Dār āl-Ma'rifa: Beirut, 2009.
22.āl-Ḏahaby, Siyar Ā'lām āl-Nubalā'. Mw'asasat āl-Risāla: Beirut, eleventh edition, 1996.
23.Ansari, Z. I. Islamic juristic terminology before Šāfiʿī: a semantic analysis with special reference to Kūfa, *Arabica,* vol. 19, Fasc. 3, 1971, pp. 255-300.
24.Aristotle, *On Rhetoric: A Theory of Civic Discourse*, trans. by G. A. Kennedy, Oxford: Oxford University Press, 2007.
25.Aristotle, Topics, In J. Barnes (ed.), *The Complete Works of Aristotle*, trans. by W. A. Pickard-Cambridge, Princeton: Princeton University Press, 1991.
26.*Avoth de Rabbi Nathan*, Edited from Manuscripts with an Introduction, Notes and Appendices by S. Schechter (Hebrew), Vienna, 1887. (Reprint, Hildesheim; New York: G. Olms Verlag, 1979.)
27.Azzan, Y. *Scripture as logos: Rabbi Ishmael and the origins of Midrash*, Philadelphia: Pennsylvania University Press, 2004.
28.Badawi, A. *Arisṭuṭālīs: āl-Khiṭaba*. Dar āl-Qalam: Beirut, 1979.
29.Berg, H. *The Development of Exegesis in early Islam*, London and New York: Routledge-Curzon, 2000.
30.Biesen, K. D. *Simple and Bold: Ephrem's Art of Symbolic Thought*, New Jersey: Gorgias Press, 2006.
31.Bravmann, M. M. *The Spiritual Background of Early Islam*, Leiden: Brill, 1972.

32.Brock, S. P. *A Brief Outline of Syriac Literature*, India: Deepka Offset Printers, 1997.
33.Cadler, N. Ikhtilâf and Ijmâ' in Shâfi'î 's Risâla, *Studia Islamica*, 58, 1983, pp. 55-81.
34.Chaumont, E. ĀL-SHĀFI'I, In C. E. Bosworth, E. van Donzel, W. P.Heinrichs and G. Lecomte (eds.), *The Encyclopaedia of Islam*, 85, Leiden: Brill, 1997, pp.181-85.
35.Coulson, N. J. *A History of Islamic Law*, Edinburgh: The University Press, 1964.
36.Danish Pazuh, M.N.T. *Mantiq Ibn āl-Muqaffa'*. Anjuman-i Shahanshahi Falsafah-i Tihran, Tehran 1978.
37.Fak̲r āl-Dyn āl-Rāzy, *Manāqib āl-'Imām āl-Šāfi'y*. Maktabat āl-Kwliyāt āl-Āzhariya: Cairo, 1986.
38.Goldfeld, Y. The Development of Theory on Qur'ānic Exegesis in Islamic Scholarship, *Studia Islamica*, 67, 1988, pp. 5-37.
39.Goldin, J. *The Fathers according to Rabbi Nathan*, New Heaven: Yale University Press, 1955.
40.Goldziher, I. *Introduction to Islamic Theology and Law*, trans. by A. and R. Hamori, Princeton: Princeton University Press, 1910/1981.
41.Goldziher, I. *The Ẓāhirīs*, trans. and edited by W. Behn, Leiden: Brill, 2008.
42.Gutas, D. *Greek Thought, Arabic Culture*, London: Routledge, 1998.
43.Hallaq, B. W. The Development of Logical Structure in Sunni Legal Theory, *Der Islam*, 64, 1987, pp. 42-67.
44.Hallaq, B. W. Non-Analogical Arguments in Sunni juridical Qiyās, *Arabica*, vol. 36, Fasc. 3, 1989, pp. 286-306.
45.Hallaq, B. W. *A History of Islamic Legal Theory*, Cambridge: Cambridge University Press, 1997.
46.Hallaq, B. W. The Authenticity of Prophetic Ḥadîth: A Pseudo-Problem, *Studia Islamica*, No. 89, 1999, pp. 75-90.
47.Hallaq, B. W. *The Origins and Evolution of Islamic Law*, Cambridge: Cambridge University Press, 2005.
48.Hallaq, B. W. *An Introduction to Islamic Law*, Cambridge: Cambridge University Press, 2009.
49.Hunt, E. J. *Christianity in The Second Century: The Case of Tatian*, London and New York: Routledge, 2003.
50.Ibn Abw Dawwd, *Kitāb āl-Maṣāḥif*. Dār āl-Bašā'īr āl-'islāmiya: Beirut, second edition, 2002.
51.Ibn Abw K̲ayt̲ama, *āl-Tāryk̲ āl-Kabyr*. āl-Fārwq āl-Ḥadyt̲ā lil Ṭibā'ā wa āl-Našr: Cairo, 2004.
52.Ibn Abw Šaybā, *āl-Muṣannaf*. Maktabat āl-Rushd: āl-Riyaḍ, 2004.
53.Ibn āl-Mūqaffa', *Risālat āl-Ṣaḥāba*. In: *Āt̲ār Ibn āl-Mūqaffa'*. Dār āl-Kutub āl-'Ilmiya, Beirut, 1989, pp. 309-24.

54.Ibn āl-Nadym, *āl-Fihrist*. Mu'asasat āl-Furqān lil Turāṯ āl-'Islāmy: London, 2009.
55.Ibn 'Asākir, *Tāryḵ Madynat Dimašq*. Dār āl-Fikr: Beirut, 1995.
56.Ibn Ḥanbal, A. *Musnad*. Bayt āl-Āfkār: āl-Riyaḍ, 1998.
57.Ibn Kaṯyr, *Manāqib āl-'Imām āl-Šāfi'y*. Maktabat āl-'Imām āl-Šāfi'y: āl-Riyaḍ, 1992.
58.Ibn Ḵaldwn, *The Muqaddimah*, 3 vol., trans. by F. Rosental, Princeton: Princeton University Press, 1958.
59.Ibn Manẓwr, *Lisān āl-'arab*. Dār Nwbilys: Beirut, 2006.
60.Ibn Muḵallad āl- Šaybāny, *Kitāb āl-Sunna*. āl-Maktab āl-'Islāmy: Beirut, 1980.
61.Ibn Sa'd, *Kitāb āl-Ṭabaqāt āl-Kabyr*. Maktabat āl- Ḵānjy: Cairo, 2001.
62.Khadduri, M. *Islamic Jurisprudence: Shāfi'ī's Risāla,* Translated with an Introduction, Notes, and Appendices, Baltimore: The Johns Hopkins Press, 1961.
63.Lowry, J. E. Does SHĀFI'Ī have a theory of 'four sources' of law? In R. Peters and B. Weiss (eds.), *Studies in Islamic law and society*, Leiden: Brill, 2002.
64.Lowry, J. E. *Early Islamic Legal Theory: The Risāla of Muḥammad ibn Idrīs āl-Šāfi'y*, Leiden: Brill, 2007.
65.Lyons, M. C. *Aristotle's Ars Rhetotica: The Arabic Version*, A new edition with Commentary and Glossary, vol. 1, Text. Cambridge: E. & E. Plumridge Ltd., Linton, 1982.
66.Lyons, M. C. Aristotle's Ars Rhetotica: The Arabic Version, *A new edition with Commentary and Glossary*, Vol. 2, Glossary. Cambridge: E.& E. Plumridge Ltd., Linton, 1982.
67.Margoliouth, D. S. Omar's Instructions to the Kadi, *Journal of the Royal Asiatic Society of Great Britain and Irland*, 1910, pp. 305-336.
68.Margoliouth, D. S. *The Early Development of Mohammedanism*, London: Williams and Norgate, 1914.
69.Marrou, H. I. *Education in Antiquity*, trans. by G. Lamb, New York: The American Library, 1956.
70.Motzki, H. The Role of Non-Arabs Converts in the Development of Early Islamic Law, *Islamic Law and Society*, vol. 6, no. 3, 1999, pp. 293-317.
71.Motzki, H. *The Origins of Islamic Jurisprudence: Meccan Fiqh before the Classical Schools*, Leiden: Brill, 2002.
72.Moubarez, H. The Development of the Semitic Logical Traditions: 1. The Hebraic Logical Tradition up till the End of third Century (In Arabic), *The Proceedings of the international conference of the oriental languages department*, Cairo: Cairo University Press, 2013, pp. 15-84.
73.Muqāṭil Ibn Sulaymān, *Tafsyr Muqāṭil Ibn Sulaymān*. Mw'asasat āl-Tāryḵ āl-'Araby: Beirut, 2002.
74.Muslim, *Saḥiḥ Muslim*. Dār āl-Kutub āl-'Ilmya: Beirut, 1991.

75.Neusner, J. *A History of The Jews in Babylonia*. vol. I. second edition. Brill: Leiden, 1969.
76.Neusner, J. *The Rabbinic Traditions about the Pharisees before 70: Part I The Masters*, Leiden: Brill, 1971.
77.Neusner, J. *The Fathers According to Rabbi Nathan: An Analytical Translation and Explanation*, Atlanta: Scholars Press, 1986.
78.Rippin, A. Literary Analysis of Qur'ān, tafsīr, and sīra: the Methodologies of John Wansbrough, In R. C. Martin (ed.), *Approaches to Islam in Religious Studies*, Tucson: The University of Arizona Press, 1985, pp. 151-163.
79.Rubin, U. Exegesis and *Hadyṯ*: the Case of the Seven *mathānī*, In G. R. Hawting and Abdul-Kader A. Shareef (eds.), *Approaches to the Qur'ān*, London: Routledge, 1993, pp. 141-156.
80.Saldarini, A. I. *The Fathers According to Rabbi Nathan version B: A Translation and Commentary*, Leiden: Brill, 1975.
81.Schacht, J. A. Revaluation of Islamic Traditions, *Journal of the Royal Asiatic Society of Great Britain and Ireland*, 2, 1949, pp. 143-154.
82.Schacht, J. *The Origins of Muhammadan Jurisprudence*, Oxford: The Clarendon Press, 1950a.
83.Schacht, J. Foreign Elements in Ancient Islamic Law, *Journal of Comparative Legislation and International Law*, Third Series, vol. 32, no. 3/4, 1950b, pp. 9-17.
84.Schacht, J. *An Introduction to Islamic Law*, Oxford: Clarendon Press, 1982.
85.Schumann, A. *Talmudic Logic*. UK: Lightning Source, Milton Keynes, 2012.
86.*Sifra*, trans. and commentary by M. Ginsberg, Atlanta: Scholars Press, 1999.
87.Sion, A. *Judaic Logic: A Formal Analysis of Biblical, Talmudic and Rabbinic Logic*, Geneva: Slatkine, 1995.
88.Street, T. Arabic Logic, In D .M. Gabbay and J. Woods (eds.), *Handbook of History of Logic, vol.1: Greek, Indian and Arabic Logic*, North-Holland: Elsevier, 2004, pp. 523-596.
89.Talmon, R. On An Eighth-Century Grammatical School in Medina: The Collection and Evaluation of the Available Material, *Bulletin of the School of Oriental and African Studies*, University of London, vol. 48, 2, 1985, pp. 224-236.
90.Tatian, Address to the Greeks, In *The Writings of Tatian and Theophilus; and The Clementine Recognitions*, transl. by B. P. Pratten, M. Dods and Thomas Smith D. D., Edinburgh: T&T Clark, 1967, pp. 1-45.
91.*The Jursalem Talmud: Second Order: Mo'ed; Tractates Pesaḥem and Yoma,* trans. And commentary by H. W. Guggenheimer, Berlin: Guyter, 2013.

92.*The Tosefta*, trans. by J. Neusner, vol. 2, Massachusetts: Henrickson Publishers, 2002.
93.Triyanta, A. Greek Philosophy And Islamic Law (The Influence of Aristotle's Logic on Analogical Qiyas in Shafi'i's Risala), *Logika*, 5, 2001, pp. 11-33.
94.Vagelophil, U. *The Syriac and Arabic Translation and Commentary Tradition*, Leiden, Brill, 2008.
95.Versteegh, K. *Landmarks in Linguistic Thought III: The Arabic Linguistic Tradition*, London and New York: Routledge, 1997.
96.Wansbrough, J. *Quranic Studies: Sources and Methods of Scriptural Interpretation*, Oxford: Oxford University Press, 1977.
97.Wegner, J. R. Islamic and Talmudic Jurisprudence: The Four Roots of Islamic Law and Their Talmudic Counterparts, *The American Journal of Legal History*, vol. 26, no. 1, 1982, pp. 25-71.
98.Wymann-Landgraf, U. F. A. *Malik and Medina: Islamic Legal Reasoning in the Formative Period*, Leiden: Brill, 2013.
99.Ziembinski, Z. *Practical Logic*, Dordrecht: Reidel, 1976.

Notes

1. The analysis of the Arabic informal logic, in a formal way, unlike the Hebrew one has not received attention. However, we have tentative attempts in [1] [43] [44].
2. Schacht [82] wrote a whole chapter about the earlier Islamic logical techniques in law such as analogy, but to integrate it in his history of Islamic legislation. So did Coulson [35], although his address for analogy is more limited [*ibid.*, pp. 40; 72-3; 59-60]. Hallaq in his history [45] is not interested in the development of such techniques but rather in introducing an outline of the logical structure for the earlier Islamic legislation and beyond. But in his *Origins and Evolution of Islamic Law* [47 ch. 5.3] [cf. Also his 48, pp. 19-27] he avoids this fault by displaying an excellent brief history of Islamic legal logical techniques. Although Wymann-Landgraf [98] has 'Islamic Legal Reasoning in the Formative Period' as a subtitle, only half of its first part addresses the informal logic [*ibid.*, pp. 85-182], while its main concern is not a history of Arabic informal logic, but is 'fundamentally concerned with Medinese praxis ('amal), a distinctive non-textual source of law which lay at the foundation of Medinese and subsequent Maliki legal reasoning' [*ibid.*, p. 3].
3. Thus, Margoliouth [67, p. 320] and Schacht [82, pp. 99-100] insisted on the Jewish influence upon the Islamic logical toolkit. Hallaq accepts only the existence of some Semitic (including Jewish) laws in Islamic law [47, pp. 4; 27-28; 194] while he rejects in his presentation of the Islamic legal and logical thinking any Hebrew influence [*ibid.*, pp. 113-18] [also, 48, pp. 19-27]. Wymann-Landgraf [98] is entirely silent about this.
4. Some call it 'Judaic Logic' [87], others 'Talmudic Logic' [85]. But we prefer to call it Hebrew in order to be compatible with the other branches of Semitic logics, i.e. 'Arabic Logic' and 'Syriac Logic'. To wit: Logic for every Semitic language.
5. For the division of *Tann'ay*itic traditions into two schools [75, pp. 156-77]. For the division of the *Tann'ay*itic methods of interpretation into two traditions ('Akiva

and Yišm'a'el), (see Ginsberg's [86] introduction to his translation of Sifra, pp. lvi-lx). And for the division of Hebrew informal logic into two traditions [72, pp. 69-73].

6. See section 3 below.

7. Tatian was an Assyrian orator and theologian who had a great influence on Syriac Christianity through his gospel harmony *Diattessaron* [49, pp. 144-75]. He was educated in a Hellenistic system [*ibid*., p. 1] which included Greek rhetoric which, in turn, included informal logic [69, pp. 148, 238-42]. Thus, in his oration to the Greeks, he uses these informal logical techniques such as analogy for proving resurrection [90, pp. 10-11].

8. Ephrem uses many informal logic techniques such as analogy [30, p. 67].

9. The *Jerusalem Talmud*. Pes. 6:1, fol. 33a says: 'From *heqqeš:* Since the continual offering is a community sacrifice and the *pesah* is a community sacrifice, just as the continual offering, a community sacrifice, overrides [the] Sabbath, so the *pesah,*a community sacrifice, overrides the Sabbath' (Neusner's [76] trans. P. 247). This inference has the following structure: A is C, B is C, C has D; then A has D and B has D. The common element is C (which has D).

10. In this paper, I shall use two editions of āl-Šāfi'y's *Risāla*. The first one is M.S.Kilani's edition [14] and I shall refer to it as '*Risāla* K'. The other one is M. Khadduri's translation of the *Risāla* [62] and I shall refer to it as '*Risāla* M'.

11. Triyanta did not decide upon which text āl-Šāfi'y depended in his identification of *qiyās* as syllogism. He just made an abstract comparison between āl-Šāfi'y's *qiyās* and Aristotle's syllogism. Thus, he says that his 'thesis only tries to compare Aristotle's syllogism to analogical *qiyās'* [93, p. 15].

12. Ibn āl-Muqaffa''s treatment of *qiyās* comes during his discussion of the difference between the judgments. Thus, he saw that that difference was due to the difference between the ancestors' opinions or was a result to 'an opinion made by its people by *qiyās* which differed and spread because of a mistake in the principle of commensurability and initiated an issue on its wrong example / رأى أجراه أهله على القياس فاختلف وانتشر بغلط فى أصل المقايسة وابتدأ أمر على غير مثاله' [53, p. 317]. It is clear here that ibn āl-Muqaffa': (a) understands *qiyās* as analogy not syllogism, (b) this understanding is different from Ishmael's school in Babylonia.

13. There are many copies of this letter beginning from the one which is in āl-Jāḥiẓ' *āl-Bayān wa āl-Tabyyn* [7] up to the one which is in Ibn Ḵaldwn's *Muqaddimah* [67, p. 307].

14. It was reported that he had a copy of the Bible or some religious book [60, Ḥ50] [52, Ḥ26828] [56, Ḥ15223].

15. '... the prophet said that 'Umar had come to him and said 'we like sayings we hear from Jews, do you think we should write some of them?' / ...عن النبى أن عمر أتاه فقال: 'إنا نسمع أحاديث من اليهود تعجبنا أفترى أن نكتب بعضها؟,''[5, Ḥ174]. (The three points before the quoted text refer to an omitted ascription chain).

16. 'Jabir said that 'Umar had copied a book from the Torah into Arabic' [6 *i* , Ḥ124. cf. also, Ḥ125-126].

17. 'Zūhary said āl-Sa'yb b. yazyd had said that the first one to have told stories had been Tamym āl-Dāry; the later asked 'Umar for that and the later permitted him' [22 *ii*, p. 443] [cf. also, 55 *xi*, p.80].

18. 'When 'Umar had consulted people he [Ka'b] preceded them' [55 *l*, p. 158].

19. '…Ya'qwb Ibn Zayd said that 'Umar Ibn āl-Ḵaṭṭāb was consulting 'Abdallāh Ibn 'Abbās in the things things / يعقوب بن زيد، قال: كان عمر بن الخطاب يستشير عبد الله بن عباس,'[61 *vi*, p.329]. It is also reported that 'some imigrators/Muhājirīn raged on 'Umar's his bringing Ibn 'Abbās closer to him than them / كان أناس من المهاجرين قد وجدوا على عمر فى إدنائه ابن عباس دونهم' [*ibid.*, p.328] [cf. also, 29, p. 130]. For his influence by the Jews see [2, p. 149].
20. Thus, we should stand with those scholars (for example: H. Birkeland, H. Gätje, C.H.M. Versteegh, F. Leemhuis and C. Gilliot) who insisted on existing of interesting in exegesis of the *Qur'ān* amongst the companions against those scholars (I.Godziher, A. Rippin and J. Wansbrough) who insisted on existing opposition of that interest. See [2, pp. 8-9] for more details and literature.
21. For the debate about dating of the collection of the *Qur'ān*, see Motzki, H. 'The collection of the Qur'ān: A reconsideration of Western views in light of recent methodological developments,' in: *Der Islam*, 78, pp. 1-34, 2001.
22. In all the reports we have previously quoted, Muḥammad was denying 'Umar's behavior, for example he said having seen 'Umar's copying a paper from the Torah 'do not ask the people of the book about anything /لا تسألوا أهل الكتاب عن شىء' [6 *i*, Ḥ125].
23. It was reported that there were oral translation of the *Torah* during Muḥammad's life: '…Abw Hurayra said that the people of the book was reading the *Torah* in Hebrew and explaining it in Arabic for the Muslims' [5 *ix*, Ḥ7542].
24. It can be said that the movement of translation had its roots in Muḥammad's era whereas it was reported that he had asked Zayd Ibn Ṯābit to have learnt Hebrew or Syriac [61 ii, p.30]. Thus, we can say that there were two persuasive traditions; one confirmed translation and borrowing from the ancient books and the other denied this. 'Umar I have chosen the first.
25. '…Ka'b was telling stories / كعب كان يقص' [55 *l*, p. 170].
26. 'Umar I was not trusting in foreign scribes, therefore he appointed Ibn 'Abbās as a secretary of what was being transmitted from the ancient books. There are many reports support this hypothesis; once Tamym said, while telling stories and 'Umar I and Ibn 'Abbās was attending, 'Fear the scholar's err… then 'Umar said to Ibn 'Abbās when Tamym finished ask him about the meaning of the scholar's err / اتقوا زلة العالم...فقال [عمر] لابن عباس: إذا فرغ فاسأله: ما زلة العالم؟' [*ibid.*, p.81]. Also, Ibn 'Abbās was beside 'Umar I during his last moments and was the link between 'Umar I and the people [61 *iii*, p. 323].
27. [61 *ix*, p. 449] [55 *l*, p. 159].
28. 'The Arabs had no books or scholarship. The desert attitude and illiteracy prevailed among them. When they wanted to know certain things that human beings are usually curious to know, such as the reasons for the existing things, the beginning of creation, and the secrets of existence, they consulted the earlier People of the Book about it and got their information from them. The People of the Book were the Jews who had the *Torah*, and the Christians who followed the religion of (the Jews). Now, the people of the *Torah* who lived among the Arabs at that time were themselves *Bedouins*. They knew only as much about these matters as is known to *ordinary People* of the Book,' [58 *i*, p. 566]. The western scholars followed Ibn Ḵaldūn steps, after adding the *Talmud* to the stock of those Jewish Bedouins.

29. The title '*Āḥbār*' is the plural of the noun '*ḥabr*' which means Rabbi. Concerning Ka'b knowing of the rabbinic books we have the following report 'Ka'b said that my father had written for me one book of the Bible and having given it to me had told me to work by it, then he had sealed *all his other books* / قال كعب: إن أبي كتب لي كتاباً من التوراة ودفعة إلي وقال: اعمل بهذا، وختم على سائر كتبه' [61 *ix*, p.449] [cf. also, [55 *l*, p. 159].

30. Ka'b said 'My father was the most knower man of what God gave to Moses, and he did not keep anything he knew away from me / كان أبي من أعلم الناس بما أنزل الله على موسى، وكان لا يدخر عني شيئاً مما يعلم' [55 *l*, p.161]. Ka'b also complained that the Rabbis blamed him for his conversion to Islam [*ibid.*, p.164].

31. āl-Ḏahaby [22 *iii*, p. 489] also says that he [Ka'b] 'was telling them [Muslims] about the Israelite books.'

32. For this classification of the authenticity of the sayings of the prophet, see [46, p.76] [29, ch. 2]. For the authenticity of the exegetical traditions including Ibn 'Abbās' ones, see: [29, ch. 3].

33. Cf. also, [29, p. 40].

34. Cf. also, [*ibid.*, p. 79].

35. This is the position of Fuat Sezgin in his *Geschichte des arabischen Schrifttums, Band I: Qur'ānwissenschaften, Hadith, Geschichte, Fiqh, Dogmatik, Mystik bis ca. 430 H.*, Leiden: Brill, 1967. And, N. Abbot in her *Studies in Arabic Literary Papyri, II: Qur'ānic Commentary and Tradition*, Chicago: The University of Chicago Press, 1967.

36. For Rippin's criticism of the alleged authenticity of the attributed books to Ibn 'Abbās, see his: 'Ibn ᶜAbbās's āl-Lughāt fi āl-Qur'ān,' in: *Bulletin of the School of Oriental and African Studies*, vol. 44, pp. 15-25, 1981; 'Ibn 'Abbās's Gharīb āl-Qur'ān,' in: *Bulletin of the School of Oriental and African Studies*, vol. 46, pp.332 333, 1983; 'Tafsīr lbn 'Abbās and criteria for dating early tafsīr texts,' in: *Jerusalem Studies in Arabic and Islam*, vol. l9, pp. 38-83, 1994; and 'Studying early tafsīr texts,' in: *Der Islam*, vol. 72, pp. 310-323, 1995.

37. See Schoeler, G., *The Oral and the Written in Early Islam*, trans. By U. Vagelpohl, London & New York: Routledge, 2006, *passim.*

38. What I mean here is that these sayings were not just sayings or aḥadyṯ, but that they expressed also practices, ideas and notions. Traditions, from an epistemological point of view, have goals, methods and specific language. (cf. Laudan, L., *Progress and its Problems: Towards a Theory of Scientific Growth*, Berkeley: California University Press, 1977; Laudan, L., *Science and Values*, California: University of California Press, 1984).

39. [13 *vi*, p. 518].

40. [26, p. 1]. Cf. also, Nuesner's [77] translation, p. 3.

41. [16 *i*, p. 219].

42. [26, p. 46]. Cf. also Goldin's [39] trans. P. 62.

43. Ibn Manẓwr tells us that 'princes were called *salāṭyn* (the plural of *sulṭān*) since rights and evidences are established by them,' [59 *xiv*, p.243] which means that that meaning of the term *sulṭān* as a king or prince was a later development.

44. Ibn Manẓwr tells us on the authority of āl-Layṯ that "*āl-sulṭān* is king's power" [*ibid.*].

45. *ḵālaṭ* the thing *muḵālaṭa* means mixed it [*ibid viii*, p.212], and *ḵalaṭ* the people and *ḵālaṭahwm* means being amongst them, and *ḵalyṭ* of the people means their tapster and the one who sits and stay amongst them [*ibid*., 215].
46. See the next subsection, item n. 2.
47. The first scholar to note the relationship between Abw āl-Jalad and Ibn ‘Abbās was I. Goldziher in his Die Richtungen der islamischen Koranauslegung, Leiden, 1952, p.66. However, Abw āl-Jalad was reported to have been ‘a reader to the Torah books and what is relating to it / صاحب كتب التوراة ونحوها’ the same report continues about Abw ‘Imrān āl-Jawny’s reciting on Abw āl-Jalad’s authority by saying: ‘recited on his authority [Abw āl-Jalad] Qatādah, Abw ‘Imrān āl-Jawny and Ward’ [12 *ii*, 2275]. And for his cooperation with Ibn ‘Abbās in interpreting the *Qur’ān* by Jewish tradition and their correspondences, see [19 *i*: 434; 723].
48. He recited on the authority of Sa‘yd b. Jubayr, ‘Aṭā‘ b. Abw Rabāḥ, ‘Ikrima, Kurayb, and Mujāhid [10 *xi*, 2467], all of them belong to Ibn ‘Abbās’ school.
49. In Ibn Sa‘d [61 *v*, pp. 88-89] it is reported on the authority of Sulaymān b. āl-Raby‘ that some people from Basra to have requested from him some advice due to he ‘had read the first book / وقد قرأت الكتاب الأول,’ i.e. the *Torah*. Also, the prophet said to him explaining a dream that he [‘Amr] had seen it: ‘if you lived you would read the two books: the *Torah* and the *Qur’ān*’. Thus, he was reading them [55 *xxxi*, p.255].
50. Ka‘b said to ‘Amr after the former asked him a question and the later answered to it ‘this is written in the Torah as you said / إنها لمكتوبة فى التوراة كما قلت’ [*ibid. xxxi*, p. 264].
51. On the authority of ‘Ikrima (one of Ibn ‘Abbās' disciples) that he heard ‘Abdallāh b. ‘Amr says that ‘Ibn ‘Abbās is the best one in knowing the past and explaining the revelation…. ‘Ikrima said, I told Ibn ‘Abbās his speech, then Ibn ‘Abbās said he had knowledge / ابن عباس أعلمنا بما مضى، وأفقهنا فيما نزل... قال عكرمة: فأخبرت ابن عباس بقوله فقال: إن عنده لعلماً’ [ibid. *xxxi*, p. 263].
52. We are told, on the authority of ‘Amr b. Qays that ‘Abdallāh b. ‘Amr said ‘it is a sign of the doomsday… that *Miṯnā* (*Mišnah*) is being read among people but nobody interprets it, then he was asked what *Miṯnā* is? He replied it is what was written but other than God’s book / من أشراط الساعة... أن تقرأ المثناة فى القوم ليس فيهم أحد يعبرها قيل له: ما المثناة؟ قال: ما كتب سوى كتاب الله’ [*ibid. xlvi*, p. 313].It should be noted here that that the speech of ‘Abdallāh b. ‘Amr has another wording which can contradict the above one. Thus, in [18 *xiii*, Ḥ14559] we have on the authority of ‘Amr b. Qays, on the authority of ‘Abdallāh b. ‘Amr also, but on the mouth of the prophet that ‘it is a sign of the doomsday … that the *Miṯnā* is being read among people / من أشراط الساعة ... يُقرأ فى القوم المثناة.’ This means, on the contrary of Ibn ‘Asākir’s text, that reading the *Miṯnā* itself is a sign of the doomsday not the non-explaining it. But this second wording is not possible because of ‘Abdallāh b. ‘Amr’s respecting of Jewish culture (There is another wording close to the second one in [3 *vii*, Ḥ4834]).
53. ‘Moses…received the *Torah* at Sinai [*ARNA*, Goldin’s [39] trans., ch. *i*, p. 3] … Joshua took over from Moses [*ibid*., p.4] … The Elders took over from Joshua [*ibid*.] … The Judges took over from the Elders [*ibid*.] … The Prophets took over from the judges [*ibid*.] …Haggai, Zechariah, ad Malachi took over from the Prophets. The Men of the Great Assembly took over from Haggai, Zechariah, and Malachi (*ibid*.) … Antigonus of Soko took over from Simeon the righteous [*ibid*.,

ch.*5*, p. 39] ...etc. Finally, Rabban Johanan ben Zakkai took over from Hillel and Shammai' [*ibid*., ch. 14, p. 74].

54. The relationship between Abw-āl-Dardā' and Ka'b was so closed that the former's wife was telling from Ka'b [51 *i*, 343], she also called Ka'b as Abw-āl-Dardā's brother [22 *iii*, p. 493]. Also, Abw āl-Dardā' said about Ka'b that he 'had great knowledge' [61 *ix*, p. 449].

55. For a biography which shows how 'Atā' was one of the adherents of Ibn 'Abbās' tradition and influenced with Jewish traditions see [10 *xx*, 3941].

56. [55 *l*, pp. 164-65].

57. 'Then we bequeathed the book to whom we chose from our worshippers / ثم أورثنا الكتاب الذين اصطفينا من عبادنا' *Q*.35:32.

58. Concerning interpretation in *ARNA* by just mention the rules of interpretation without any details, see [Goldin's [39] trans., p. 74, and with citing RS, see*:* *ibid*., P. 154]. Concerning indicating to the importance of interpretation, see [*ibid*., p. 5, 91].

59. It should be noted that Abw āl-Dardā' also, one of the translation movement supporters said on the authority of Ibn Abw Qilāba 'you will not understand the *Qur'ān* entirely until you can see aspects for it / لن تفقه القرآن كل الفقه حتى ترى للقرآن وجوهاً' [61 *ii*, p. 308].

60. Bravmann [31, p. 185] sees that 'certainly, the principles of *ra'y* and *'ilm* cannot be considered as having been suddenly introduced by 'Umar (or his immediate predecessors), rather it *may be assumed* that the Arab mind had been familiar with these principles in a considerably earlier period' (Italics are mine). But this is just an assumption, while our reconstruction is based on facts and parallel texts.

61. For a serious study about the jurisprudence of Ibn 'Abbās' students, see [71].

62. Hishām Ibn Yūswf the judge was one of āl-Šāfi'y's teachers in Yemen [37, p. 44].

63. 'He obtained (knowledge) from Ibn 'Abbās, Abw Hurayra… 'Abdallāh Ibn 'Amr… and Ṭāwws', 'The Abundance of his knowledge was from the scripts of the people of the book', 'he was a judge on Ṣan'ā' [22 *iv*, p. 545].

64. 'He memorized from … Ibn 'Abbās', 'and he was buying books for his brother' [22 *v*, 311-12].

65. Most Islamic law scholars concentrated on the influence of Medina school of *fiqh* on āl-Shāfi'ī, or as Motzki puts it 'The proportion and the importance of Meccan *fiqh* in the work of āl-Šāfi'y has not yet been properly appreciated by research. Until now it has always been assumed that the decisive influence on āl-Šāfi'y emanated from Malik and Medinan jurisprudence. One of the reasons for this assessment is probably to be sought in the fact that almost nothing was known of Meccan *fiqh*' [71, p. 292]. In the present paper, I did not commit to this mistake. Instead, I concentrated on Medina's linguistics as it will be shown below. Moreover, I have to refer that *ra'y* techniques was also prevailed in Medina (see for the nature of these techniques; [82, pp. 113-119] [98, pp. 145-182], which means (in addition of influence of 'Umar's translation movement on Medina scholars and transmission of *RS* 1-3; 6 rules to the Medina traditions) More influence of *RS* on āl-Shāfi'ī's informal logic.

66. I say that āl-Šāfi'y borrowed only the term qiyās of the Iraqis grammarians not its content, that because there is a difference between the grammarians *qiyās* and the jurists one, or as Versteegh explains: 'the *qiyâs* of the Arabic grammarians represents a totally different concept: it is a method to explain apparent deviations

from the rules in certain phenomena by referring to their resemblance to other phenomena. The result is an increased regularity because the rules are applied to as many phenomena as possible. This kind of analogical reasoning is different from the concept of 'analogy' in Western linguistics, which serves as an instrument to explain irregularities by showing how they developed by interference from other phenomena' [95, p. 35]. And it is a known fact the borrowing of terms amongst sciences.

67. He is reported in many sources to have made a poem which started by saying 'Grammar is nothing but *qiyās* which is followed / إنما النحو قياس يُتبَع' [9 *xiii*, p. 355].

68. āl-Šāfi'y is reported to have said that 'he who would like to be great in grammar should depend on āl-Kisā'y /من أراد أن يتبحر فى النحو فهو عيال على الكسائى' [55 *lx*, 116-17].

69. This is reported by [3, p. 107 ff.]. In addition, āl-Šāfi'y wrote many polemical essays against Iraqis jurists, for example; *Kitāb āl-Radd 'ala Muḥammad Ibn āl-Ḥasan*, in [15 *ix*, pp. 85-170]. Cf. also [34, p. 182].

70. āl-Šāfi'y has been to Iraq twice, the first time for a trial in which he learnt from the Iraqis (around 796), and the second one for teaching (813) [34, p. 182].

71. There are here two problems/questions; (1) did Aristotle's *On Rhetoric* was translated before the end of the second century A.H., the time of āl-Šāfi'y's activities? (2) Did āl-Šāfi'y has knowledge of the Hellenistic tradition? Concerning the first question, most scholars who wrote on the ancient Arabic translation of Aristotle's *On Rhetoric* believed that it was translated about the end of the second century A.H. (for example, Badawi's [28] introduction to his publication of the translation, p. ز; Lyons' [65] introduction for his edition, p.i, where he puts its date (p. vi) at 731). Only U.Vagelophl [94] believed that it was translated later at āl-Kindy's (805-873) circle [*ibid.*, pp.130; 165; 180] based mainly on terminology, but this is not acceptable, because the most important terms are not kindian, such as παράδειγμα which was rendered as proof or *burhān* [66, p.110] while āl-Kindy kept this term, i.e. *burhān* for ἀπόδειξις [Rescher, N. *Studies in the History of Arabic Logic*. University of Bitsburgh Press, 1963, p. 14]. Concerning the second question, we have in āl-Bayhaqy's book about āl-Šāfi'y a report about āl-Šāfi'y, although says that āl-Šāfi'y had read Aristotle's books in medicine [4 *i*, p. 133] which is absurd, but reflects his knowing of Aristotle.

72. Lowry sees that there are only four rules, or as he puts it: 'in any event, Šāfi'ī views the permissible forms of *qiyās* as three: the *argumentum a fortiori*, *ma'nā*-based *qiyās*, and *shabah*-based *qiyās*,' [64, p. 154], again the *argumentum a fortiori* divides into two; 'the *argumentum a maiore ad minus* and *a minore ad maius*,' [*ibid.*, p. 153]. This is also Hallaq's view [45, pp. 23, 29]. But, in fact, the *argumentum a fortiori* has three forms not two as we shall show.

73. If it is permissible for you to eat three apples that does not mean it is permissible for you to eat more.

74. We may connect this with Schacht's observation about the religious and ethical nature of Islamic law and jurisprudence [82, p. v].

75. What is between the brackets is *TAR* L's reading.

76. Cf. Khadduri's [62, p. 79] trans. '[Analogy's] conformity [to precedent] should be based on two conditions.'

77. Khadurri translates '*ma'nā*' here as meaning not reason (*Risāla* M, p. 290)

78. Lowry also criticizes Hallaq but because the *ratio legis* is a lawful technique for resolving ambiguities while ‘in Islamic law, the immediate purpose of the *ma‘nā/‘illā* is not to resolve ambiguities in the law, but to extend a statute of known meaning to a case of first impression.’[64, pp. 150 – 151, n.132].
79. Lowry criticized Hallaq for his confusing the *a simili* with **Sh.5** as ‘the *argumentum a simili* thus seems closer to Šāfi‘ī’s concept of *ma‘nā*-based *qiyās* [**Sh.4**]’ [64, p. 152, n. 133]. Thus, Lowry seems to have fallen at the same mistake by regarding āl-Šāfi‘ī’s aim was the purpose not meaning.
80. The Syriac translator rendered the Greek word πίστις as *taṣdyq*. For more details, see [66, p. 115].
81. We should note here that the Syriac translator(s) rendered the Greek word ἀπόδειξις / demonstration by the Arabic word *taṯbyt* or *taṯabut*. Cf. [66, p. 21. And p. 173, for more details].
82. The Syriac translator rendered the Greek word ἐπαγωγή /induction as *i‘tibār*. See for more details [66, pp. 58, 239].
83. The Syriac translator rendered the Greek word συλλογισμός / syllogism as سلجسة, سلجسموس, سلوجسمة, سلوجسموس. See for more details [66, pp. 132, 213].
84. The Syriac translator(s) rendered the word παράδειγμα as *burhān* or proof in most of the places. See for more details [66, pp.110, 167].
85. The Syriac translator(s) rendered the Greek word ἐνθύμημα as *tafkyr*. See for more details [66, pp.56, 259].
86.
‘ونحن قائلون الآن فى التثبيت وما يرى تثبيتاً. فالتثبيت كما هو فى الديالقطيقية منه: الإيفاغوغى-وهو الاعتبار- ومنه ما نرى [يرى] اعتباراً ومنه السلجسة. ومنه ما نرى [يرى] سلجسة. وبهذه الحال [يوجد ها هنا أيضاً] فإن البرهان شيء من الاعتبار، والتفكير شيء من السلجسة يوجد ها هنا أيضاً، والتفكير الذى يرى: سلجسة الريطورى، وبالبرهان الاعتبار الريطورى. وقد أعنى بالتفكير: السلوجسموس الريطورى، وبالبرهان الاعتبار الريطورى يرى [تُرى]’ [*TAR*B, p.11; *TAR*L, p. 9].
87.
‘وأما الإقناع خاصة فقد يكون فيه من الكلام على جهة البرهان غير قليل. وإنما يكون الشغب الأكثر فى تلك التفكيرات’ [*TAR*B, p. 12; *TAR*L, p. 10]
88.
‘وقد يؤتى بالتفكيرات من الصادقات ومن الدلائل’ [*TAR* B, p. 14; *TAR* L, p. 12].
89.
‘فالدلائل والصدق والرواسم هن مقدمات الريطورية’ [*TAR* B, p. 18; *TAR* L, p. 17].
90. Also, he says at [*TAR* B, p. 178; *TAR* L, p. 169] ‘فأما أن يكون كل شيء من الرسوم غير ذى سلوجسموس فقد تبين لنا فى أنالوطيقى,’ without any clarification.
91. ‘ومن الرواسم كالجزئى [كالجزؤى]، ومنها كالكلى. فلتكن الرواسم ها هنا كما لو قال قائل: إن الحكماء عدول، لأن سقراطس كان حكيماً وعدلاً. فهذا الآن رسم، وهو له إن كان هذا القول حقاً وليس باضطرارى، لأنه ليس سلوجسماً [سلوجسمياً]’ [*TAR* B, p. 14; *TAR* L, p. 13].
92. What are between < and > is Badawi’s additions, and it seems to be reasonable. Lyons edited the text as following: ‘ونحو آخر من قبل العلامة، فان هذا ايضاً بلا سلجسة...او لو قال قائل ان ديانوسوس * * لانه شرير، فهذا غير ذى سلوجسموس* * شرير’ [*TAR* L, p. 164]. What are between two asterisks is lacunae in the original ms.
93. The *apodeixis* syllogism is inferred from [24, 1357a: 29-30].
94. [*TAR* B, pp. 6-7; 11; 15].
95. The word ἀπόδειξις or demonstration even was rendered as *tathbyt* as we said before.
96. Demonstration does not aim to persuasion at Aristotle.

97. My translation seems to be incomprehensible, that because the Arabic passage is also so. I tried to render this incomprehensibility in the English translation too. It should be noted that I did not translate *bi āl-ākṯar* as at the most part, as it would be expected. The reason will be clear at the next few pages.
98. Khdduri's note n. 1, p. 67 in: *Risāla* M.
99. For God's *Bayān* see [*Risāla* K: 53; 54], for the messenger's *Bayān* see [*Risāla* K 58]. Cf. also, [64, p. 23 ff].
100. 'ومنه: ما فرض الله على خلقه الاجتهاد فى طلبه/one of it [*Bayān*] consists of what God commanded his creatures to seek through *'ijtihād*' [*Risāla* K: 59] [*Risāla* M, p. 68]. Cf. [64, p. 23 ff].
101. *Bayān* is including also (1) linguistic manners and styles [*Risāla* K: 174-176]; cf. [*TAR*'s third treatise on Style], (2) RS: 4-5 or the general/عام and the particular/خاص [*Risāla* K: 173, and passim].
102. Cf. Also, [15 ix, p. 77], where he provides an example for a blind that needs for demonstration.
103. Cf. Also, [*ibid.*, pp. 8; 11; 19-20; 32; 33; 34; 35].
104. 'والسنة منها خاصة، ومنها عامة' [*TAR* B, p. 46. Cf. also p. 64] [*TAR* L, p. 50. Cf. also p. 67]
105. ' فالخاصة منها هى المحدودة فى أناس، أعنى عند كل واحد منهم... وأعنى بالعامة تلك التى هى فى الطبيعة' [*TAR* B, p. 64. Cf. also p. 70] [*TAR* L, p. 67. Cf. also p.73].
106. This is the concept of *sunna* in *TAR*. But it has other ramifications which will seem to be in opposition to āl- Šāfi'y's concept. For TA the general *sunna* is not written, while the particular *sunna* is written (some of it in reality) [*TAR* B, p. 46; 64] [*TAR* L, p. 50; 67]. This seems to be in opposition to āl-Šāfi'y's concept, because, for him, the *Qur'ān* is the book (written) in which there are 'الفرائض المنصوصة / the texted duties' [*Risāla* K: 97] while the prophet's *sunna* is his practice which is 'بلا نص كتاب / without a texted book' [*Risāla* K: 100]. But if we contemplate a little, we shall discover that there is no opposition, Because *TA*'s non-written general *sunna* expresses absolute laws like the *Qur'ān*'s: ' هو الشئ الذى يزكيه [يزكنه] الكل بالطباع/ it is the thing which everyone approves [appealed to] it naturally' [*TAR* B, p. 64; *TAR* L, p.67], while his particular *sunna* expresses laws which should not contradict the general one 'إن كانت السنة المكتوبة مضادة للأمر، قد ينبغى أن نستعمل السنة العامة / if the written *sunna* was in contradiction with the things, then may we use the general one' [*TAR* B, p. 71] [*TAR* L, p.73], this is just as the prophet's *sunna* in āl-Šāfi'y's concept for it [*Risāla* K: 307]. In addition, the prophet's *sunna*, for āl-Šāfi'y, is *Aḥadyth* or the prophet's fixed speech, i.e. written. (It is known thanks to Schacht [81, p. 145] that āl-Šāfi'y triumphed for *Āḥadyṯ* movement in his time)
107. See the above note.
108. [Ms.23a-23b]. It must be noted here the different reading of Lyons where he reads: ' حكيماً ما هو أحداً / some wise man who is unique, as: 'حكيماً ماهراً جداً/a very clever wise man' [*TAR* L, 75b: 22-23, p. 74.]. However, this does not effect in the significance of the sentence in general, i.e. it should be there some wise man. But on my reading which accords to the Arabic *Organon* manuscript, this wise man should be only one man, a unique one. It should be noted also Badawi's different reading for another word in that sentence. Thus, he reads: 'يرذل / be getting bad,' as: 'يردك / comes to you' [*TAR* B, p.72]. It should be noted also the great difference in meaning between the [Ms.23a-23b] and the Aristotelian text [1375b: 23-24]: 'And [one

should say] that to seek to be wiser than the laws is the very thing that is forbidden in those laws that are praised'.

109. This happens during his arguing against *'istiḥsān* and Iraqi school, thus he says: 'فإن قلتم: لأنهم لا علم لهم بالأصول / if you say because they have no knowledge of elements/usūl' [15 *ix*, p. 74] and his intention by these elements is the *Qur'ān* and *sunna* as it is shown by the next paragraphs. He also calls the knowledge of the *Qur'ān* and *sunna* 'علم الأصول / science of the elements' [*15 ix*, p. 77]. Cf. Also, [84, p. 60]. However, some scholars [35, pp. 55-60] [33, p. 78] [45, p. 22] supposed without any textual justification that āl-Šāfi'y had four elements (or sources). Lowry [63] refused to consider that āl-Šāfi'y had any theory about elements or sources [*ibid.*, pp. 24, 50], because, from his point of view, whenever āl-Šāfi'y speaks about elements or sources, then his talking either messy or out of context [*ibid.*, pp. 32-33]. Lowry arrived to this conclusion as a result of his gathering of lists of āl-Šāfi'y's sentences about elements [*ibid.*, pp. 31- 32]. But most of what he gathered are not sentences about elements so far as Lowry's believing so. Most of the sentences in Lowry's lists do not contain the word usūl/elements (for example, [*Risāla* K: 397; 881; 1101]. Thus, Lowry also like the other mentioned scholars does not have textual evidence for his claim.

110. For example: 'فلا يجوز أن يقال لقول: فرضٌ إلا لكتاب الله، ثم سنة رسوله / So it is not permissible to regard anything as a duty save that set forth in the *Qur'ān* and *sunna* of His Apostle' [*Risāla* M, p. 112]. See also [*Risāla* K, 266; 281; 293, and *Passim*].

111. Schacht [48, pp.17-19]. For a more detailed analysis and meanings of the term *sunna*, see [23, pp. 259-282].

112. 'And He [God] said: God has sent down to thee the Book and the Wisdom, and has taught thee what thou did not know before; the bounty of God towards thee is ever great [Q. IV, 113]… So God mentioned His Book – which is the *Qur'ān* – and Wisdom, and I have heard that those who are learned in the *Qur'ān* – whom I approve – hold that wisdom in the *sunna* of the Apostle of God' [*Risāla* M, p. 111; *Risāla* K: 250 252].

113. For the primary meaning of the term *ijtihād*, see [31, pp. 188-194]. And for its development [45, pp. 19-20].

114. āl-Šāfi'y says about the *a fortiori*: 'فأقوى القياس / and the strongest *qiyās*' [*Risāla* K: 1483].

115. [*TAR* B, pp. 11, 13-14] [*TAR* L, pp. 10,12], their counterparts passages in *On Rhetoric* are [24, 1356b 15-16; 1357a 31-33] respectively.

116. It is interesting that neither Hallaq [43] [45] nor Lowry [64, pp. 32-3; 147 ff.] recognized inferring by sign at āl-Šāfi'y. However, Lowry identified it as 'in the nature of estimation based on incomplete information, driven by necessity, and evaluated in terms of purely pragmatic consideration' [64, p. 147]. But as I shall show that this is not correct.

117. [82, pp. 99-100]. Also, [64, p.153, n.138]. Our result is confirmed also by H. Motzki [70] statistical research about the role of non- Arabs converts in the Islamic formative scholarship. According to this statistical work, their role was weak in comparison to the native Arabs from the Arabian Peninsula.

118. For the influence of Hellenistic rhetoric on the Jewish or Hebraic informal logic, see: Daube, D., 'Rabbinic methods of Interpretation and Hellenistic Rhetoric,' in: *Hebrew Union College Annual*, 22, 1949, pp. 239–264.

119. [22 *ii*, p.448].

120. For Ka'b's son and their knowledge of the ancient books, see [61 *ix*, p. 455].

121. The other misunderstanding of Aristotle because of translation in philosophy is the attribution of theology of Aristotle (in fact, extracts from the *Enneads* of Plotinus) to Aristotle. For more details, see: Rowson, E.K., 'The Theology of Aristotle and Some Other Pseudo-Aristotelian Texts Reconsidered,' in: *Journal of the American Oriental Society*, 112, 1992, pp. 478-484.

1. Introduction

Connecting Sacred and Mundane: From Bilingualism to Hermeneutics in Hebrew Epitaphs

Michael Nosonovsky

College of Engineering and Applied Science,
University of Wisconsin-Milwaukee,
Milwaukee, WI 53201,
the United States of America
nosonovs@uwm.edu

1. Introduction

Gravestones play a prominent role among the monuments of Jewish culture still present in Eastern Europe, where Jewish civilization has thrived for centuries. Most of the gravestones have inscriptions in Hebrew. The oldest Ashkenazi gravestones in Eastern Europe are dated with the first part of the 16th century C.E. The total number of Hebrew inscriptions constitutes tens of thousands. Despite their abundance, Hebrew gravestone inscriptions (or epitaphs) are rarely studied by philologists or anthropologists as a literary genre or a phenomenon of culture [13], [14], [18].

The oldest Jewish gravestone inscriptions in Europe are dated with the first centuries before the Common Era. However, most of these oldest epitaphs, as well as most of the inscription from the first millennium C.E., are in Greek or Latin, with only occasional Hebrew words included sometimes [7]. The phenomenon of elaborated Hebrew epitaphs emerged at the turn of the millennia [11]. The appearance of such elaborated texts coincides with the emergence of the rabbinical Judaism in Europe at about the 10th century C.E., as opposed to the earlier *Ga'on*ic Judaism with its centers in Babylonia and in Palestine. Writing epitaphs in Hebrew was a part of a more general process of creating a sophisticated rabbinical culture with Hebrew language playing a prominent role in several areas of the communal life including, but not limited to, the liturgy and religious education [16].

Hebrew epitaphs are related to the rabbinical literature, and in many instances they use the same formulas or lexica as the latter. However, the epitaphs are seldom studied from the viewpoint of the rabbinical logic and hermeneutics.

In this paper, I will discuss the genre of the Ashkenazi Hebrew epitaphs as a hermeneutic phenomenon and will show that the main function of the epitaphs is to connect the ideal world of Hebrew sacred texts (as presented or symbolized by the Hebrew language and the Written Torah, the culture of written texts, and normative, canonical Judaism) to the world of everyday 'mundane' or 'profane' life of the Jewish community (as presented or symbolized by the Aramaic or Yiddish languages and the Oral Torah, colloquial culture, and a folk religion). The actualization of a sacred text is a central problem of hermeneutics, and thus the methods of connecting the sacred to the mundane in the epitaphs are at the very center of the Judaic hermeneutics in general. The material of this study was collected during numerous field trips to Ukraine and other parts of Eastern Europe since the early 1990s [15].

2. Epitaphs Between the Sacred and Profane

The epitaphs occupy an intermediate position between the ideal world of the sacred texts and the real world of the everyday life of a Jewish community at several levels.

2.1. Absolute Coordinates: Name, Date, and Marker of a Place

Almost every epitaph involves four necessary elements [12, 13, 15]:

First is an *introductory phrase*. In most cases the introductory phrase is פה נטמן "here lies" (usually abbreviated as פנ). Besides that, sometimes, הציון הזה "this sign," עד הגל הזה "this stone is a witness," and some other formulas are used. The introductory formula refers to the burial place and it seems redundant, because the gravestone itself marks the place. As I have suggested earlier [12], [14], this formula corresponds to the function of the epitaph as a marker of a place, where a certain contact with the soul of the deceased is possible. It is important also to mark the ritually impure place of the burial, for example, because the *Kohanim* are forbidden to go there.

Syntactically, the introductory phrase can be viewed as a subject part of a sentence 'Here lies X'. However, in many cases the introductory formula is separated from the rest of the text. For instance, the abbreviation פנ is often written on top of a monument separately from the rest of the inscription. The abbreviation פנ is usually present on a Jewish gravestone even if the rest of the inscription is written in a different language, such as Russian. This indicates that starting the mid-18th century, the introductory formula plays a symbolic role of a marker of a Jewish grave, similarly to, for example, a Star of David on the gravestones of the 20th century.

Second is the name of the deceased person. The name is given in its complete form following a 'title' and often a list of virtues: '[description of virtues] title X [nicknamed N] *ben/bat* title Y, blessing.' The titles range from a simple ר *R[eb]* [= 'a man'] to elaborated pleonastic titles, such as the abbreviated הה מוהרר = הרב הגדול מורנו הרב רבי ('The g[reat] R[abbi], ou[r teacher,] R[abbi] R[eb]'). A description of virtues can also range from a straightforward one to an elaborated one. The name is usually presented in its official form, the way a person would be called in an official document, such as a *ketubba* or *geṭ*, or when a person is called to read the Torah. The official form of the name is discussed in the treatise *Giṭṭin*. The standard blessing after the father's name is זל (=זכרונו לברכה 'his memory is for blessing').

Third is the date of death, which is given in accordance with the Hebrew calendar and the Era from the Creation. The practical value of remembrance of the date of death is that the person can be commemorated on that day of the year (a custom known as *yohrẓeit* in Yiddish). Sometimes, a chronogram is used: a biblical verse with certain letters marked in it, so that the sum of numerical values constitutes the year.

Fourth is a final blessing formula, almost always תהי נפשו צרורה בצרור החיים 'May his/her soul be bound in the bundle of life' usually abbreviated to תנצבה.

A typical epitaph looks somewhat like this:

פ"נ
איש תם וישר
ר' יצחק ב"ר אברהם
י"ב אדר תקל"ב לפ"ק
תנצבה

Here lies a simple and righteous man (Job 1:1) R[abbi] Isaac s[on of] R[abbi] Abraham [died on] 12 *Adar* (5)532 a[ccording to the] M[inor] E[ra] (=1772 CE), M[ay] H[is Soul] b[e Bound] i[n the Bundle of] L[ife].

In this epitaph, the expression איש תם וישר ("a simple and righteous man") is used as a praise formula in front of the name of the deceased. The title 'Rabbi' does not imply that the person had a rabbinical ordination. It is just a form of politeness or respect. The so-called פרט קטן 'minor era' implies stating the Hebrew year from the Creation of the world without indicating a millennium.

Although these four elements are found in virtually every Hebrew epitaph from Eastern Europe, their functional value is not clear. Why would one, for example, say 'here lies' on a gravestone? Isn't it obvious that a gravestone marks a grave of a person whose body lies under the stone? Why are the date of death, name, and gender such important individual characteristics, unlike, say, an occupation?

One possible answer to this question is that time, place, and individuality constitute an absolute system of coordinates to which the person is related. The mystical *Sefer Yeẓirah* ('Book of Creation') mentions three categories: עולם *'olam* ('world'), שנה *šanah* ('year'), and נפש *nefeš* ('soul') as a symbolic representation of the space, time, and individuality (or subjectivity). Relating a person to these coordinates by designating his own place, moment in time, and name constitutes a hermeneutic act of connecting with the Absolute.

2.2. Biblical Quotations

Various biblical verses are used in the epitaphs, and their function may be different. Often a verse mentioning a Biblical character with the same name as the deceased is used. Below is an example of an epitaph from the town of Buczacz (1792 C.E.):

> ותקח מרים את הטוב בידה ידה ששלחה לאביון ותנוח שם מרים תקבר פה ך"ג שבט תקנ"ב
>
> And Miriam took the good in her hand, the hand that she prostrated to the poor, and Miriam died there, and she was buried here 23 *Ševat* (5)552.

Three Biblical quotations are found in this epitaph: וַתִּקַּח מִרְיָם אֶת-הַתֹּף בְּיָדָהּ 'And Miriam took… the drum in her hand' (*Exodus* 15:20), וְיָדֶיהָ שִׁלְּחָה לָאֶבְיוֹן 'prostrated her hand to the poor' (*Proverbs* 31:20), which means she was generous in giving charity; the verse is from the description of אשת חיל 'a righteous wife" in Pr 31; וַתָּמָת שָׁם מִרְיָם, וַתִּקָּבֵר שָׁם "And Miriam died there and was buried there' (*Numbers* 20:1).

In the example above, the purpose of the first quotation is to compare *Miryem* from Buczacz with Biblical Miriam. The word תֹּף *tof* ('drum') is substituted by a similarly sounding word טוב *ṭov* ('good'). The second quotation from the popular liturgical poem אשת חיל ('a righteous wife') based on *Proverbs* 31, which is recited on Saturday Eve, stresses that this *Miryem* from Buczacz was a righteous wife like a Biblical ideal. The third verse compares the death of *Miryem* from Buczacz with that of Biblical Miriam, with the word שָׁם *šam* ('buried there') substituted with פה *poh* ('here'). The verse ותקח טוב בידה ('and she took good in her hand') constitutes a chronogram which yields the year 552 from the Creation or 1791/2 C.E. when numerical values of the letters are summed up. This compliments the regular way of indicating the year תקנ"ב.

Biblical quotations are actively used when virtues of the person are discussed. The purpose of listing the virtues is to witness in favor of the deceased in the heavenly court. One of the euphemisms of the death is נתבקש לישיבה של מעלה 'He was called to the meeting of the heavenly court.' Thus the epitaph itself serves as a guardian angel for the dead. The connection between the deceased and his or her surviving relatives works in both directions: his/her merit can protect those living, זכותו יגן עלנו 'his merit will protect us' or even זכותו יליץ עלינו ('His merit will be accounted for us'). The praise section of the epitaph is called הלצה ('praise', the same word can mean 'rhetoric') while the epitaph itself is מליץ, a guardian angel in the heavenly court.

The most common praising formula in the male epitaphs is איש תם וישר 'a simple and righteous ma'", based on *Job* 1:1. The standard formula in female epitaphs is אשה חשובה וצנועה 'a modest and important woman'. This formula does not have a Biblical source, but the word צנועה ('modest') has certain gender-related implications, while the expression אשה חשובה ('an important woman') is discussed in *Pesaḵim* 108a, which states that only an 'important' women should recline during the Passover Seder. Moses Isserles (1520 – 1572) further states that 'in our time' every woman is an important woman [2].

2.3. Traditional Jewish Bilingualism and Orthography Code-Switching the Epitaphs

The sociolinguistic concept of the Traditional Jewish bilingualism was developed by Max Weinreich [16]. According to his view, two Jewish languages, such as Hebrew and Yiddish, have two different sociolinguistic functions. In an ideal scheme, Hebrew is a written language used predominantly in written communication. This is not limited to liturgy, Torah studies, and religious treaties. Hebrew is also used for the needs of practical written communications including the correspondence, bookkeeping, communal paperwork (the so-called *pinqasim* or books of records of various community institutions). Yiddish is a language of predominantly oral communication. This scheme applies to the pre-modern Jewish society of Eastern and Central Europe. The actual or real scheme of bilingualism is different from the ideal one in that on rare occasions Hebrew is used for oral communication, and Yiddish is used for writing, including entertainment literature (mostly intended for women). Note that Hebrew is considered a male language (all boys learn it in a *ḥeder*, an elementary school), whereas Yiddish is considered of interest for women, who were usually not proficient in Hebrew (and often illiterate) and thus unable to participate in Hebrew written communication. Yiddish was considered a *mamelošn* (mother's language) while Hebrew was associated with the culture of Talmudic and rabbinical studies.

While Hebrew and Yiddish constitute two distinct languages (the first one is Semitic, whereas the second one is Germanic), there were many forms of texts which could be considered intermediate between pure Hebrew and Yiddish. These are either Hebrew texts with a large amount of Yiddish borrowed words or Yiddish text rich with the Hebrew component words. Examples of such texts would include the so-called Scribal Yiddish (the language of some communal documents written in Yiddish with about 50% or more Hebrew inclusions), secret languages or 'cryptolects' of some merchants (e.g., *Lakudeš* of late medieval/early modern cattle traders in Germany), the language of Talmudic discussion, rich of Hebrew, and many others. Furthermore, since Yiddish has a significant Hebrew/Aramaic component (10% to 25% of its vocabulary, according to various estimates), in a certain context almost every Hebrew word or expression can be a part of Yiddish. Therefore, while a sophisticated linguistic conceptual apparatus has been developed (including such concepts as 'Whole Hebrew vs. Merged Hebrew'), it is sometimes impossible to distinguish between a 'foreign' Hebrew word borrowed in a Yiddish text from a 'native' Yiddish word of Hebrew origin [17].

Although Hebrew and Yiddish both use Hebrew letters, they use radically different orthography. Hebrew orthography is a consonant one with letters representing only consonant phonemes (with some exceptions). Yiddish developed a phonemic orthography with letters representing both consonant and vowel phonemes and/or sounds. Thus, Hebrew letter *'ayin* in Yiddish designates [e], letter *komeẓ-'alef* designates [o], *pasaḥ-ẓvey-yuden* is [ay], and so on. Despite that, orthography can hardly be an indicator of whether the word is in Hebrew or in Yiddish. This is in part because Yiddish lexica of the Hebrew component is written in Hebrew orthography (despite being a part of Yiddish). Furthermore, Yiddish orthography is used in Ashkenazi Hebrew texts when foreign words of non-Yiddish origin are used [14].

Epitaphs are written almost exclusively in Hebrew. Yiddish epitaphs are rare. However, the use of orthography code-switching represents the same trend: the traditional Hebrew (consonant) orthography is used for words and concepts of Biblical origin, while the phonetic or phonemic (Yiddish) orthography is used for profane or non-biblical realities. Example:

התורני מהורר משה במ' יעקב שטערקב**ע**רגר

A Torah man, R. Moses son of Jacob Šterkberger (1666 C.E., Trostyanec).

Note that in Germanic last name "Šterkberger" letter ע *'ayin* is used for [e] (not שטרקברגר as it would be spelled in accordance to the consonant Hebrew orthography).

An interesting example of how different orthographies relate to the sacred texts and to the everyday life is found in one of the oldest Ashkenazi inscriptions from Eastern Europe, the 1520 C.E. epitaph from Busk [7].

> נתן פאר תחת אפֿר כי פה נטמן איש נאמן ר' יהודא בן ר' יעקב דמתקרי ליודא
>
> Gave jewelry instead of the ash (cf. Is 61:3), because here lies a reliable man, R. Yehuda, son of R. Jacob, who was nicknamed Ide (Busk 1520).

Ide and Yehuda (often spelled יהודא with *'alef* to avoid a combination of letters constituting the God's name) are essentially the same name. Although in accordance to the modern Hebrew pronunciation they would be pronounced differently, the Ashkenazi Hebrew dialect reading would be the same. The juxtaposition of these two names makes sense only as a written (not oral) comparison between (Biblical) יהודה and יודא from Busk.

We can make an important conclusion that the use of Hebrew or Yiddish orthography marks whether a particular word (and realities designated by the word) are found in the Hebrew sacred text or if the word is only related to everyday mundane reality.

Thus we observe the same pattern of the actualization of a sacred text, or the bridging between the realm of the sacred texts and the realm of the everyday life, whereas the epitaph constitutes a tool to construct such a bridge.

2.4. Between the Canonical and Popular Religion

The Hebrew religious law (*halakah*) does not stipulate what should be written in an epitaph [5], [8]. Furthermore, the very custom of writing and reading epitaphs is considered by Talmudic sages somewhat undesirable and, perhaps, it is associated with Hellenism or other pagan beliefs. The sages said:

> אין עושין נפשות לצדיקים דבריהם הם זכרם
>
> Do not build a monument for the righteous, their words are their monument (*Babylonian Talmud*, *Mekilt'a* 11:7).

Reading epitaphs is mentioned among ten activities which distract a learner or even weaken his memory:

עשרה דברים קשים ללימוד העובר תחת האפסר [הגמל] וכל שכן תחת גמל [עצמו] והעובר בין שני גמלים והעובר בין שתי נשים והאשה העוברת בין שני אנשים והעובר מתחת ריח רע של נבילה והעובר תחת הגשר שלא עברו תחתיו מים מ' יום והאוכל פת שלא בשל כל צרכו והאוכל בשר מזוהמא ליסטרון והשותה מאמת המים העוברת בבית הקברות והמסתכל בפני המת ויש אומרים אף הקורא כתב שעל גבי הקבר

> Ten things adversely affect one's study: Passing under the bit of a camel and much more so under the camel itself, passing between two camels, passing between two women, the passing of a woman between two men, passing under the offensive odor of a carcass, passing under a bridge under which water has not flowed for forty days, eating bread that was insufficiently baked, eating meat out of a soup-ladle, drinking from a streamlet that runs through a graveyard, and looking into the face of a dead body. Others say: He who reads an inscription upon a grave (*Babylonian Talmud*, *Horayot* 13b).

One can conclude from this, that reading epitaphs was considered an idle and undesirable activity and perhaps even that the epitaphs were not intended to an occasional human reader, but rather for the eternity. The use of sophisticated chronograms to denote the year in some inscriptions, which significantly complicate deciphering and increase the possibility of a mistake, also suggests that providing information about the year to an occasional reader was not a priority of the composers of the inscriptions.

Although the Jewish religious law does not stipulate what should be included into an epitaph, the epitaphs are generally perceived as something belonging to the realm of sacred or religious, as most activities related to death and its rituals. Thus the epitaphs fill a niche between the official religion and folk religious practice, bridging the gap between these two existential areas [14].

There are several functions of an epitaph. First, the gravestone serves as a marker of a ritually unclean place so that the *Kohanim* (decedents of the biblical priests, who are prohibited from touching the dead body or entering a cemetery) avoid it. In addition, the gravestone marks the place where some contact with the soul of the dead is possible. Second, an epitaph is a prayer. By reading an inscription one also reads the prayer for the dead. Some epitaphs in some regions use entire commemorative prayer *'El male' raḥamim* ('God full of Mercy'). Third, an epitaph is evidence of the virtues of the dead and of the sorrow of the survivors, to help for a good decision of his/her fate in the heavenly court. A didactic function of reminding about the death to survivors, which is very common for Christian and Ancient (cf. Latin '*Sta, viator*', 'Traveler, pause') epitaphs, is rare in Jewish epitaphs. Most epitaphs have no narrator and no intended reader. The figure of an intended reader is absent from the epitaphs as well. God is the intended reader.

2.5. Between the Professional and Folk Literature

Looking at the epitaphs as a literature phenomenon, one finds a situation very similar to that in the case of the epitaphs as a religious phenomenon. Gravestone inscriptions are obviously related to the big literature, of which the epitaph is a traditional genre. Furthermore, there are poetic epitaphs which are related to the traditional Hebrew genres of קינה *qinah* ('elegy') and הספד *hesped* ('lamentation'), which, in turn, are related to Arabic elegy (الرثاء *riṯā'*, a part of a traditional قصيدة *qaṣīda'*), as well as to European poetry genres.

One of the main differences between the professional and folk literature is that a folk text has neither a single author nor a canonical version. There are many authors who contribute to the shaping of such a text which usually exists in many versions.

Some epitaphs have had known authors. However, the majority of these short texts are composed by anonymous authors using the formulas of previous epitaphs. There is evidence that in some places collections of standard parts and formulas of epitaphs existed, which were based on earlier inscriptions. Relatives of the deceased could select parts of these previous epitaphs to carve on the gravestone to commemorate the person. This is a mechanism very similar to how a folk text exists by combining a new version of the text from the parts of earlier versions.

It is well established by the structural anthropology, that there is a limited number of plots in a folk fairy tale. In an epitaph, there is in essence only one single plot: a person of good virtues has died on a particular day and has been buried at a particular place, with the hope that his soul will be bound in the 'bundle of life.'

3. Hermeneutics of the Epitaphs

The way of how an epitaph handles biblical quotations is quite sophisticated. Although at the surface level the Bible is being cited, a more scrutinized analysis shows that rabbinical or liturgical text, which cite the Bible, are indeed cited in many cases.

For example, the common final blessing תנצבה (תהי נפשו צרורה בצרור החיים) 'May his/her soul be bound in the Bundle of Life' is technically a reminiscence to *1 Samuel* 25:29. However, the blessing has a radically different meaning from the original verse in the *Book of Samuel*:

> וַיָּקָם אָדָם לִרְדָפְךָ, וּלְבַקֵּשׁ אֶת-נַפְשֶׁךָ; וְהָיְתָה נֶפֶשׁ אֲדֹנִי צְרוּרָה בִּצְרוֹר הַחַיִּים, אֵת יְהוָה אֱלֹהֶיךָ, וְאֵת נֶפֶשׁ אֹיְבֶיךָ יְקַלְּעֶנָּה, בְּתוֹךְ כַּף הַקָּלַע
>
> And though man be risen up to pursue thee, and to seek thy soul, yet the soul of my lord shall be bound in the bundle of life with the Lord

> thy God; and the souls of thine enemies, them shall he sling out, as from the hollow of a sling.

The verse in the Book of Samuel does not imply the afterlife, while 'a soul bound in the bundle of life' means staying safe and alive. The Talmudic interpretation of this verse is different. It is concerned about the fate of the body and of the soul after death and it starts with the discussion of a different verse, *Ecclesiastes* 12:7:

> Our Rabbis taught: 'And the dust return to the earth as it was, and the spirit return unto God who gave it' (*Ecclesiastes* 12:17): Render it back to him as He gave it to thee, [viz.,] in purity, so do thou [return it] in purity... The Holy One, blessed be He: concerning the bodies of the righteous He says, 'He entereth into peace, they rest in their beds' (*Isaiah* 57:2); while concerning their souls He says, 'yet the soul of my Lord shall be bound up in the bundle of life with the Lord thy God' (*1 Samuel* 25:29). But concerning the bodies of the wicked He says, 'There is no peace saith the Lord, unto the wicked" (*Isaiah* 48:22); while concerning their souls He says, and 'the souls of thine enemies, them shall he sling out, as from the hollow of a sling' (*1 Samuel* 25:29).
>
> It was taught, R. Eliezer said: The souls of the righteous are hidden under the Throne of Glory, as it is said, 'yet the soul of thine Lord shall be bound up in the bundle of life' (*1 Samuel* 25:29). But those of the wicked continue to be imprisoned, while one angel stands at one end of the world and a second stands at the other end, and they sling their souls to each other, for it is said, 'and the souls of thine enemies, them shall he sling out, as from the hollow of a sling' (*1 Samuel* 25:29) (*Babylonian Talmud*, *Šabbat* 152b).

According to this interpretation, the Bundle of Life is a certain place under the Throne of Glory, from which the souls are taken when placed into the bodies and to which the souls of righteous people return after their death [1]. The Talmud also says that angels greet the souls of righteous people by these words, 'May his/her soul be bound in the Bundle of Life.'

Due to this interpretation, the verse is cited in rabbinical and liturgical literature. The *Yizkor* commemoration prayer says: 'May his soul be bound in the bundle of life together with the souls of Abraham, Isaac, Jacob, Sarah, Rebecca, Rachel, and Lea, and with the rest of righteous men and women, who are in the Garden of Eden.'

An epitaph with the formula תנצבה essentially cites the commemorative prayer, which, in term, cites the Talmudic interpretation of the Biblical verse, rather than the verse itself. Thus the citation is indirect and it employs the scheme:

The Bible → Talmudic interpretations → Liturgical texts → Epitaphs.

Another example is the above-mentioned epitaph of Miriam from Buczacz. The phrase ותקח מרים את הטוב בידה 'And Miriam took the good in her hand' is a paraphrase of the Biblical verse וַתִּקַּח מִרְיָם אֶת-הַתֹּף בְּיָדָהּ "And Miriam took... the drum in her hand" (*Exodus* 15:20). The word תֹּף *tof* ('a drum') is substituted by a similarly sounding word טוב *ṭov* (pronounced *tof* in a Yiddish dialect, 'the Good').

One could assume that the pun was invented by the author of the epitaph. However, the case can be more complicated, since a similar formula with the same pun (*ṭov* instead of *tof*) was found in another epitaph from Warsaw (geographically quite far away) [5]. An independent invention of the same pun is unlikely. It is much more probable that in both cases the phrase was borrowed from a certain written source:

The Bible → a rabbinical source → Epitaphs.

These two examples illustrate a general principle: Biblical verses are usually quoted in the traditional texts through the lenses of Rabbinical texts and commentaries.

Another important hermeneutic feature of the epitaphs is their above mentioned relation to the internal Jewish bilingualism. While the 'Internal Jewish Bilingualism' is a scholastic concept developed by academic scholars, particularly, Yiddish linguists such as Max Weinreich, Uriel Weinreich, and Joshua Fishman, the theory of the Hebrew-Aramaic bilingualism (and, to a lesser extent, of the Hebrew-Yiddish bilingualism) was also elaborated by Rabbinical authors.

It is not just that Hebrew is a male and Yiddish is a female language in a symbolic sense or that Hebrew is the language of the Written Torah, while Aramaic is the language of the Oral Torah. Hebrew is called לשון קודש *lašon-qodeš* ('the sacred language') while Aramaic is called לשון תרגום *lešon targum* ('the language of the Translation'). Torah verses are supposed to be studied three times פעמיים מקרא פעם תרגום 'Twice the Scripture, once the [Aramaic] Translation.' This is not a random requirement. The ability to translate a text from the Sacred Language into a spoken language constitutes an important level of understanding the text.

Furthermore, the Aramaic language was viewed as an intermediate layer between the Hebrew language and the seventy languages of the peoples of the world (according to a traditional view, there are seventy nations in the world). Thus according to the Lurianic Qabbalah and, in particular, Rabbi Isaiah Horowitz (*Šela ha-Qadoš*, 1565 – 1630), the Aramaic language corresponds to the intermediate layer קליפת נגה (*qelippat nogah*) between the holy and the profane. The Talmud states that the 'Ministering Angels' (מלאכי

השרת) do not understand Aramaic. This is because otherwise there would be a temptation to equate it in status with Hebrew:

> A King talks about his needs to his servants, but he rarely talks to his ministers and only in a regal manner, so that nobody would think that they are equal to him. And about the servants nobody would assume that they are equal to the King, so there is no concern. Therefore, the ministering angels need every language and there is no concern, but with Aramaic there is a concern [2].

Judah Loew ben Bezalel (Maharal of Prague, d. 1609) has developed an elaborated theory, according to which the Aramaic language is a universal language of mankind but it does not belong to any particular nation (among the 'seventy nations of the world'), whereas Hebrew is a particular language of the Jewish people. Maharal writes:

> May the Prayer be recited in any language? Behold Rab Judah has said: A man should never pray for his needs in Aramaic. For R. Johanan declared: If anyone prays for his needs in Aramaic, the Ministering Angels do not pay attention to him, because they do not understand that language! (*Babilonian Talmud*, *Soṭah* 33a)
>
> The principal meaning is that the Ministering Angels do not understand the Aramaic language at all, as it is not even called 'a language'. As I explained on *Megillah* 10b on 'And I took a name from Babylonia...,' they do not have writing and language. The Aramaic language is not a part of the seventy languages, although it is a language, it is not among the seventy created by the Holy One, blessed be he. Why Aramaic is not among the seventy languages? Because it is said in *Sukkah* 52a about the Chaldeans that 'they will not be a people'... The Torah paid respect to the Aramaic language; however, it does not belong to the seventy languages of the peoples of the world. This is because among the angels there are seventy appointed as ministers over the peoples of the world, however, the angels have no connection to the Aramaic language [3].

Maharal further claims that Aramaic was the language of Adam, the first human (and thus this language is universal), and that Aramaic is the language of the messianic future world, explaining the rule 'the Scripture twice, the [Aramaic] Translation (*Targum*) once':

> The Translation is the degree of the World to Come because it is not considered a language at all, as it is said 'And I took a name from Babylonia...' (*Megillah* 10b) is about the Chaldeans who have no writing and language of their own. As we explained in a different place, the Aramaic language or the language of Babylonia is not

considered a language. Its essence is thought, and thought corresponds to the highest degree of the World to come, this is 'Translation once'. In addition, the Ministering Angels do not understand Aramaic, and 'Translation once' is because it corresponds to the World to Come, as it is known that it belongs to Israel and not to the angels [4].

'Rabbi Juda said on behalf of Rava: Adam, the first man, spoke Aramaic' (*Babilonian Talmud, Sanhedrin* 38b) The meaning is that neither the Holy Language nor the rest of the seventy languages were appropriate for him. Because the Holy Language is a particular language of one nation, and the seventy languages as well. For Adam to master every language that originated from him, a particular language was inappropriate. However, he had the Aramaic language [3].

Rabbi Nachman of Breslov (1772 – 1810) wrote that the world was left imperfect in order to leave for a man space to finish some work and to improve the world thus co-creating the world together with the Lord [10]. This is similar to how, when a baby boy is born uncircumcised and thus 'imperfect', the circumcision should be performed. Only with the *Targum* (Aramaic translation) the holy language would become perfect. Biblical Joseph had a perfect knowledge of Hebrew, which involved the ability to translate into other languages. This is indicated by Joseph's ability to interpret dreams, as the word תרדמה *tardemah* ('dream') has the same *gemaṭri'a* as the word תרגום *targum* ('translation').

Other Chassidic Rabbis claimed that in the modern time, Yiddish played the same role as Aramaic in the time of Talmud. The Rebbe from Vilednik said that by filling the Germanic language with Hebrew words (which is the case in Yiddish) the Jews bring the holiness to a non-Jewish language and thus accelerate the coming of the Messiah [19]

We see how the idea of translation from the holy language is related to more general concepts of the actualization of a sacred text and its interpretation, which is one of the functions of an epitaph.

4. Conclusion

Hebrew epitaphs are rarely studied as Jewish religious texts. Despite that, epitaphs demonstrate various features similar to the rabbinical and other Jewish traditional texts and genres. The most prominent among these features is the actualization of the sacred text by relating it to the everyday realities. This is achieved by proper biblical quotations and by orthography code-switching. The techniques are somewhat similar to the rabbinical hermeneutic approaches. Biblical quotations are often indirect so that the epitaphs cite liturgical and rabbinical texts citing biblical verses, rather than directly citing the biblical verses.

One of the central themes of the Jewish culture is its relationship to texts and, in particular, to texts in different languages. An important feature of this relationship is its bilingualism, with Hebrew being the language of the sacred texts and Aramaic or Yiddish being the language of everyday life. The translation from the holy language into the language of the everyday use is considered an important tool of the actualization of the sacred texts. While epitaphs are written in Hebrew, the traces of Hebrew/Yiddish orthography switching can be found in them when they switch between the biblical and mundane realities.

To summarize in one sentence, Hebrew epitaphs are a bridge between the realms of the canonical texts and of the everyday life of the Jewish community, which employ traditional rabbinical hermeneutic tools for the actualization of the sacred texts.

References

1. Fogelman, M. Tehe nišmato ẓerura bi-ẓeror ha-ḥayim, *Sinay*, 49, 1961, pp. 176–180 (in Hebrew).
2. Isserles, Moses ben Israel 'Oraḥ Hayim, 472.4 gloss 2 Lemberg: .S.L. Kugel, 1866
3. Judah Loew ben Bezalel (ha-Maharal from Prague), *Hidduše 'Aggadot,* Soṭah 33a, Jerusalem: 1972 (in Hebrew).
4. Judah Loew ben Bezalel (ha-Maharal from Prague), *Tiferet Yiśra'el*, 13, Kiryat Yoel: 2007 (in Hebrew).
5. Heilman, S. *When a Jew Dies*, Berkley: University of California Press, 2001.
6. Horowitz, Isaiah (Šela), *Šney luḥot habrit*, Pesaḥim, Maẓa Šemura Jerusalem : E. Munk, 1992 (in Hebrew).
7. Horst, Van der, P. W. *Ancient Jewish Epitaphs: an Introductory Survey of a Millennium of Jewish Funeral Epigraphy (300 BCE – 700 CE)*, Kok Pharos: Kampen, 1991.
8. Kraemer, D. *The Meanings of Death in Rabbinical Judaism*, London, New York: Routledge, 2000.
9. Krajewska, M. Cmentarze żydowskie w Polsce: nagrobki i epitafia, *Polska sztuka ludowa*, 1-2, 1989, pp. 27–44.
10. Naḥman of Bratzlav, *Liqute Moharan*, New York, 1966, *Liqute Moharan 1:19.*
11. Nahon, G. *Inscriptions hebraiques et juives de France medievale*, Paris: Belle Lettres, 1986.

12. Nosonovsky, M. Hebrew epitaphs of the 16th century from Ukraine, *Monuments of Culture: New Discoveries – 1998*, Nauka, Moscow, 1999, pp. 16-27 (in Russian).
13. Nosonovsky, M. The scholastic lexicon in Ashkenazi Hebrew and orthography, *Pinkas. Journal of the Culture and History of East European Jewry* , 2, Zara, Vilnius, 2008, pp 53-76.
14. Nosonovsky, M. Folk beliefs, mystics and superstitions in Ashkenazi and Karaite tombstone inscriptions from Ukraine, *Markers*, 26, 2009, pp. 120-147.
15. Nosonovsky, M. Old Jewish Cemeteries in Ukraine: History, Monuments, Epitaphs, In. M. Chlenov (ed.), *The Euro-Asian Jewish Yearbook - 5768 (2007/2008)*, Moscow: Pallada, pp. 237-261.
16. Weinreich M. *History of the Yiddish Language*, New Haven, CT: Yale University Press, 2008.
17. Shapira D. Yiddish–German, Slavic, or Oriental?, *Karadeniz Araştırmaları*, 6, 2010, pp. 127–140.
18. Wodziński, M. *Groby cadyków w Polsce. O chasydzkiej literaturze nagrobnej i jej kontekstach*, Wrocław: Towarzystwo Przyjaciół Polonistyki Wrocławskiej, 1998.
19. Yiśra'el Yosef Dov Ber of Vilednik, Še'arit Yiśra'el, *Zemanim, Šavuot* 6 (in Hebrew).

Using Lotteries in Logic of *Halakhah* Law. The Meaning of Randomness in Judaism

Ely Merzbach

Department of Mathematics,
Bar-Ilan University,
Israel
ely.merzbach@biu.ac.il

Today, a lottery is seen as a wholly blind process, totally without meaning. However, in Judaism it has a lot of meanings until now. Let us begin with some examples:

***Babylonian Talmud, Sanhedrin* 17a**

> The Rabbis taught: But there remained two men in the camp (*Numbers* 11). Some say: Their names remained in the urn. When the Holy One, blessed be He, said to Moses, Gather seventy of the elders of Israel, Moses said: 'How shall I do it? If I choose six out of each tribe, there will be two too many; if I select five, ten will then be wanting. If I choose six out of one and five out of another, I shall cause jealousy among the tribes.' What did he do? – He selected six men from each tribe, and brought seventy-two slips, on seventy of which he wrote 'Elder', leaving the other two blank. He mixed them up in an urn, and said: 'Come draw your slips.' To each who drew a slip bearing the word 'Elder', he said, 'Heaven has already consecrated you.' To him who drew a blank, he said: 'Heaven has rejected you, what can I do?'

Already from this text, we learn that result of the urn depends of 'Heaven'. The lottery is not blind, but depends of the God's will.

Our next example deals with the *Yom Kippur* sacrifices:

***Babylonian Talmud, Yom'a* 39a, 39b**

> Our Rabbis taught: Throughout the forty years that Simeon the Righteous ministered, the lot would always come up in the right hand;

from that time on, it would come up now in the right hand, now in the left...

Our Rabbis taught: During the last forty years before the destruction of the Temple, the lot did not come up in the right hand.

The probability of obtained 40 consecutive times the same result is very low. It is as if as obtaining the same face throwing a coin 40 consecutive times (1/2 at the power 40). This example shows not only the Divine intervention in human history, but also delivering messages regarding the behavior of a person or community.

Babylonian Talmud, Bab'a Batr'a **122a**

The land was divided by lot, for it is said (*Numbers* 26), "only by lottery". It was only divided by use of the *Urim* and *Tumim*, as it said, "According to the lot." How was this done? Eleazar was wearing the *Urim* and *Tumim*, while Joshua and all Israel stood before him. An urn with the tribes' names and an urn with the boundaries were placed before him. Animated by the Holy Spirit, he exclaimed: 'Zebulun' is coming up and the boundary lines of Acco are coming up. Then he mixed the urn of the tribes well and Zebulun came up in his hand. And he mixed the urn of the boundaries well and the boundary lines of Acco came up in his hand. Animated again by the Holy Spirit, he exclaimed: 'Naphtali' is coming up and the boundary lines of Ginosar are coming up. He mixed the urn of the tribes well and Naphtali came up in his hand. He mixed the urn of the boundaries well, and the boundary lines of Ginosar came up in his hand. And he did this with each tribe.

The *Rašbam* explains:

They needed two lotteries, one for the tribes, and one for the borders. You could not say: what I draw now be for Reuven, because if you do, the division is not being done by lottery, as the text says 'only by lottery.'

The probability is the following:

$$\frac{1}{(12)^2}\cdot\frac{1}{(11)^2}\cdots\frac{1}{(2)^2}=\frac{1}{(12!)^2}=\frac{1}{(479\cdot 10^{10})^2}\approx\frac{1}{10^{25}}$$

Sharing the land of Israel was very important, and we need the Divine intervention for this.

Babylonian Talmud, Sanhedrin **43a**

> Our Rabbis taught: ...When the Holy One, Blessed be He, said to Joshua, Israel has sinned, he asked Him, 'Master of the Universe, who has sinned?' 'Am I an informer?' He answered, 'Go and cast lots.' Therefore, he went and cast lots, and the lot fell upon Aḵan. He said to him: 'Joshua, will you convict me based on a lottery? You and Eleazar the Priest are the two greatest men of the generation, yet if I were to cast lots upon you, the lot might fall on one of you. I beseach you, he replied, cast no aspersions on the lots, for the Land of Israel is to be divided by lots, as it is written (*Numbers* 26), the Land shall be divided by lot.

From these examples, we can understand the different Biblical events, which stand out in the history of the Jewish People, the *ḥazal's* relation to these events, and their importance in figuring out the purpose of the world. We see that Judaism's special understanding of random occurrences in the world (unlike rationalistic cultures, on the one hand, or Eastern cultures on the other hand) integrates order and randomness. We will explore the meaning of the connection between these two factors.

Despite the variety found across the *ḥazal* different interpretations of the *Torah*, I think that there is universal agreement amongst them about the theological meaning of chance as the hidden workings of God. It must be emphasized that in Judaism chance is always meaningful, in that it reveals to man the desire of God or in intended to reveal to him the path he should follow. Chance is the exact opposite of doubt. Chance takes several different forms: accident, chance, fate, luck, speculation, magic, and more. There is a chasm between the way *ḥazal* and the wise men of Greek looked at chance and fate.

In some cases, the use of lottery is forbidden, because it means using a holy tool for his own interests:

***Babylonian Talmud, Sanhedrin, Mišnah* 3:24b**

> These are ineligible; those who gamble with dice... Rabbi Yehuda said: 'When is this true, when they have no other occupation, but if they have another occupation, they are eligible... What is wrong with gamblers?... Rabbi Šešet says... because they are not involved with settling the world.

The reason for this is that since lottery is a holy tool in the hands of God, we cannot use it for our personal interest.

On the other hand, it is lawful for a person to buy a lottery ticket, as explained by an important Rabbi:

Rabbi Ya'qov Ariel, *Q&A in the Tent of the Torah*

Following the Jewish law, it is permitted to participate in national lotteries. This is because at the time of the lottery, the loser has already paid for their ticket, and the winner takes his prize from a sum that has been prepared for dispersion as prize money. However, it seems that wasting 20% of his income on this is the limit.

Concerning property, the lottery can work as an act of transfer of ownership. In certain cases, the result of utilizing a lottery can replace the process of acquisition:

Babylonian Talmud, Bab'a Batr'a 106b

It was taught: Rabbi Yossi said: 'When brothers divide an inheritance, as soon as the lot for one of them is drawn, all of them acquire possession of their shares. On what grounds? – Rabbi Eleazar said: Just like the possession of the Land of Israel. As that began by lot, so here also it is by lot. However, there the division was made through the ballot box and the *Urim* and *Tummim*; shouldn't the division here also be through the ballot box and the *Urim* and *Tummim*? Rabbi Aši replied: Because of the mutual benefit, the lot suffices here because in return for the benefit of mutual agreement they determine to allow each other to acquire possession by the lot alone.

Šulḥan A'ruḵ, ḥoŠen MiŠpat 175:2-3

After deciding to use a lottery for a division, once one lot has been decided, the division will be made for all…

If two brothers divided an inheritance, and then a third brother, who they did not know about, appears, the division is annulled. Even if there were three fields, and each brother took one, and divided the third field between them. When the third brother came and they cast lots, even if the third field goes to him, any of the three brothers can nullify the lottery, and then a new lottery must be held for all of them. Even if the third brother receives part of each of the other fields and is satisfied, either of the other brothers can annul the lottery since it was done in error.

Many *halakhic* decisions are patently dependent upon the *poseq's* (adjudicator's) understanding of what a lottery is. Rabbi Yair Baḵraḵ (18th century) wrote the book *Ḥavat Yair* that is a famous Responsa book:

Ḥavat Yair, Section 61

> Once, twelve people held a lottery for a silver goblet. They put 12 slips of paper, each with one of their names on it in one box, and they put in a second box, 11 blank slips and one that said *mazal tov*. An infant drew one slip from each box, and the one that came out together with the *mazal tov* would receive the goblet. As it happened, the *mazal tov* came up on the sixth draw. One of the remaining people checked the box with names, and it turned out that one of the names had been omitted, and there had been only 11 slips in the box. The participants called for annulling the lottery, but the one who won said they had no reason to complaint, this only increased their chances; and to one whose name was omitted he will do a compromise and compensate him.

Nevertheless, the Rabbi answered that it is a false lottery (not holy); then it is invalid.

We see from this story that the lottery must be done in a perfect way in order to be holy and to be accepted by God.

There are different approaches, to using lotteries in the courts or for community decisions. Another example is the following problem concerning elections, written by the previous chief Rabbi of Israel Rabbi Ovadia Yosef in the 80':

Rabbi Ovadiya Yosef

> There was a city where a committee of 36 people prepared to choose someone to be rabbi of their city. As they were two wise men candidates for the position, the votes split, so each one received 18 votes. The committee decided, by itself, to cast lots, and one of the men was chosen. The second wise man appealed, saying one could not rely on a lottery, that they must convene again and choose a rabbi, and whomever they chose was the one God wanted appointed. The lottery was cancelled, because the two wise men did not know about it and they did not agree before it was cast.

In some cases, it is possible to casting lots even for capital crimes. Let's begin with Maimonides:

Rambam, *Hilkhot Yesodei HaTorah*, Chapter 5, Halakah 5

> If gentiles say to a group of women: Give us one of you and we will defile her, and if you do not we will defile all of you. They should all be defiled, and not give over a soul of Israel.
> If gentiles say: Give us one person and we will kill him, and if you do not we will kill all of you, you should not turn anybody over to them.

Latter Rabbi Yehuda Haḥasid wrote:

Sefer Haḥasidim, Section 679

> People traveling on the open seas and a fierce wind arises which seems likely to destroy the ship or to sink it, and other boats are passing safely, so they know that someone on the boat is a transgressor and they are being punished for him. They have the right to cast lots. If the same person was chosen three consecutive times, he is the guilty one, and they have the right to throw him into the sea... Proof is from the story of the prophet Jonah...

Sefer Haḥasidim, Section 702

> People traveling on the open seas and a fierce wind arises, they have no right to cast lots, because if they fall on someone, they would be required to cast him into the sea, and it is not right to do as was done to Jonah son of Amitai.

The *poseq* Rabbi Eliezer Waldenberg explains:

Q&A ẓiẓ Eliezer, Chapter 18, Section 48b

> There is no contradiction, because Section 679 speaks of a case where the other boats are passing safely. This is a proof that someone on the ship is guilty in God's eyes, which is not the case in Section 702, where there is no external proof that there is someone guilty on this one ship...

Moreover, the *poseq* Rabbi Moshe Feinstein gives the following rule:

Igrot Moše, *Ḥošen Mišpat*, Chapter 2, Section 78

> If two people are sick and need medical care, which one should a doctor treat first, if they both reached him at the same time? Then they should follow the order listed in the *Babylonian Talmud* (*Horayot* 13a), and if the doctor is not familiar with the list, he should use a lottery.

To this day, there is no precise definition of randomness. A random event is thought to be something that happens with no meaning and no clear cause. In the modern world, the holiness of the random is completely absent. There is a branch of mathematics called Probability Theory, which deals with the quantitative aspects of randomness, developing axioms, and investigating concepts such as independent (unconditional) events, stochastic processes, and borderline occurrences. Despite the success of Probability Theory, not a word has been said about the deeper meaning of the accidental. Computer scientists try to develop algorithms, which are able to produce pseudo-random numbers, but the creative powers of man are incapable of creating true randomness. Apparently the creation of randomness demands a higher level of complexity than which is actually known to man.

The special relationship of *ḥazal* to randomness is not confined merely to the realms of philosophy and thought, but also carries with it fundamental implications for the way man lives his daily life. This can be seen in many laws regarding lotteries. It would appear that due to Judaism's absorption of Western culture over tens of generations, these laws are not frequently encountered today.

There is a wide range of discussions about lotteries by *ḥazal*. For example, in *Yalqut Šim'oni* (*midraš*ic text) it says:

> There are many names for lotteries: *ḥeleš*, luck, fate, trial. The children of Esau suffered from all of them. Amalek was struck with weakness, as it says: 'and Yehoshua weakened…' (*Exodus* 17:13) The fourth kingdom will be struck with trial in the future, as it says: 'birth pangs will come upon him' (*Hosea* 13:13).

In the *Tanak̲* (Bible), the word lottery appears to have different meanings. It is used first to describe using physical objects to make decisions in times of doubt. It also refers to things, which are determined by one's fate or personal destiny. Fate also implies one's lot in life, or fortune, as in *Daniel* 12:13: 'and you will receive your fate in the end of days.'

Of course, there is a direct connection between the two meanings: just as it is impossible to know the results of a lottery, also the future of a person is neither known nor predictable. While you can debate whether the future of a person is predictable, when one uses the phrase 'fate', one usually means, consciously or unconsciously, that the results of the activity include an unknowable factor.

There are many verbs that are used together with 'lottery' in the *Tanak̲*: 'cast,' 'threw,' 'shot,' 'hurl,' 'fell,' 'came up,' 'came out,' 'was.' This diversity teaches us the richness of the lottery, and how important and central it is in all manner of fields in the life of humankind. Lottery as a masculine noun reminds us in the *Torah* of the control and indisputable influence of the Creator.

In this work we focused on the first and original meaning in Hebrew of the word, which today is usually referred to as 'lottery,' and in religious language, is frequently called 'holy lottery' or 'righteous lottery.'

As mentioned above, there are practical implications to a discussion on randomness. The flood of gambling lotteries (such as *Lotto, Toto, Mif'al HaPayis*) which have spread across many countries in the world, and the question of establishing legal casinos arouses ruminations, especially amongst the religiously traditional population. What is the *Torah*'s position regarding these games, and towards people who invest considerable amounts of time and money in them?

Another king of lottery is what is referred to today (erroneously, it would seem), as 'The Gaon of Vilna's Lottery', making personal decisions based on lotteries. For example, Rabbi Yosef David Azoulai (The Ḥida) from the 18th century wrote the following:

Q&A Ḥaim Ša'al, II, Section 38, Item 4

It is permitted to open the *Torah* and look at the verse that comes up (to make a decision). Where it says that one should not open a Bible in the manner of lotteries refers to the case where a person is roving from house to house-offering women and men to cast lots, as some people do (fortunetellers). However, if a person wants to do it for himself or herself, it is permitted.

There are many stories about the Gaon of Vilna's Lotteries:

1. *Rabbi Moshe Feinshtein*: Once a question arose in his family as to whether they should travel to a certain place. He opened a Bible and the verse that appeared was (*Exodus* 10:11) 'And the men went out,' and the answer was clear (Baer Miriam).
2. *Rabbi Lapyan* told that before he travelled from Lithuania to England, he tried the Gaon of Vilna's lottery, as he had learned if from the '*ḥafetz ḥaim*', asking whether to travel or not. The answer that came up was the verse (*Genesis* 46:4) 'I will go down to Egypt with you, and I will bring you back up.'
3. Lottery to determine the identities of the slain from the Company 35 in the Israel army: *Rabbi Aryeh Levine* conducted this lottery. See the book *A ẓadiq in Our Time* written by S. Raz.

Throughout the generations, there were differences of opinion regarding the use of lotteries. There was a disagreement, for example, that was recorded in verse between Rav Ibn Ezra and Rav Yehuda from Modena, regarding the nature of dice games. Rav Ibn Ezra wrote this about them:

Playing with dice/ the hit is fresh/ the end is destruction/ cursed in the gates.
He will disperse his money/ and increase his sin/ revolt against his creator/ in vows and lies.

> He thinks he will profit/ he will never succeed/ and if he deceives his brother/ his days will be bitter.

Rav Yehuda from Modena responded in kind:

> Playing with dice/ his occupation is clean/ his cup overflowing/ his fate is weighed in the gates.
> If his Maker chooses/ he will lose his capital/ if this is his sin/ speaking lies.
> He will lose or win/ like a successful businessperson/ and will become accustomed / to sweetening the bitter.

But lotteries don't deal only with games, and there is an opening to introduce lotteries into judicial proceedings and legal decisions, by way of a law that forbids a judge from leaving a decision as a '*din ḥaluq*', which is to say, a partial decision, as a result of his inability to decide because he lacks sufficient proof. For example, the *RoŠ* (*Rabenu HaŠer*), the great adjudicator of all of Western Europe in the 14th century, in one of the most difficult matters brought to him for adjudication by the Queen of Spain:

> I have explained all this at length in order to show that it is not within my purview nor is it legitimate to leave a decision as a *din ḥaluq* (*ḥaluq* means partial, incomplete). A judge must complete the decision in order to create peace in the world. Therefore, the Sages gave permission to the judges to decide as they see fit in a place where the facts and evidence do not lead to a clear decision. Sometimes this will be a judge decision without reason, proof, nor evaluation, and sometimes as a compromise.

Rabbi Joseph Karo, (in the *Šulḥan 'Aruḵ, Ḥošen Mišpat)* also rules in the same manner:

> A judge has the power to decide by compromise, in a place where he is unable to come to a clear decision.

Today we are used to thinking that we, the human race, are subject to not only chance or fate, but that we ourselves actually create our own fate. This does not mean that we have no control over our own lives. We always have free choice to do what we wish. This outlook means to say that the existentialist view of freedom sees our lives as having a certain direction or chosen tendency. Looking backwards, a person does not see his own life as wholly random.

The intention of this research was to demonstrate that from a traditional Jewish point of view, randomness has a deeper meaning. This fact become clear, by analyzing the way that *ḥazal* relates to randomness, and their understanding of events in which uncertainty is included.

The importance of the meaning of randomness appears into both philosophy and deed. In Judaism, there is a deep connection between thought and deed, and they cannot be disconnected one from the other. Nonetheless, and their study help us to develop a deeper understanding of these concepts and their purpose.

With all the above examples, we come to a better understanding of the nature of the world, its development, and the meaning of miracles and randomness. These concepts lead to the concept of blessing and the use of statistics, which are not examined here in. It is clear that these concepts affect our understanding of free will, and the accompanying apparatuses, such as *Purim*, *Amaleq*, luck, and the *Urim* and *Tumim* (the Cohen's breastplate).

Practical considerations in casting a lottery following Jewish law:

A. A perfect lottery: The lottery must be conducted on all the involved items. Usually there is one group of items, so a single lottery is sufficient. However, if there are more than one group of items involved, then you must use more than one lottery, one for each group.

B. A fair lottery: A lottery must be fair. There must be equal chances for each side in the dispute, or in scientific language, the distribution of the results should be a uniform distribution.

C. The appearance of the lottery: The lottery must appear to be fair and not a trick conducted by the participants. Everyone is present at any of the stages of the lottery: preparation of the slips, mixing, etc. It turns out that the appearance of fairness is extremely important, and one cannot use a lottery in a place where the community present does not sense that it is a fair lottery.

Purposes of the Lottery:

1. Divine intervention in human history.
2. Delivering messages regarding the behavior of a person or community.
3. Leaving free will in Man's hands.
4. Variations in the process of renewal and continuity of life.
5. Prevention of prediction of natural phenomena in the long term.

Conclusions

A person cannot refuse to follow the results of a lottery, because the results come from the Heaven… One who refuses to obey a lottery is as one who violates one of the Ten Commandments. 'We see that in the *Torah* and the *Prophets* and in the *Writings* that they relied on lotteries when they were conducted without man's calculations or intervention', as it is said: 'One should cast the lottery discreetly, for the decision is from Go' (*Proverbs* 16:33). '…Since it is obvious that a fair lottery will reflect God's will, while it will not be not the case if a dishonest lottery is performed' (*Ḥošen Mišpat* 175).

Hebrew law uses a lottery for decisions only when it is conducted perfectly. The lottery joins in the search for the truth, and every casting of lots must be to further God's will.

'The lot brings an end to strife, and separates the contentious' (*Proverbs* 18:18). The commentators explain: 'The lottery will terminate the contention over the separation of property, because the lottery will determine each one's portion.'

Let us conclude by the following: Art's purpose is to transform the unexpected into the necessary. A lottery's purpose is to transform the necessary into the unexpected.

References

1. *Babylonian Talmud.*
2. Yaakov Ariel, *Q&A in the Tent of Torah*, Jerusalem.
3. Yosef David Azoulai (The *ḥida*), *Q&A ḥaim Ša'al,* Jerusalem.
4. Yair Bar<u>k</u>a<u>k</u>, *ḥavat yair (Responsa book)*, Jerusalem.
5. Moshe Feinstein, *Igrot MoŠe,* New York.
6. Yehuda Haḥasid, *Sefer ḥasidim,* Jerusalem.
7. Joseph Karo, *Shulḥan 'Aru<u>k</u>, ḥoŠen MiŠpat,* Jerusalem.
8. Simha Raz, *A Tzadik in Our Time,* Lina ed. 1974, Jerusalem.
9. Eliezer Waldenberg , *Q&A ẓiẓ Eliezer*, Jerusalem.
10. *Yalqut Šim'oni,* Jerusalem.

Probabilistic Foundations of Rabbinic Methods for Resolving Uncertainty

Moshe Koppel

Departament of Computer Science,
Bar-Ilan University,
Israel
moishk@gmail.com

1. Introduction

The modern theory of probability is twice removed from Rabbinic laws concerning uncertainty. First, in its current form the theory of probability is simply the study of a particular class of functions and is not concerned with assigning probabilities to real-world events. Second, even if on the basis of certain stipulations, the theory is applied to actual events, it remains descriptive and not prescriptive. Nevertheless, certain philosophical issues which have arisen as a result of attempts to explicate the meanings of probabilistic statements are highly relevant to a proper understanding of Rabbinic approaches to uncertainty. In this paper, I will attempt to present a unified overview of Rabbinic laws concerning uncertainty. I will use ideas taken from the study of foundations of probability where these ideas seem helpful but will try to refrain from belaboring the analogy for its own sake.

One historical point needs to be emphasized. The modern theory of probability has its roots in the work of Pascal and others in the 17th century. It would be utterly anachronistic to attribute to the 1st century sages any foreknowledge of these developments. Moreover, doing so does not purchase any explanatory power with regard to Rabbinic approaches to uncertainty. At the same time, the claim that the ancients were bereft of any systematic thinking with regard to uncertainty is both arrogant and demonstrably false. I will use modern ideas about the foundations of probability as a starting point for identifying which probabilistic insights do and do not lie at the root of Rabbinic pronouncements on such matters.

Nevertheless, my approach in this article is unabashedly ahistorical: rather than chart a chronological progression of ideas or identify conflicting schools of thought, I will attempt to harmonize a broad range of sources. Where a *Tann'ayitic* or *'Amor'aic* source permits multiple interpretations, I will not outline all views but rather select the most straightforward or consensual interpretation. Likewise, I will relate to the central ideas discussed in the vast post-Talmudic literature – both classical [2], [9] and contemporary [1], [3], [4], [6], [7], [10], [13] – devoted to Rabbinic laws concerning uncertainty but, for the sake of offering as straightforward and unified a treatment as possible, I will cite opinions of the commentators in an extremely selective manner. The fact that I marshal the support of a particular commentator regarding a particular point should in no way be taken to mean that I can claim such support regarding related points.

In the first part of this article, I will use the distinction between two types of majority principles – *rub'a d'it'a qaman* (literally: a majority which is in front of us) and *rub'a d'leyt'a qaman* (literally: a majority which is not in front of us) – to motivate a discussion of distinct definitions of probability. This will lay the groundwork for the explication of a number of thorny Rabbinic concepts involving uncertainty and indeterminacy.

2. Interpretations of Probability

The *Talmud* in *Ḥullin* 11a-11b interprets the phrase (*Exodus* 23:2) 'incline after the majority' (*'aḥarey rabim l'haṭot*) to mean that decisions of a court are decided by majority. This is then generalized to the above-mentioned principle of *rub'a d'it'a qaman* (henceforth: *RDIK*), which includes other cases such as that of 'nine stores,' i.e., a piece of meat is found in the street and all that is known is that it comes from one of ten stores, nine of which sell *košer* meat. In such cases we apply the principle that 'that which is removed, was removed from the majority' (*kol d'pariš me-rub'a pariš*; henceforth: *pariš*). The *Talmud* states that this inference covers only the principle of *RDIK*, of which Sanhedrin and 'nine stores' are offered as typical examples, but not the parallel principle of *rub'a d'leyta qaman* (henceforth: *RDLK*). The *Talmud* offers a number of examples of *RDLK* where the majority is followed because it would be impossible to function normally or adjudicate cases without doing so (but concludes that precisely because of that impossibility these cases can't serve as a basis from which to infer a general principle of *RDLK*). Several cases of *RDLK* that are illustrative are that the husband of one's mother (at the time of conception) may be presumed to be one's father, that a child may be presumed to be potentially fertile and that a murder victim may be presumed not to have been suffering from a prior life-threatening condition.

What is the precise difference between *RDIK* and *RDLK*? Although the names are suggestive, the *Talmud* offers no explicit definition of *RDIK* and *RDLK* and no rationale for treating them differently. We might, however, shed considerable light on the distinction by considering an interesting philosophical debate dating back to the 1920's which covers similar conceptual territory. The rest of this section will consist of a slightly lengthy diversion through that territory.

Let's consider carefully what exactly we mean when we say that the probability of some event is p/q. Early (the 17th and 18th century) work in probability was motivated to a large extent by games of chance (coins, cards, dice). Thus, when somebody said that 'the probability of the event H is p/q' it was understood that what was meant was that the event H obtained in p out of q equally likely possible outcomes. Thus, for example, when we say the probability that the sum of two throws of a die will be exactly six is 5/36, we mean that there are 36 equally likely possible throws and 5 of them have the desired property. Similarly, in the case of the found meat, there are ten possible sources for the meat and nine of them are *košer*, so we might say that the probability that the meat is *košer* is 9/10. This understanding of probabilistic statements is usually called the 'classical' interpretation [5].

What is interesting for our purposes is that the classical interpretation turns out to be inadequate as a definition of probability. This became obvious once insurance companies began using probability theory to compute actuarial tables. What does it mean to say that 'the probability that a healthy forty-year-old man will live to the age of 70 is p/q'? What are the q equally likely possible outcomes, p of which find our insurance policy holder celebrating his seventieth birthday? No such thing. This led philosophers such as Reichenbach [8] and von Mises [11] to suggest the 'frequentist' interpretation of probability: the statement that 'the probability that a healthy forty-year-old man will live to the age of 70 is p/q' means that of the potentially infinite class of hypothetical healthy forty-year-old men, the proportion who will see seventy is p/q.

It is important to understand that according to each of these interpretations, the classical and the frequentist, there is always some subjective aspect in assigning a probability to an event. In the case of classical probability, this subjective element is rather benign: we need to define the underlying 'equally likely' cases, or what is called in formal parlance, the 'sample space.' For example, in the case of 'nine stores,' we might just as plausibly use as our sample space the three shopping malls in which the stores are concentrated or perhaps the ten thousand pieces of meat that are unequally distributed among the stores. The choice of which sample space is most appropriate is ultimately a matter that must simply be stipulated. It is tempting to imagine that the 'right' sample space is the one in which the various elements are equally probable. But obviously, this formulation is circular since it is the very notion of probability that we are trying to define. To be sure, in many cases, there is a rather obvious first choice of sample space. For example, in tossing a die, we would naturally identify the six possible faces as our sample space. This intuition rests on some sort of 'indifference principle' (why should one face be more likely than another?). But such indifference principles have proved remarkably resistant to precise formulation. Ultimately, the assignment of sample space is a matter of stipulation.

If in the case of classical probability, assigning a probability to an event requires a bit of judgment, in the case of frequentist probability such an assignment is fraught with judgment. Think of the example in which we wish to determine the probability that a particular child is potentially fertile (actually in the situation described in the *Talmud* we wish only to determine that this probability is greater than ½). We wish to do so by invoking some rule that says: there is some reference class *A* in which this child is a member and the expected proportion of members of *A* which are potentially fertile is *p*/*q*. This expected frequency is in turn determined by our past experience with members of class *A* and the frequency of fertility they exhibited. But what class *A* is appropriate? Should *A* be the class of all young mammals or all human children or perhaps the class of all children who share this child's medical history or the class of children who share this child's medical history and genetic stock? If we define the class too broadly we run the risk that our experience with the class is irrelevant to the particular child in question. If we define it too narrowly we run the risk that our experience with the class is too limited to provide any reliable information with regard to the class in general. And if we define it bizarrely (say, the class consisting of this child and all major household appliances), the results are, well, bizarre. The selection of the reference class *A* as well as the determination that our experience with samples from that class is sufficient to project some statistical law onto the whole class are matters of judgment.

Consider now the extreme case of a probabilistic statement such as 'the probability that the United States will attack Iraq within two months is 60%.' The problem with such statements is that the events in question belong to no natural class since the ensemble of relevant facts renders the case unique. It is implausible that we mean to say that in 60% of cases like this an attack occurs, because there aren't any cases quite 'like this.' Since according to the frequentist interpretation every probabilistic statement must refer to some class, these statements are utterly meaningless within the frequentist framework and indeed are rejected as such by von Mises and others.

One attempt to salvage such statements as meaningful has involved yet another interpretation of probability, the 'subjectivist' interpretation. According to this interpretation, the statement that the probability of some event is *p*/*q* is taken to reflect the degree of certainty with which some rational observer is convinced of the correctness of the statement, as might be reflected in a betting strategy. Unlike the previous interpretations, such an interpretation does not require the identification of any relevant class. For example, for someone to say that the probability that the United States will attack Iraq within two months is 60% is simply to say that they regard as fair either side of a bet with 3:2 odds in favor of such an attack occurring.

To summarize, there are at least three different kinds of probabilistic statements: classical, frequentist and subjective. For each type, any instance of such a statement is meaningful only to the extent that at least one potentially fuzzy factor can be plausibly defined. In the classical case this factor is a sample set, in the frequentist case it is a reference class, and in the subjectivist case it is simply the strength of a hunch.

In the following sections, we will see how various Rabbinic methods can be best understood in relation to these different types of probabilistic statements. Moreover, we will see that different ways of resolving the fuzzy aspects of probabilistic statements can neatly account for certain apparent anomalies. In the next section, we will explain differences between the conditions and consequences of *RDIK*, on the one hand, and those of *RDLK*, on the other. After that we will clarify when *RDIK* is applied and when a converse rule (*qavu'a*) is applied and will elucidate the difference between uncertainty (*safeq*) and indeterminacy.

3. *Rub'a d'itt'a qaman* and *rub'a d'leyt'a qaman*

We will define the principle of *RDIK* more precisely in the next section but for now it is enough to define it roughly as follows: A random object taken from a set a majority of the members of which have property P, may be presumed to have property P. As so defined, the principle does not require any (but perhaps the most naive) probabilistic notions. Nevertheless, it is evident that the classical interpretation is fully adequate for a probabilistic formulation of *RDIK*: *RDIK* amounts to specifying the members of the set as a sample space and following the result with probability greater than ½. Note that *RDIK* refers specifically to a set of q concrete objects, p of which have some property, while the classical definition of probability refers more generally to q possible outcomes (which may be abstract).

The classical interpretation is, however, clearly irrelevant to the examples of *RDLK* we have seen. The frequentist interpretation, on the other hand, squares with *RDLK* perfectly [7]. Simply put, all examples of *RDLK* are statistical laws: most children born to married women are fathered by their husbands, most children are ultimately fertile, most people are not about to die, etc.

The identification of *RDIK* with the classical interpretation and *RDLK* with the frequentist interpretation will help us clear up a number of difficulties, as we shall see presently. We should note in advance, however, that the case should not be overstated. While the Rabbis certainly distinguished between two distinct kinds of majority that can be neatly embedded in full-blown theories of numerically quantifiable probability, it does not follow – and we are not suggesting – that the Rabbis were in conscious possession of any such theory.

Let us begin with the question of which is stronger, *RDLK* or *RDIK*. Later commentators have marshaled proofs for each possibility, the most salient of which follow.

The strength of *RDLK* relative to *RDIK* can be clearly seen in the following: It is well-established that we do not convict in capital cases based on mere likelihood (*Babylonian Talmud*, *Sanhedrin* 38a). Thus, consider the case of an abandoned baby boy, called an *'assufi*, whose mother is one of a given set of women one of whom is a non-Jew. In this case, there is a *RDIK* in favor of the child's Jewish maternity. While such a child may be regarded as a Jew for certain purposes, a woman who eventually marries him cannot be convicted of adultery, since 'we do not administer the death penalty on the basis of uncertainty' (Maimonides, *Hil. Issurei Biah* 15:27). Nevertheless, consider another case of uncertain maternity, in which a woman has a relationship with a child that is typical of that of mother and son but, as is generally the case, there are no witnesses to the birth. In this case, there is a *RDLK* in favor of the woman's maternity. If she and the 'son' are witnessed having sexual relations, they can be convicted for incest, since 'we administer the death penalty on the basis of presumptions' (Maimonides, *Hil. Issurei Biah* 1:20). Clearly, *RDLK* in these cases is stronger than *RDIK*.

In other cases, however, the weakness of *RDLK* relative to *RDIK* is evident. For example, the *Babylonian Talmud* (*Yevamot* 119b) cites the view of Rabbi Meir that a majority-based argument generally does not trump even a mere contrary status quo. Thus, for example, dough of tithes that was last known to be ritually clean but was found in the proximity of a child who is contaminated cannot be burned (as would ordinarily be done for contaminated tithes), according to Rabbi Meir, on the basis of a *RDLK* that children typically pick at dough in their vicinity (*Babylonian Talmud*, *Qiddušin* 80a), since this (*RDLK*-type) majority argument is inadequate to overcome the status quo of the dough being clean. The Tosafists (*Yevamot* 67b s.v. *'ein ḥošešin*, *Yevamot* 119a s.v. *kegon*) marshal proofs that this principle holds only with regard to *RDLK*, but that *RDIK* always trumps a status quo presumption. Moreover, according to R. Yochanan, in the case of the dough even the Rabbis who disagree with R. Meir would concede that the dough can't be burned on the basis of this *RDLK*. Nevertheless, they would not so concede in a case of *RDIK* (see *Babylonian Talmud*, *Qiddušin* 80a and the gloss of Rashi s.v. *im rov*). Thus, in these cases *RDLK* is weaker than *RDIK*.

We might be able to reach a definitive answer regarding which is stronger, *RDIK* or *RDLK*, by explaining away one or the other set of proofs.

But to do so would be to answer the wrong question. To understand the crucial difference between *RDIK* and *RDLK*, let's recall the difference between the classical interpretation of probability and the frequentist interpretation.

In the case of classical probability, the part that is left to judgment is rather limited. Typically, a rather straightforward sample space is taken for granted. Once that's taken care of, assigning a probability is a simple matter of calculation. In fact, in the limited case of *RDIK*, the cases need only be counted. In the case of frequentist probability, however, selecting a reference class and then estimating frequencies within the class requires a substantial investment of judgment. With what confidence can we assert that for some class A the event in question occurs with some sufficiently high frequency? Answering this question, even loosely, is inevitably a matter of judgment. Hence, *RDLK* can only be established based on rabbinic judgment.

Consequently, if you've seen one *RDIK* you've seen them all – unless there is some countervailing principle that prevents its application, *RDIK* is a decision procedure that resolves, but does not dispel, uncertainty in favor of the majority regardless of whether p/q is .99 or .51. That is, in applying the principle of *RDIK* we acknowledge that there is uncertainty but the *RDIK* allows us to decide in favor of the majority much in the way that a majority vote settles a case in court. Invoking *RDIK* is not sufficient, however, to achieve the degree of certainty necessary to establish the facts of a capital case.

Unlike *RDIK*, however, there are various types of *RDLK*. The apparent contradiction regarding the relative strengths of *RDIK* and *RDLK* simply reflects the fact that different applications of *RDLK* have different strengths (both in terms of the strengths of the laws themselves and in terms of the strength of the evidence for the laws). Since *RDLK* is always a product of rabbinic judgment, it stands to reason that they exercise this judgment variably. There are three types of decision rules and, depending on rabbinic judgment, *RDLK* can be any one of them.

The middle type is the one we have seen in the case of *RDIK* – a resolution procedure. These are often referred to as '*hak̲ra'ah*.' (This term, as well as the parallel terms below, was first proposed in [9].) An example of this is the *RDLK* that most births are not of healthy males (*Babylonian Talmud*, *Ḥullin* 77b).

There are stronger decision rules which simply render irrelevant the minority possibility – some examples of *RDLK* are treated as certainties in the sense that we proceed *as if* the uncertainty has not simply been resolved but rather has been dispelled altogether. These are often referred to as '*beirur*'. It is about these that we say 'we administer the death penalty on the basis of presumptions' – in capital cases certainty is required and these examples of *RDLK*, unlike any example of *RDIK*, do indeed provide certainty for legal purposes (at least regarding the establishment of relevant background facts [2, section 4:8]; tying a defendant to a particular act requires witnesses).

Finally, there are weaker decision rules that are merely 'defaults' in the sense that they are applied only as last-resort tie-breakers when no more substantive decision rule is available. These are often referred to as '*hanhagah.*' The typical example of a default rule in rabbinic law is a status quo argument. In some cases, *RDLK* is established merely as a default rule so that at most it can neutralize, but not defeat, another default rule such as status quo. For R. Meir, most cases of *RDLK* are of this variety.

4. *Rub'a d'itt'a qaman* and *qavu'a*

Let's now return to the principle of *RDIK* and attempt to define it more precisely. We have already seen that according to the *Talmud* (*Babylonian Talmud*, *Ḥullin* 11a), this principle covers both the case of majority vote in Sanhedrin and that of 'nine stores' where the meat is found on the street. Moreover, the *Talmud* often invokes the related, though clearly not identical, principle that a mixture of permitted and forbidden objects may sometimes be assigned the status of the majority (*biṭul b'rov*).

The generalization from the case of majority vote to cases such as 'nine stores' is not inevitable – the case of voting is more a procedural issue than one of resolving uncertainty. According to Talmudic principles [12, section 5:7], if a prophet declared the questionable piece of meat to have come from the minority, his claim might be decisive, but if he ruled in accord with the minority position in the Sanhedrin, we would ignore him (*Babylonian Talmud*, *Bab'a Meẓy'a'* 59b). Similarly, it has been argued [2, section 3:4] that the extension to *biṭul b'rov* is not inevitable, as the *Talmud* seems to assume. Clearly, the *Talmud* is operating with a majority principle sufficiently general to cover all of the above cases.

Before we consider what this principle might be, let's consider the remarkably similar situation with regard to another decision principle, namely, that 'that which is fixed is as half and half' *(kol qavu'a k'meḥẓah al meḥẓah dami*; henceforth: *qavu'a*). Like *RDIK*, the case identified in the *Talmud* as the 'source' case of *qavu'a* is a procedural matter. Someone throws a stone into an assembly of nine Israelites and one Canaanite, intending to kill whichever person the stone happens to hit. The question is whether this unspecific intention is sufficient intention to kill an Israelite to warrant conviction for murder of an Israelite (a distinct offense from that of killing a Canaanite). The Rabbis apply the principle of *qavu'a* to determine that the Israelite majority does not render the intention sufficient (*Babylonian Talmud*, *Ketubot* 15a). What exactly the principle might be requires explanation. But note that in this case there is no doubt that the actual victim was indeed an Israelite and not a Canaanite. The issue under discussion is only whether the intention to kill 'some member of this group' can be regarded as the intention to kill an Israelite. Thus, there is no uncertainty regarding any of the facts of this case and no decision-method for resolving empirical uncertainty is called for.

The *Talmud* then cites as the classic example of *qavu'a*, the parallel case to that of 'nine stores' that we considered above: 'If there are nine stores which sell *košer* meat and one which sells non-*košer* meat and someone took [meat] from one of them but he doesn't know from which one he took, the meat is forbidden.'

The parallelism between *RDIK* and *qavu'a* is remarkable. In both, the 'source' case involves court procedures and includes no elements of actual uncertainty and in both the standard case is a version of 'nine stores' in which the central issue is apparently one of uncertainty. This suggests that *RDIK* and *qavu'a* do not directly concern uncertainty, but rather are dual principles regarding mixed *sets* which cover cases of uncertainty as a by-product.

The principle of *RDIK* might thus be formulated this way:

> Given a set of objects the majority of which have the property *P* and the rest of which have the property not-*P*, we may, under certain circumstances, regard the set itself and/or any object in the set as having property *P*.

The principle of *qavu'a* is the opposite of this:

> Given a set of objects some of which have the property *P* and the rest of which have the property not-*P*, we may, under certain circumstances, regard the set itself, and consequently any object in the set, as being neither *P* nor not-*P* but rather a third status. We can call this status *hybrid*, or perhaps, *indeterminate*.

It is important to note that *RDIK* comes in two varieties: *RDIK* can assign a single status to the entire mixed set (as in the case of *biṭul b'rov*) or it might assign a status directly to an individual object in the set (as in *pariš*). *Qavu'a*, on the other hand, comes in only one variety: a hybrid status must be assigned to a set and then only indirectly to an individual item in the set. When *qavu'a* is invoked, each individual item in the set loses its individual identity and is regarded simply as a fragment of an irreducibly mixed entity. It is not treated as an individual of *uncertain* status but rather as a part of a set that is *certainly* mixed. Given this, we are ready to answer the central question: When do we apply *RDIK* and when do we apply *qavu'a*?

Roughly speaking, the idea is that when an object is being judged in isolation, it must be assigned a status appropriate to an individual object;

when it is judged only as part of a set, it can be assigned some new status. *Qavu'a* can only be invoked in the latter case. To see this distinction very starkly, consider two scenarios in each of which we have before us a box containing nine white balls and one black ball.

Scenario 1: I reach into the box, pull out one ball without showing it to you and ask: What is the color of this ball?

Scenario 2: I don't reach into the box, but instead ask: What is the color of a random ball in this box?

In the first case, if you were to answer, say, 'black,' your answer would be either true or false, but either way would be an appropriate response to the question that was asked. There is a determinate answer to the question, although this answer is unknown to you. In the second case, the answer 'black' (or 'white') is neither true nor false, since there is no determinate answer to the question. You could say nothing more specific than that the box contains both white and black balls.

Obviously, the case of the stone-thrower considered above is analogous to scenario 2 – asking about the status of an unspecified member of the group is like asking about the color of an unspecified ball. The appropriate level at which to assign status in this case is the level of the set, not the level of the individual, and the set is indeed mixed. This is the sort of case in which *qavu'a* can be invoked.

By contrast, a piece of meat that is found in the street is clearly analogous to scenario 1 – the status of a particular item is in question. This is the kind of case in which *RDIK* is invoked. Admittedly, the case of a piece of meat bought in one of the stores might plausibly be regarded as analogous to scenario 1 since the act of buying could be considered analogous to pulling out a specific ball. However, the Rabbinic principle is, somewhat counter-intuitively, otherwise: apparently, the critical moment is the one *prior* to actually encountering the piece in question. When the piece is found on the street, it is judged as an individual because prior to the moment that it is found, it is already no longer 'in the set.' When the piece of meat in question is bought in the store, prior to its being bought it is indeed 'in the set.'

The distinction between *qavu'a* and *RDIK* might be restated in terms of the issue of sample space selection considered above. *RDIK* assumes the "standard" sample space. In the case of the meat found in the street, that sample space is the set of stores. But *qavu'a* entails the selection of a non-standard, but entirely sensible, sample space: the single element consisting of the entire set of stores. This single item is mixed.

Let us now spell out in detail the precise method for determining when to apply *RDIK* and when to apply *qavu'a*.

First, there are a number of cases in which *qavu'a* cannot be invoked because a hybrid status is inappropriate.

In the case of a vote in Sanhedrin which is, by definition, a mechanism for rendering a decision.

If uncertainty regarding the status of an individual object that belonged to the set arose only after the object had been isolated from the set (*pariš*), then it is this object alone that must be assigned some status. While a member of a set consisting of objects some of which are *P* and some of which are not-*P* can be assigned a hybrid status *as part of the set*, an individual object being assigned a status on its own cannot. Thus, we need to choose either *P* or not-*P* for this object and we choose the majority of the set from which it comes. For example, in the case of 'nine stores' in which the meat is found on the street, the isolated piece of meat is assigned either the status '*košer*' or the status 'non-*košer*.'

Similarly, if the set is somehow 'incohesive,' so that each object in it is regarded as having left the set, we apply *RDIK* and not *qavu'a*. Thus, for example, a set of travelers passing through a town do not constitute a set for purposes of *qavu'a*, while the residents of the town do (*Babylonian Talmud, Ketubot* 15b; *Babylonian Talmud, Yom'a* 84b).

Finally, if it is not certain that the set contains any objects that are, say, not-*P*, the set cannot be assigned a hybrid status (formally, it is said to lack the necessary condition of *'itḥazeq 'issur'a*) and *RDIK* is invoked rather than *qavu'a*. Thus, the *Toseft'a* (*Ṭaharot* 6:3) considers a case in which we are given a mixture of ten loaves, including one loaf that is ritually unclean, that is eaten in two rounds of five loaves each. Those who eat in the first round are rendered ritually unclean because at that point the set certainly contains one unclean loaf, but those in the second round are not unclean because by then the set might not contain an unclean loaf.

To summarize: in all cases in which we are not assigning a status to a mixed set, *qavu'a* is not invoked but rather *RDIK*. Note that although in these cases the membership of the doubtful item in the set, or the cohesiveness of the set itself, may be inadequate for invoking *qavu'a*, this does not diminish the relevance of the set for purposes of *RDIK*. Thus, for example, even though the piece of meat found on the street cannot be assigned a hybrid status because it is not part of the set, the fact that the meat is known to have originated in the set still renders the composition of the set (i.e., the majority) relevant to determining the status of the piece.

When the above rule does not apply (that is, the issue is the status of a mixed set), there are cases in which *RDIK* is not applicable. In particular, for the case of a mixed set we cannot invoke *RDIK* whenever *biṭul b'rov* is not possible.

First, if the objects in the set are each identifiable as either *P* or not-*P* (*nikar bimkomo*). For example, in "nine stores" the status of each store is known, it is only the origin of a particular piece of meat that is in doubt. Clearly, in such a case, we can't define the set as either *P* or as not-*P*; as a set, it is both.

Second, if individual objects in the set are each regarded as sufficiently significant that the status of each cannot be subordinated to the status of the set or if *biṭul b'rov* is inapplicable for any other reason. Thus, given a herd of oxen including one that has been sentenced to death and is forbidden for use, we can't invoke *biṭul b'rov* due to the significance of living creatures and hence we invoke *qavu'a* by default (*Babylonian Talmud, Zevaḥim* 73b).

Third, if the set includes an equal number of objects that are *P* as are not-*P*. In such a case, *biṭul b'rov* is obviously not possible.

In all the above cases, the set fails to take on a single status as a set and hence the principle of *qavu'a* can be invoked: the set is assigned a new hybrid status (*P* and not-*P*) as are individual objects drawn from the set.

Finally, if neither of the above rules apply (so that we have a mixed set where *biṭul b'rov* is possible), *RDIK* is invoked. This is the ordinary case of *biṭul b'rov*. It is important to note that, as in the case of *qavu'a*, *biṭul b'rov* applies when the set is being judged as a set. *Biṭul b'rov* is simply applied prior to *qavu'a*. Thus, by the time *qavu'a* is considered the set is no longer a mixed set but rather a uniform set.

5. *Qavu'a* and *safeq*

The crucial distinction between uncertainty (*safeq*) regarding an individual object and *qavu'a*, which is a *definite* hybrid status assigned to a set, cannot be over-emphasized. When *qavu'a* is invoked, it is the definite mixed status of the entire set that concerns us and not the uncertain status of any individual item in the set. It is generally the failure to appreciate this distinction that leads to the conclusion that *qavu'a* is completely counter-intuitive.

Let's consider for a moment the alternative, more common, explication of *qavu'a* as merely a leveling of the playing field in which the case is treated as a symmetric *safeq*. On this understanding, which I reject, the sample space would contain two elements: *košer* and non-*košer*. According to my explanation, in cases of *qavu'a*, the sample space consists of a single element: the entire mixed set. Might not the phrasing "that which is fixed (*qavu'a*) is as half and half" suggest that the rule is in fact that we assign each status a probability of ½, that is, that we have a sample space consisting of *two* elements? Why do I reject this possibility?

First of all, because such a rule would be arbitrary and the one I argue for is perfectly sensible. Moreover, the notion that 'half and half' refers to a probability of ½ is utterly anachronistic. The assignment of probabilities to the range [0,1], so that ½ is in the middle, is a relatively recent convention. The phrase 'half and half' refers rather to set composition and not to probability. Specifically, it refers to the third case in Rule 2 of the *qavu'a/RDIK* rules above in which *qavu'a* applies to a mixed set that includes an equal number of objects that are *P* as are not-*P*. The point of the rule that 'that which is fixed (*qavu'a*) is as half and half'' is that in all cases that satisfy the conditions for *qavu'a*, *RDIK* is not invoked just as it is obviously not invoked in the case where there is no majority.

Finally, there are important halakhic differences between cases which are deemed *safeq* and cases where *qavu'a* is applied. For example, if a person had before him two indistinguishable pieces of meat, one *košer* and one non-*košer* – a case of *qavu'a* – and he ate one of them, he is obligated to bring a special sacrifice known as *asham taluy*. But if he had before him one piece, possibly *košer* but possibly non-*košer* – a case of *safeq* – he is not so obligated (see Maimonides, *Hil. Šegagot* 8:2). Similarly, if a mouse takes a piece from a mixed pile of pieces of leaven and of matzah, in a manner such that the principle of *qavu'a* would apply, into a house which has been inspected for Passover, the house must be re-inspected. But if it took a single piece of which has an even chance of being leaven or matzah into the house – this is a *safeq* – the house need not be re-inspected (see Maimonides, *Hil. Ḥameẓ u-Maẓah* 2:10-11). In the case of *safeq*, we can presume that an inspected house remains free of leaven since one possible resolution of the uncertainty regarding the subsequent events is consistent with this presumption. In the case of *qavu'a*, however, there is no uncertainty to resolve. Rather, some object of known mixed status has certainly been brought into the house; this is enough to nullify the presumption.

Now that we have established that cases of *qavu'a* are not cases of *safeq*, which cases are in fact *safeq*? The status of an object is *safeq* when it is not judged as part of a set (so that *qavu'a* and *biṭul b'rov* do not apply) *and* it has not been removed from a set with a majority (so that *pariš* does not apply) *and* it does not belong to some reference class for which some statistical law is known (so that *RDLK* does not apply). A simple example of *safeq* is one in which a piece of meat is found in the street and might have come from one of two stores, one *košer* and one non-*košer*.

In such cases, second-order default rules might be invoked to determine a course of action. These second-order rules involve the nature and severity of the prohibition in question and relevant presumptions, a detailed discussion of which is beyond the scope of this article.

Acknowledgement

This paper is a revised and abridged version of M. Koppel, Resolving uncertainty: a unified overview of rabbinic methods, *Tradition*, 37, 2003, pp. 27-51.

References

1. Beck, J. Shtern, V. The Talmudic concepts of making decisions under uncertainty, *BDD*, 15, 2004, pp. 37-64.
2. Heller, A. L. *Shev Shmaat'ta* (in Hebrew), Lemberg: Rapaport, 1804.
3. Koppel, M. Inclusion and Exclusion (in Hebrew), *Higayon*, 1, 1989, pp. 9-11.
4. Koppel, M. Further comments on *rov* and *qavu'a* (in Hebrew), *Higayon*, 4, 1997, pp. 49-52.
5. Laplace, P. S. *A Philosophical Essay on Probabilities*, transl. from French 6th ed. [1840], London: Wiley, 1902.
6. Moscovitz, L. On the principles of majority (*rov*) and *itḥazeq isura* (in Hebrew), *Higayon*, 4, 1997, pp. 18-48.
7. Rabinovitch, Nachum L. *Probability and Statistical Inference in Ancient and Medieval Jewish Literature*, Toronto: Univ. of Toronto Press, 1973.
8. Reichenbach, H. *The Theory of Probability*, Berkeley: University of California Press, 1949.
9. Shkop, S. *Sha'arei Yosher*, Warsaw: Hutner, 1928.
10. Taylor, N. The definition of *rov* in rabbinic law (in Hebrew), *Higayon*, 4, 1997, pp. 53-65.
11. Von Mises, R. *Probability, Statistics and Truth*, New York: Dover, 1957.
12. Wasserman, E. *Qunṭeres Divrei Soferim*, Pietrikov: Folman, 1924.
13. Werblowsky, Y. *Rov* and probability, *Higayon*, 4, 1997, pp. 5-22.

On the Babylonian Origin of Symbolic Logic

Andrew Schumann

University of Information Technology and
Management in Rzeszow,
Rzeszow,
Poland
andrew.schumann@gmail.com

1. Introduction

Conventionally, Aristotle (384 – 322 B.C.) is considered a father of symbolic logic. In this paper, I try to show that this statement is false, since the Greek logic (the Aristotelian logic as well as the Stoic one) was based on a Sumerian-Akkadian legal hermeneutics. So, the origin of symbolic logic should have been connected to establishing a logical tradition of the Sumerian-Akkadian jurisprudence at first.

The legal tradition of the *Talmud* is a direct continuation of the Babylonian tradition. The majority of the legal terminology in *Mišnah*itic Hebrew as well as in Talmudic Aramaic was taken from Akkadian. The Akkadian root words were considered indicators of a high-level literary language. For example, the Akkadian term of *alaktu* to denote 'a way' or even 'a spiritual road,' most probably, became a root word for the Hebrew term of *halakah* (Hebrew: "way," "law"). The point is that, according to the Bible and the *Talmud*, the Jewish community after the Babylonian captivity (i.e. since ca. 587 B.C.) enjoyed a fairly high status in Babylonia, e.g. "Mordecai sat in the king's gate" (*Esther* 2:21). We can assume that many Judahites served as judges or scribes at the house of the Achaemenid kings and, therefore, they learned the Akkadian-Aramaic legal tradition well and, then, they became "Talmudists."

The relative law formulations ("if a crime, then a punishment") allowed the Sumerians and Akkadians to differ general cases/notions from particular cases/notions and to use a naïve set theory. The analysis of Old-Babylonian and New-Babylonian business correspondence and trial records shows us many examples of difficult logical schemata as results of applications of some inference rules to law codes. The main idea of Babylonian trial was that any trial must be final in problem decision and its verdict must be complete and be inferred from the list of arguments (facts and documents): "If facts and documents, then a trial verdict." In case the set of arguments is not complete for inferring a final decision, the court takes a conditional verdict: "If facts and documents, then if an additional document that is missing, then a trial verdict" (that is logically equivalent to the following sentence: "If facts and documents and an additional document that is missing, then a trial verdict"). For instance: "Five branded sheep were seen in the flock of Kīnaya. Zēriya testifies against Kīnaya, proving that Kīnaya stole three of the sheep. The assembly decrees that Kīnaya must repay those sheep thirtyfold. Kīnaya claims that the remaining two sheep were given to him by a shepherd. Kīnaya must present the shepherd to the administrators of the Eanna. If he does not present the shepherd, then Kīnaya must repay the Eanna thirtyfold for those two sheep, as well [29 October, 547 B.C.]" [2, p. 52].

After the detailed analysis of Babylonian business correspondence and trial records we can assume that the Babylonians used inference rules which are analogous to the Talmudic *middot* (Hebrew: "logical rules"), first of all to the Hillel rules. Thus, we can claim that symbolic logic appears first not in Greece, but in Mesopotamia and this tradition was grounded in the Sumerian/Akkadian jurisprudence and the *Talmud* preserves this tradition for us until today. The only known codification of the Greeks is the *Law Code of Gortyn* (Crete, the 5th century B.C.). It was made within the Babylonian legal tradition. In this way the Greek logic was established within a Babylonian legal hermeneutics. Hence, a Sumerian-Akkadian symbolic logic was first over the world.

2. Particulars and Generals in Legal Reasoning

There are the following two logical notions which are fundamental for our logical reasoning in the everyday life: 'particular' (representing a case or species) and 'general' (representing a genus). In the meanwhile, a particular A is regarded as a case of an appropriate general B so that this general B is implied by this particular A just logically. For instance, the following conditional statement is ever true: "If it is a silver fir (A), then it is a tree (B)" ("Each silver fir (A) is a tree (B)"), where "silver tree" is a particular and "tree" is a general. Hence, if the implication $A \Rightarrow B$ is semantically true, it means that A is a particular case from B and B is a general characteristics for A.

The idea how to differ particulars and generals and how to use this difference for constructing true implications is not so easy. There is only one culture that has born this idea to life. That was the Sumerian-Akkadian culture. Let us exemplify the fact that it was not so simple to think up this logical foundation for any implication. In the Chinese language, we can correctly utter: "A horse is a horse, two horse is a horse" (*yī mă mă e, èr mă mă e*). Hence, we do not differ there (i) "a horse" as a real horse that can serve as a particular instance (subject) for our reasoning and (ii) "a horse" as a general notion that can be a general characteristics (predicate) for real items. In fact, Mohists syllogisms are rather sophisms which were based on mixing particulars and generals in this exemplified way.

In the Sumerian and Akkadian codes of laws, for the first time there were introduced some general notions as generalizations of particulars. The word to denote a generalization is *mimma* or *mimma šumšu* (Akkadian: "whatever"), e.g.: *mimma mala iddinu ītelli* (*Laws of Hammurabi* §113, §116, see [5]) "Whatever he originally gave as the loan." Implicitly, it means that suitable Hammurabi laws §113 and §116 concerning all the items given as the loan cover all the cases: "If there is whatever he originally gave as the loan, then rules §113 and §116 should take place." Let us assume that somebody gave an ox as the loan. Then we can apply the following composite implication: "If he gave an ox as the loan (A), then it is the case of whatever he originally gave as the loan (B). From this it follows that rules §113 and §116 of the *Law Code of Hammurabi* should be applied for giving this ox as the loan (C)." Formally: $((A \Rightarrow B)\ \&\ (B \Rightarrow C)) \Rightarrow (A \Rightarrow C)$. Hence, this *mimma* ("whatever") assumes a logically correct construction of conditional propositions (implications) with a logical rule of transitivity of implication. All the same is as it holds in the modern symbolic logic.

The expressions "a man who..." (*awīlum ša...*) and "a woman" (*sinništum*) from the *Laws of Hammurabi* are related to all human beings according to their gender. Both expressions are another form to denote a generalization. Each actor is examined as a particular case of *awīlum* or *sinništum* covered by appropriate rules of the *Laws of Hammurabi*. Also, there are many other expressions in Akkadian denoting "whoever" such as *mannummê* and *attamannu*.

Thus, the Sumerian-Akkadian codes of laws allow us to appeal to general notions assuming that they cover all the particular instances. As a result, in these codes, for the first time the implication as a kind of logical proposition with a correct semantics was introduced. Each article of the code, i.e. each rule, is formulated in the form of implication: "If/when (Akkadian: *šumma*) this or that occurs, this or that must be done as a trial judgment." The Semitic legal tradition (including the *Talmud*) is a continuation of the Sumerian and Akkadian law formulations. So, in the Bible we can find out the following three ways of law formulations which are typical for non-Jewish Aramaic legal texts, also:

(1) 'Casuistic': "If/when (non-Jewish Aramaic: *hn* or *'m*) this or that occurs, this or that action must be undertaken or this or that punishment must

be inflicted." This *hn* or *'m* is a derivation from the Akkadian *šumma*. An example from the Bible is as follows:

> If [*w 'im*] he has not been redeemed in any of those ways, he and his children with him shall go free in the jubilee year (*Leviticus* 26:54).

(2) 'Apodictic': "Thou shall not... (non-Jewish Aramaic: prohibitions in the second person singular of the imperfect, sometimes by using the negative particle *l'*)." A Biblical example:

> Do not [*l'o*] deal basely with your countrymen. Do not [*l'o*] profit by the blood of your fellow: I am the Lord (*Leviticus* 19:16).

(3) 'Relative': "The man who... (non-Jewish Aramaic: *'īš zī* or *gəbar zī* or *'enāš zī*)" or "Whoever ... (non-Jewish Aramaic: *zī* or *mn*)." This *zī* or *mn* is a derivation from *awīlum* and *sinništum*. Some examples from the Bible:

> And the Lord said to Moses: Whoever [*mī*] sinned against Me, him shall I erase from My book (*Exodus* 32:33).

> If [*kī*] a man [*'īš*] has a wayward and defiant son, who does not heed his father or mother and does not obey them even after they discipline him (*Deuteronomy* 21:18).

> And whoever [*we **kol** hanefeš*] does any work throughout that day, I will cause that person to perish from among his people (*Leviticus* 23:30).

It is worth noting that in the *Torah*, the word *kol* (Hebrew: "all") is often used for expressing the notions "whoever" and "whatever." It is a loanword derived from the following Akkadian words: *kala*, *kali*, *kaluma* ("everything," "everyone," "everybody").

Hence, the Sumerian/Akkadian legal style was integrated in the broader context of Near Eastern juridical terminology.

The only Greek law code preserved until now is the *Law Code of Gortyn* (see its text in [8]) written in the Dorian dialect and dated to the first half of the 5th century B.C. It was a codification of the civil law of the ancient Greek city-state of Gortyn located in southern Crete. It is a type of stone inscription on the wall of a public civic building in the agora of Gortyn. Its script style is called boustrophedron, in which alternate lines must be read in opposite directions rather than from left to right, or right to left. This code contains the articles formulated in the form of implications αἰ δέ... (the Dorian dialect of Old-Greek: "and if...") in the way of

Sumerian/Akkadian legal tradition. This text includes also expressions for general notions such as ὅς κ'... ("whosever...") and ὅτι δέ τίς κ'... ("and whatever anyone..."), etc.

In the Stoic propositional logic established by Chrysippus (c. 279 – c. 206 B.C.), the general notions are expressed in the way of legal tradition by the terms "whatever" and "whoever" as well as it was done in the *Laws of Hammurabi* first, and later in the Greek law codes like the *Law Code of Gortyn*. For instance, the well-known proposition "Man is a rational, mortal animal" (ἄνθρωπός ἐστι ζῷον λογικὸν θνητόν) was reformulated in the following manner: "**Whatever** thing is man, that thing is a rational, mortal animal" (εἴ τί ἐστιν ἄνθρωπος, ἐκεῖνο ζῷόν ἐστι λογικὸν θνητόν) (Sextus Empiricus, *Against the Ethicists* 9). Another example of Stoic universal affirmative propositions: "**Whosoever** are men, they are either Greeks or barbarians" (τῶν ἀνθρώπων οἱ μέν εἰσιν Ἕλληνές οἱ δὲ βάρβαροι) (Sextus Empiricus, *Against the Ethicists* 11).

The main difference of the Stoic formulation of universal affirmative propositions from the Aristotelian one is that the Stoic formula is interpreted as an implication immediately: "Whatever is *A*, it is *B*" is understood as "If *A*, then *B*." All the same as it took place in the Sumerian/Akkadian legal culture.

A general notion is called "idea" (ἰδέα) or "eidos" (εἶδος) in Greek. Unfortunately, we do not know how these terms were used in the Greek legal hermeneutics, because no Greek legal commentaries or trial records were preserved. Nevertheless, we know very well how the Sumerian/Akkadian difference between generals and particulars is applied in the Talmudic legal commentaries. In the *Talmud*, there are the following two significant logical terms: 'general' (*klal*) and 'particular' (*praṭ*), traditionally involved into commentaries.

Let us consider a conventional Judaic legal commentary on the following Biblical verse:

> Thou shalt not covet thy neighbour's house, thou shalt not covet thy neighbour's wife, nor his manservant, nor his maidservant, nor his ox, nor his ass, nor any thing that *is* thy neighbour's (*Exodus* 20:17).

Rabbi Yišm'a'el pays our attention on that "Thou shalt not covet thy neighbour's house" is a general concept (*klal*) that is followed by several particular instances (*praṭīm*): "Thy neighbour's wife, nor his manservant, nor his maidservant, nor his ox, nor his ass." And at the end of the verse we again face a general (*klal*): "Nor any thing that *is* thy neighbour's." According to Rabbi Yišm'a'el, this sequence started from a general and gone to a particular and then again to a general is a case for applying the Judaic inference rule that is called 'general-particular-general' (*klal u-praṭ u-klal*):

> "You shall not covet your neighbor's house" – general [כלל]. "And his man-servant, and his maid-servant, and his ox, and his ass" – particular [פרט]. General-particular [כלל ופרט] (The rule is:) There exists in the general only what exists in the particular. "And all that belongs to your neighbor" – reversion to the general. (This leaves us with) general-particular-general (The rule is:) You deduce only what is in accordance with the particular, viz.: Just as the particular is something which is acquired and bestowed, so, all that is acquired and bestowed (comes under "You shall not covet," [and not coveting another's learning]). But then, why not say: Just as the particular speaks of movable property, which does not serve as surety, so, all such property ([and not land] comes under "You shall not covet")? Since it is written (in this context) in the second Decalogue "his field," (we must revert to) "Just as the particular is something which is acquired, etc.") Or, just as the particular does not enter your domain except with the acquiescence of the owner, so all such things (are subsumed in "You shall not covet") to exclude one's coveting another's daughter for your son or his son for your daughter. I might think that (if one covets) in speech, (he is in transgression of "You shall not covet;" it is, therefore, written "You shall not covet the silver and gold upon them and take, etc." Just as there, he is not (in transgression of "You shall not covet") until he performs an act, so, here (*Mekhilta d'Rabbi Yishmael* 20:14:3, translated by Rabbi Shraga Silverstein).

Thus, for the first time, particulars and generals started to be distinguished logically in the Sumerian/Akkadian legal hermeneutics. The Sumerians and Akkadians founded a legal system for which trial decisions had to be reached by deducing them from the law code by applying the following two inference rules which are basic now for the modern symbolic logic, too: *modus ponens* and *modus tollens*. Recall that *modus ponens* is formulated as follows: if two sentences A and $A \Rightarrow B$ are true, then the sentence B is true, also. The rule of *modus tollens*: if the sentence $A \Rightarrow B$ is true and the sentence B is false, then the sentence A is false, too. Each law code contains implications $A \Rightarrow B$ which are examined as true forever. Each court should have considered a factual case C of indictment that was verified by testimonies or signed documents and then the court should have found out an appropriate general A for this C. After that the court judgment can have deduced a verdict B by *modus ponens* applied two times:

$$\frac{A \Rightarrow B;\ C \Rightarrow A;\ C}{B.}$$

The latter sentence is a verdict what should be done (which punishment B should be chosen) according to the rule $A \Rightarrow B$ from the code of laws.

If the situation C of indictment was not suitable for the legal rule $A \Rightarrow B$ from the code, *modus tollens* was applied one time:

$$\frac{C \Rightarrow A;\ A \Rightarrow B;\ \neg A}{\neg C.}$$

Hence, the task of any court is to examine all the facts, such as testimonies or signed documents, for verifying the indictment C or falsifying its general case A within an appropriate law $A \Rightarrow B$. Therefore, 'making a decision by a court' was called *dīna parāsu* in Akkadian, where *dīna* means "law" and *parāsu* means "to separate," "to divide," or "to get a particular." In other words, the direct meaning of *dīna parāsu* is to deduce something from a law or to make a particular case within a law. Thus, *dīna parāsu* became the first word denoting a deduction as such in human languages. 'Examining the facts' was called *warkata parāsu* in Akkadian. It is worth pointing out that 'giving a decision by an omen' was called *dīna šakānu* – "to establish a law." Omens in Akkadian were formulated by conditional propositions "If... then..." too and *dīna šakānu* meant to put forward a conditional law.

Let us return to the Talmudic difference between a particular (*praṭ*) and a general (*klal*). The logical term *klal* came from the Akkadian word *kalû* ("all" or "totality"), in Hebrew *kol*, while *praṭ* with the meaning *paraṭ* ("to separate," "to divide," or "to get a particular") came from the Akkadian word *parāsu*. In Hebrew there is another term *paras* to denote the verb "to separate" and "to divide." It came from the Akkadian *parāsu* also. Nevertheless, for denoting a logical notion to be a particular or an individual case only *paraṭ* is used. The meaning of *dīna parāsu* as a deductive trial judgment was shared in Judaism. So, there is the following well-known Judaic rule: "We do not make decisions as generals (*ha**klal**ōt*)" (אין למדין מן הכללות), since "We make decisions only as particulars (*ha**praṭ**īm*)" – we should follow *dīna parāsu* in all our judgments.

The ability to distinguish particulars from generals purely logically is not so easy. In Indian philosophy this ability appeared quite late (only after the Pāli Canon, i.e. after the 1st century A.D.). For instance, in the *Yamaka*, belonging to the *Abhidhammapiṭaka* of the Pāli Canon, there are considered many possible pairs of different abstract entities A and B within the following four possible answers to the question 'Is A B? But is B A?': (i) 'All A are B' and 'All B are A' (it means, A and B are generals); (ii) 'All A are B' and 'Not all B are A' (i.e. 'Some B are not A') (it means, A is particular and

B is general); (iii) 'Not all *A* are *B*' (i.e. 'Some *A* are not *B*') and 'All *B* are *A*' (it means, *A* is general and *B* is particular); (iv) 'Not all *A* are *B*' (i.e. 'Some *A* are not *B*') and 'Not all *B* are *A*' (i.e. 'Some *B* are not *A*') (it means, *A* and *B* are particulars). The answers allow us to affirm whether *A* and *B* are general or particular. Hence, on the one hand, in the *Yamaka*, the Indian author knows what is general, and what is particular, but, on the other hand, he does not know how to infer from the difference between particulars and generals. He does not use any inference rule. In the Pāli Canon, the only book, whose author knows how to infer from distinguishing particulars and generals correctly indeed, is the *Milindapañha* written in Hellenized Gandhāra.

The textual evidence illustrated above that the logical thinking appeared in India and China much, much later than in Babylonia is explained by different understandings of legality in these cultures. While in Babylonia there holds the Akkadian concept of law, *dīna* (Hebrew: *dīn*), as a legal proceeding made by logical deductions, in India there was the Hindu concept of law, *dharma* (Pāli: *dhamma*), and in China – the Chinese concept of law, *dào*, quite close to the *dharma*. While *dīna* is formalizable logically, *dharma* as well as *dào* is not at all, by their primary definitions.

The *Edict* of Aśoka, the Indian emperor of the Maurya Dynasty who ruled almost the whole Indian subcontinent from c. 268 to 232 B.C., became the first law document as such, issued in India. It is worth noting that it was written down on the stone wall or stele, too – in the Babylonian (Sumerian/Akkadian) style that was obviously borrowed. This text was written in a Prakrit close to Pāli. But several translations of the *Edict* into some other languages were published simultaneously with the main text. The Greek and Aramaic versions of this *Edict* excavated in Kandahar are unique, because they can be regarded as an outer cultural commentary to the concept of *dhamma* of Aśoka, proposed by a Greek scholar/philosopher and by an Aramean legist/"Talmudist." Let us consider first the Greek commentary:

1. δέκα ἐτῶν πληρη[....]ων βασι[λ]εὺς
2. Πιοδασσης **εὐσέβεια[ν** ἔδ]ε[ι]ξεν τοῖς ἀν-
3. θρώποις, καὶ ἀπὸ τούτου εὐσεβεστέρους
4. τοὺς ἀνθρώπους ἐποίησεν καὶ πάντα
5. εὐθηνεῖ κατὰ πᾶσαν γῆν• καὶ ἀπέχεται
6. βασιλεὺς τῶν ἐμψύχων καὶ οἱ λοιποὶ δὲ
7. εἴ τινες ἀκρατεῖς πέπαυνται τῆς ἀκρα-
8. σίας κατὰ δύναμιν, καὶ ἐνήκοοι πατρὶ
9. καὶ μητρὶ καὶ τῶν πρεσβυτέρων παρὰ
10. τὰ πρότερον καὶ τοῦ λοιποῦ λῶιον
11. καὶ ἄμεινον κατὰ πάντα ταῦτα
12. ποιοῦντες διάξουσιν.

> Ten years being completed king Piyadassi [*A.Sch.*—Aśoka] showed piety (i.e. Dhamma) [*A.Sch.* —εὐσέβεια] to men. And from that time [onwards] he made men more pious. And all things prosper throughout the whole world. And the king refrains from [eating] living beings, and indeed other men and whosoever [were] the king's huntsmen and fishermen have ceased from hunting, and those who were without control [over themselves] have ceased as far as possible from their lack of [self-] control, and [have become] obedient to father and mother and to elders, such as was not the case before. And in future, doing all these things, they will live more agreeably and better than before [7, p. 260 – 261].

The Greek scholar translated the *dhamma* as εὐσέβεια that means piety. So, establishing *dhamma* in the Empire by Aśoka meant, for the Greeks, establishing a priority of religious customs in the everyday life.

The Aramean jurist was more rigorous in his commentary than the Greek author:

1. שנן 10 פתיתו עביד זי מראן פרידארש מלכא קשיטא מהקשט
2. מן אדין זעיר מרעא לכלהם אנשן וכלהם אדושיא הובד
3. ובכל ארקא ראם שתי ואף זי זנה כמאכלא למראן מלכא זעיר
4. קטלן זנה למחזה כלהם אנשן אתהחסינן אזי נוניא אחדן
5. אלך אנשן פתיזבת כנם זי פרבסת הוין אלך אתהחסינן מן
6. פרבסתי והופתיסתי לאמוהי ולאבוהי ולמזישתיא אנסן
7. איך אסרהי חלקותא ולא איתי דינא לכלהם אנשיא חסין
8. זנה הותיר לכלהם אנשן ואוסף יהותר.

> Ten years having passed, our Lord the king Piyadassi [*A.Sch.*—Aśoka], decided to instruct men in Dhamma. Since then, evil among men has diminished in the world. Among those who have suffered it has disappeared, and there is joy and peace in the whole world. And even in another matter, that which concerns eating, our Lord the king kills very few animal.
> Seeing this the rest of the people have also ceased from killing animals. Even those who catch fish, their activity has been prohibited. Similarly those that were without restraint have now learnt restraint. Obedience to mother and father, and elders, and conformity with the obligations implied in this, is now in practice. There are no more trials for men of piety. Thus the practise of Dhamma is of value to all men, and it will continue to be so [7, p. 260 – 261].

This translation of the Aramaic text is not adequate absolutely. The much more correct translation is as follows:

> 1. For ten years penitence was made by Our Lord, Prīyad'arš [פרידארש], the king, showing [מהקשט] a straight way [קשיטא].

2. Since that time evil decreased for all men [*klhm 'nšn*] and he destroyed all the confrontation.
3. And a foundation [*štī*] arose on the whole earth [*wbkl 'rq'*]. And besides, it is in respect to the food: for Our Lord, the King, little
4. is slaughtered. Seeing this all men have ceased [to do it]. And those men who [*zī*] were catching living beings [*zwny'*],
5. have been forbidden [to do it]. Thus, who were bound, those ceased to
6. be bound. And good obedience [is observed] to his mother and to his father and to the elder men
7. as destiny imposed upon him. And the law [*dīn'a*] does not exist in respect to anyone who is strong.
8. This benefited all men and will benefit all them.

Hence, the Aramean "Talmudist" translated the *dhamma* of Aśoka in the following two manners: (i) the *dhamma* is a simple/straight way proposed by the King Prīyad'arš (פרידארש מלכא קשיטא מהקשט); (ii) this way is not a law [*dīn'a*]; as a result, if we follow the *dhamma*, we do not need any legal proceeding [the same term *dīn'a*] at all (ולא איתי דינא לכלהם אנשיא חסין). It means that the *dhamma* is before any law and cannot be formalizable as the Akkadian *dīna* (i.e. as the Aramaic *dīn'a*). In the *Talmud*, there is a concept of 'fundamental ethics' called 'road of the earth' (*dere<u>k</u> 'ereẓ*, ארץ דרך) which denotes the ethics before the Judaic legality that is called *dīn Torah* (Hebrew: "the law of the *Torah*"). Respectively, this Hebrew concept of the 'road of the earth' is close to the *dhamma* as it was understood by the author of the Aramaic version of the *Edict*.

In the Hebrew Qabbalah, the Aramaic word *dīn'a* denoting a law has rather negative connotations linking legality just to prohibitions, too. The matter is that since the 1st century A.D. the post-Akkadian approach to legality with an emancipation from the strong *dīn'a* has taken place in the Aramaic world including Judea of that time; according to this approach, ethics started to be considered more important than any law. This post-Akkadian approach was very well expressed in Christianity, first Syrian/Aramaic.

Thus, *dhamma* cannot be formalized by series of implications. So, it is out of any logic in principle. This evidence was well seen by the author of the Aramaic version of the *Edict* of Aśoka, also. Therefore, we cannot find out any implication in this *Edict*. This text is out of logic.

To sum up, we know that the Achaemenid Dynasty ruled the northern part of India for about 200 years before the Greco-Macedonian foray into India in ca. 327 B.C. And this dynasty was based on the Akkadian legal tradition with the Aramaic language got official over the whole Achaemenid Empire. Therefore, the Aramaic commentary to the *Edict*, mentioned above, is so significant. This commentary shows that Aśoka performed the following social reforms: (i) he approved a priority of religious customs in decision-making (he established a kind of theocracy); (ii) he rejected the Achaemenid *dīn'a* and validated emancipation from the law.

Nevertheless, the Akkadian-type legality came back later to India due to sharing the Hellenistic legal culture that was so close to the Semitic one. Since Alexander the Great's invasion of the Indus Valley, there have been founded several Hellenistic states in India: Bactria or the Indo-Greek Kingdom (from the 3rd century B.C. to the 1st century B.C.), the Indo-Scythian Kingdom (from the 1st century B.C. to the 1st century A.D.), the Kushan Empire (from the 1st century to the 4th century A.D.). In these states Greek was used as an official language; first of all, it was used for edicts, trading and receiving taxes. At the same time, Gāndhārī played the role of sacral language for liturgy and philosophy.

The change of the official language in the Kushan Empire from the Greek language to the Bactrian one is fixed in the Rabatak inscription of the *Edict* of Kaniṣka, the king of the Kushan Empire. This *Edict* was issued in 127 A.D. and it was found in 1993 at the site of Rabatak, near Surkh Kotal in Afghanistan. So, Kaniṣka was the first who replaced the use of Greek by the "Aryan" language after the 400-years history of the Greek and Greco-Scythian communities in the North-West of India. In fact, this "Aryan" language was Bactrian – one of the Old-Eastern-Iranian dialects with many loanwords from Greek.

The text of the *Edict* was written in the Greco-Bactrian script:

[– – –]νο βωγο στοργο Κανηϸκε κοϸανο ραϸτογο λαδειγο χοαζαοαργο βαγο
εζνογο κιδι ασ[ο] Νανα οδο ασο οισποανο μι βαγανο ι Ραοδανι αβορδο κιδι ιωγο χϸονο
νοβαστο σαγωνδι βαγανο σινδαδο οτηια ι ιωναγγο οασο οζοαστο ταδηια αριαο ωσταδο αβο ιωγο χϸονο αβο [ι] Ιυνδο φροαγδαζο αβο ϸατριαγγε ϸαορε αγιτα κοο-
αδηανο οδο ι ωζοπο οδο [ι Ζ]αγηδο οδο ι Κωζαμβο οδο ι Παλαβοτρο οιδρα αδα αβο ι Ζιριτ-
αμβο σιδηιανο προβαο οδο μανδαρο ι στορανο αβο ι σινδο ωσταδο οτηια αρουγο
Ιυνδο αβο ι σινδο ωσταδο. ταδι ϸαι Κανηϸκε αβο ϸαφαρο καραλραγγο φρομαδο
αβεινα [...]ο βαγολαγγο κιρδι σιδι β {^{2}vac.}^{2} αβο ριζδι αβο μα κα {^{2}vac.}^{2} ραγα φαρειμοανο β-
αγανο κιδι μαρο κιρδανε ι μα ν ο[φ]αρρο Ομμα οοηλδι ια αμσα Νανα οδο ια αμ-
σα Ομμα Αορομοζδο μοζδοοανο Σροϸαρδο Ναρασαο Μιιρο. οτηια ουδοα-
νο πιδογιρβο φρομαδο κιρδι ειμοανο βαγανο κιδι μασκα

νιβιχτιγενδι οτ-
ηια φρομαδο αβειμοανο þαονανο κιρδι αβο Κοζουλο Καδφισο þαο αβο ι φρ-
ονιαγο οδο αβο Οοημο Τακτοο þαο αβο ι νιαγο οδο αβο Οοημο Καδφισο þαο αβο
ι πιδα οδο αβο ι χοβσο αβο Κανηþκο þαο. τα σαγωνδι þαονανο þαο ι βαγοποο-
[ρο] α[...] φρομαδο κιρδι ταδι þαφαρε καραλραγγε κιρδο ειο βαγολαγγο
[...] ο καραλραγγο οδο þαφαρο καραλραγγο οδο Νοκονζοκο ιαþτο ο-
α[στο πι]δο ια φρομανο ειμιδβα βαγε κιδι μαρο νιβιχτιγενδι ταδανο αβο þαονανο þαο αβο Κανηþκε κοþανο αβο ιαοηδανι ζορριγι λρουγο αγγα[ο]αγγο οανινδ-
ο π[...]ινδι οδ {²vac.}² δι βαγοποορο ασο ιωγο χþονο αβο ιο α χþονο ιυνδο αρουγο π-
αδα[χþανο] ι βαγολαγγο αβο ιωγο χþονο ασπαδο ταδι αβο ι αριαμοσο χþονο αγγαρ {²vac.}²
[...π]ιδο þαο φρομανα αβισο ι παþηνα λαδο αβισο ι ρα[...]λαδο αβισο [...]
[...]þα ι μαδ {²vac.}² α αβο βαγανο λαδο οδο [...]ο[...]αχαδ[...]βαγο[...]
[– – – – –]

(the reconstruction of the *Edict* is cited from [6, p. 77 – 81]).

[1] … of the great salvation, Kanishka the Kushan [*A.Sch.*— Κανηþκε κοþανο], the righteous, the just, the autocrat, the god [2] worthy of worship, who has obtained the kingship from Nana and from all the gods, who has inaugurated the year one [3] as the gods pleased. And he *issued a Greek *edict (and) then he put it into Aryan. [4] In the year one it has been proclaimed unto India, unto the *whole of the realm of the **kshatriyas*, that (as for) [5] them – both the (city of) … and the (city of) Saketa, and the (city of) Kausambi, and the (city of) Pataliputra, as far as the (city of) Sri-Campa [6] – whatever rulers and other *important persons (they might have) he had submitted to (his) will, and he had submitted all [7] India to (his) will. Then King Kanishka gave orders to Shafar the *karalrang* [8] *at this … to make the sanctuary which is called B … ab, in the *plain of Ka …, for these [9] gods, (of) whom the … *glorious Umma leads the *service here, (namely:) the *lady Nana and the [10] lady Umma, Aurmuzd, the gracious one, Sroshard, Narasa, (and) Mihr. [interlinear text: … and he is called Maaseno, and he is called Bizago] And he likewise [11] gave orders to make images of these gods who are written above, and [12] he gave orders to make (them) for these kings: for King Kujula Kadphises (his) great [13] grandfather, and for King Vima Taktu, (his)

grandfather, and for King Vima Kadphises [14] (his) father, and *also for himself, King Kanishka. Then, as the king of kings, the *devaputra* [15] … had given orders to do, Shafar the *karalrang* made this sanctuary. [16] [Then …] the *karalrang*, and Shafar the *karalrang*, and Nukunzuk [led] the worship [17] [according to] the (king's) command. (As for) *these gods who are written here – may they [keep] the [18] king of kings, Kanishka the Kushan, for ever healthy, *secure, (and) victorious. [19] And [when] the devaputra, the *ruler of all India from the year one to the year *one *thousand, [20] had *founded the sanctuary in the year one, then *also to the … year … [21] according to the king's command … (and) it was given also to the …, (and) it was given also to the …, (and) also to [22] … the king gave an *endowment to the gods, and … [6, p. 77 – 81].

1-3 The year one of Kaniṣka, the great deliverer, the righteous, the just, the autocrat, the god, worthy of worship, who has obtained the kingship from Nana and from all the gods, who has laid down (i.e. established) the year one as the gods pleased.
3-4 And it was he who laid out (i.e. discontinued the use of) the Ionian [*A.Sch.*—Greek] speech and then placed the Arya (or Aryan) speech (i.e. replaced the use of Greek by the Aryan or Bactrian language).
4-6 In the year one, it has been proclaimed unto India, unto the whole realm of the governing class including Koonadeano (Kaundinya) and the city of Ozeno (Ozene) and the city of Zageda (Saketa) and the city of Kozambo (Kausambi) and the city of Palabotro (Pataliputra) and so long unto (i.e. as far as) the city of Ziri-tambo (Śri-Champa).
6-7 Whichever rulers and the great householders there might have been, they submitted to the will of the king and all India submitted to the will of the king.
7-9 The king Kaniṣka commanded Shapara (Shaphar), the master of the city, to make the Nana Sanctuary, which is called (i.e. known for having the availability of) external water (or water on the exterior or surface of the ground), in the plain of Kaeypa, for these deities – of whom are Ziri (Śri) Pharo (Farrah) and Omma.
9-9A To lead are the Lady Nana and the Lady Omma, Ahura Mazda, Mazdooana, Srosharda, who is called ... and Komaro (Kumara) and called Maaseno (Mahasena) and called Bizago (Visakha), Narasao and Miro (Mihara).
10-11 And he gave same (or likewise) order to make images of these deities who have been written above.
11-14 And he ordered to make images and likenesses of these kings: for king Kujula Kadphises [*A.Sch.*—Κοζουλου Καδφιζου or Κοζολα Καδαφες; Kharoṣṭhī: Kujula Kasasa; Ancient Chinese: 丘就卻, *Qiujiuque*; reigned 30–80 A.D.], for the great grandfather, and for this grandfather Saddashkana (Sadaṣkaṇa), the Soma sacrificer, and for king V'ima Kadphises [*A.Sch.*—Οοημο Καδφισης, Early Middle

Chinese: 阎膏珍, *Jiam-kaw-trin*; reigned 90–100 A.D.], for the father, and for himself (?), king Kaniṣka.
14-15 Then, as the king of kings, the son of god, had commanded to do, Shaphara, the master of the city, made this sanctuary.
16-17 Then, the master of the city, Shapara, and Nokonzoka led worship according to the royal command.
17-20 These gods who are written here, then may ensure for the king of kings, Kaniṣka, the Kushana, for remaining for eternal time healthy, secure and victorious ... and further ensure for the son of god also having authority over the whole of India from the year one to the year thousand and thousand.
20 Until the sanctuary was founded in the year one, to (i.e. till) then the Great Arya year had been the fashion.
21 ... According to the royal command, Abimo, who is dear to the emperor, gave capital to Pophisho.
22 ... The great king gave (i.e. offered worship) to the deities (this translation is taken from [4]).

No law codes from the Hellenistic states in India, unfortunately, were preserved. However, there are many indirect evidences that they were of the Greek-Semitic style. So, there are excavated some early business and taxation documents in Greek and many later real estate, trading, and taxation documents written in Bactrian in the Greco-Bactrian script and prepared in the Hellenistic way, e.g. they were made from leather, which is absolutely untypical for India. These documents are evidences that in the North-West of India, most probably, a Hellenistic codification of the civil law was implemented.

The Hellenistic legal context is a good explanation of the fact why the *nyāya* school of logic as well as the Buddhist (*yogācāra*) logic were simultaneously founded in the 2nd century A.D. in Gandhāra, the center of the Kushan Empire, namely in the region, where the Greek language was official for more than three centuries.

The Akkadian-Aramaic legality with a good tradition of logical deductions for legal hermeneutics was continued by the Greek legal culture and, then, this Hellenistic culture flourished also in Gandhāra. The tradition of that legality was so influential among the neighbor regions. For instance, the Kushan way of legality was implemented also in the Kingdom of Khotan, the Scythian Buddhist kingdom existed from the 3rd century to the 4th century A.D. and located on the branch of the Silk Road in the modern Xinjiang, China. In this kingdom Gāndhārī, the sacral language of the Buddhists of Gandhāra, was official. At the Tarim Basin site of Niya there were excavated many documents written in Gāndhārī in the Kharoṣṭhī script, where a law code is mentioned:

> His majesty, *etc*. [...] Sugita informs us that he paid a price for a woman Sugisae. The price was forty-one rolls of silk. When this sealed wedge-tablet reaches you, forthwith you must carefully inquire in person, whether she was really bought. A **decision** must be made **according to law**. Against the law officials must not take possession of that woman. If you are not clear about it there, there will be a decision when they appear in our presence at the **royal court** [1].

In turn, the legality of the Kingdom of Khotan influenced on the Chinese legal tradition trough the *mahāyāna* Buddhism. For example, in Buddhism there are the following 'ten evil acts' (十悪): (i) the three physical evil acts: killing, stealing, and sexual misconduct; (ii) the four verbal evils: lying, slander, coarse speech, and empty chatter; (iii) and the three mental evils: greed, anger, and foolishness. This Buddhist reflexion on evils influenced on defining the 'ten abominations' (十惡), fundamental for the Chinese traditional legality, first formulated in the legal documents of the Northern Qi ruled northern China from 550 to 577. They are as follows: (i) plotting a rebellion (謀反) against the ruler or parent; (ii) plotting a great sedition (謀大逆), first of all, damaging the royal temples or palaces; (iii) plotting a treason (謀叛); (iv) a contumacy (惡逆) including harming or murdering the parents and grandparents or husband's elder relatives; (v) a depravity (不道) – murdering three or more innocent people in one family; (vi) a great irreverence (大不敬) towards some sacral things and a disrespect to the Emperor or his family; (vii) a lack of filial piety (不孝), including maltreating the parents or grandparents; (viii) a discord (不睦) – harming the husband or elder relatives; (ix) an unrighteousness (不義) – a petty treason including murdering local government officials; (x) an incest (內亂).

Let us draw our first conclusions:

1. For the first time, the logical notions 'particular' ('species') and 'general' ('genus') and appropriate logical inference rules including *modus ponens* and *modus tollens* were proposed for legal proceedings in the Sumerian/Akkadian culture.

2. The Akkadian concept of *dīna* (Aramaic *dīn'a* and Hebrew *dīn*) implicitly assumes a formalization of law and a logical technique with deducing verdicts from the law code and verified facts.

3. The Greek tradition of logic is much younger than the Babylonian one and it appeared due to adopting the Semitic legal tradition with a deductive logic for the Greek legal proceedings.

4. The logical techniques of the *Talmud* are quite authentic to the original logic established by the Sumerians and Akkadians first.

5. The *nyāya* school of logic as well as the Buddhist (*yogācāra*) logic was founded in the 2nd century A.D. in Gandhāra because of adopting a Hellenistic legal tradition in this country.

3. On the Semitic Roots in the Law Code of Gortyn

The text of the *Law Code of Gortyn* is an important evidence that the civil laws were interpreted by the Greeks in the way of the Akkadian concept of *dīna* (Aramaic *dīn'a* or Hebrew *dīn*): (i) from this code, a legal proceeding is contextually reconstructed as almost the same as the Semitic legal proceedings; (ii) in this code, we see a formalization of laws that is very similar by their articles to the Semitic codifications first proposed by the Akkadians.

Let us consider first some similarities to Semitic legal proceedings. For instance, there is a requirement in the *Law Code of Gortyn* to support the own position at a court by a testimony from a minimum of two witnesses: "In the presence of two free adult witnesses" [8, p. 39]. The same number occurs in the Neo-Babylonian trial records (see [2]). Sometime there can be an additional witness, but in the Semitic legal tradition, it was accepted that two witnesses are a sufficient amount of testimonial evidence. The Judaic law requires the same amount of two, as it is seen in the Judaic commentaries to the following Biblical verse:

> One witness shall not rise up against a man for any iniquity, or for any sin, in any sin that he sinneth: at the mouth of two witnesses, or at the mouth of three witnesses, shall the matter be established (*Deuteronomy* 19:15).

The most principal thing in similarities to the Semitic juristic culture is that a judge in the *Law Code of Gortyn* is assumed to be an expert in deducing verdicts from the implications of the code by logical inference rules (first of all, by *modus ponens* and *modus tollens*). That is the same as it was supposed in the Semitic legal proceedings.

Also, there are many direct similarities to Semitic law formulations. For example, among Semitic tribes there was a tradition of levirate marriage, according to that if a man dies and he has no son or daughter, then the wife of the dead man shall not get married to a stranger, but her husband's brother shall take her for himself as a wife:

> If brethren dwell together, and one of them die, and have no child, the wife of the dead shall not marry without unto a stranger: her husband's brother shall go in unto her, and take her to him to wife, and perform the duty of a husband's brother unto her (*Deuteronomy* 25:5).

In the *Law Code of Gortyn* the levirate marriage is defined as follows:

> The heiress is to be married to the brother of her father [*A.Sch.*—husband?], the oldest of those living. And, if there be more heiresses and brothers of the father, they are to be married to the next oldest.
> And if there should not be kinsmen of the heiress as is defined, she may hold all of the property and be married to whomsoever she may wish from the tribe. And if no one from the tribe should wish to marry her, the relatives of the heiress are to proclaim throughout the tribe: "Does no one wish to marry her?" And if anyone should marry her, (it should be) within thirty days from the time they made the proclamation; but if not, she is to be married to another, whomsoever she can. And if a woman becomes an heiress after her father or brother has given her (in marriage), if she should not wish to remain married to the one to whom they gave her, although he be willing, if she has borne children, she may be married to another of the tribe, dividing the property as is prescribed; but if there should be no children, she is to be married to the groom-elect, if there be one, and take all the property; and if there is not, as is prescribed [8, p. 45 – 46].

The *Law Code of Hammurabi* (see Figure 1) is one of the oldest well-preserved Babylonian law codes. It is dated to ca. 1728 – 1686 B.C. Thus, archeologically, it is regarded as one of the first well-detailed samples for all known Semitic legal traditions. The *Law Code of Gortyn* is much younger. So, it is dated just to the 5th century B.C. Nevertheless, it is readily shown that a majority of the laws of Gortyn are similar to the laws of Hammurabi. It means that the Gortyn Greek laws have, obviously, Semitic roots.

For example, in the *Law Code of Hammurabi* the status, whether somebody is a slave, is a documented fact that can be ever proved by a court:

> **§282** If a slave should declare to his master, "You are not my master," he (the master) shall bring charge and proof against him that he is indeed his slave, and his master shall out off his ear [5, p. 132].

A fugitive slave can be seized, but only to be led him or her back to his or her owner immediately:

> **§17** If a man seizes a fugitive slave or slave woman in the open country and leads him back to his owner, the slave owner shall give him shekels of silver.
> **§18** If that slave should refuse to identify his owner, he shall lead him off to the palace, his circumstances shall be investigated, and they shall return him to his owner [5, p. 84 – 85].

It is prohibited to hold a fugitive slave in captivity:

§19 If he should detain that slave in his own house and afterward the slave is discovered in his possession, that man shall be killed.
§20 If the slave should escape the custody of the one who seized him, that man shall swear an oath by the god to the owner of the slave, and he shall be released [5, p. 84 – 85].

In the *Law Code of Gortyn* we see a prohibition to hold a fugitive slave in captivity, also, and it is well expressed, too, that the decision, whether somebody is a slave indeed, belong only to the court:

> Whosoever may be likely to contend about a free man or a slave is not to seize him before trial. But if he make seizure, let (the judge) condemn him to (a fine of) ten staters for a free man, five for a slave of whomsoever he does seize and let him give judgment that he release him within three days; but if he do not release him, let (the judge) condemn him to (a fine of) a stater for a free man and a drachma for a slave, for each day until he do release him; and the judge is to decide on oath as to the time; but if he should deny the seizure, unless a witness should testify, the judge is to decide on oath. And if one party contend that he is a free man, the other party that he is a slave, whichever persons testify that he is a free man are to prevail. And if they contend about a slave, each declaring that he is his, the judge is to give judgment according to the witness if a witness testify, but he is to decide on oath if they testify either for both or for neither. After the one in possession has been defeated, he is to release the free man within five days and give bade the slave in hand; but if he should not release or give bade, let (the judge) give judgment that the (successful party) be entitled, in the case of the free man to fifty staters and a stater for each day until he releases him, in the case of the slave ten staters and a drachma for each day until he gives him bade in hand; but at a year's end after the judge has pronounced judgment, the three-fold fines are to be exacted, or less, but not more [8, p. 39].

According to the *Law Code of Hammurabi*, if somebody forcibly seizes and rapes a virgin, then, first, the fornicator shall give "triple" the silver as the value of the maiden to her father and, second, her fornicator shall marry her, if her father agrees, and shall have no right to divorce her:

Figure 1. The stele of the Law Code of Hammurabi, Louvre Museum; *by courtesy of Vladimir Sazonov*.

§A 55 If a man forcibly seizes and rapes a maiden who is residing in her father's house, [...] who is not betrothed(?), whose [womb(?)] is not opened, who is not married, and against whose father's house there is no outstanding claim – whether within the city or in the countryside, or at night whether in the main thoroughfare, or in a granary, or during the city festival – <…> If he (the fornicator) has no wife, the fornicator shall give "triple" the silver as the value of the maiden to her father; her fornicator shall marry her; he shall not reject(?) her. If the father does not desire it so, he shall receive "triple" silver for the maiden, and he shall give his daughter in marriage to whomever he chooses [5, p. 174 – 175].

There is almost the same rule in the *Torah*:

If a man comes upon a virgin who is not engaged and he seizes her and lies with her, and they are discovered, the man who lay with her shall pay the girl's father fifty [shekels of] silver, and she shall be his wife. Because he has violated her, he can never have the right to divorce her (*Deuteronomy* 22:28-29).

In the *Torah*, almost all the sexual contacts beyond the marriage incur the death penalty:

If a man is found lying with another man's wife, both of them – the man and the woman with whom he lay – shall die. Thus you will sweep away evil from Israel. In the case of a virgin who is engaged to a man – if a man comes upon her in town and lies with her, you shall take the two of them out to the gate of that town and stone them to death: the girl because she did not cry for help in the town, and the man because he violated another man's wife. Thus you will sweep away evil from your midst. But if the man comes upon the engaged girl in the open country, and the man lies with her by force, only the man who lay with her shall die, but you shall do nothing to the girl. The girl did not incur the death penalty, for this case is like that of a man attacking another and murdering him (*Deuteronomy* 22:22-26).

The same highest penalty is supposed in the *Law Code of Hammurabi* for different sexual misconducts:

§129 If a man's wife should be seized lying with another male, they shall bind them and throw them into the water; if the wife's master allows his wife to live, then the king shall allow his subject (i.e., the other male) to live.
§130 If a man pins down another man's virgin wife who is still residing in her father's house, and they seize him lying with her, that man shall be killed; that woman shall be released.

> **§131** If her husband accuses his own wife (of adultery), although she has not been seized lying with another male, she shall swear (to her innocence by) an oath by the god, and return to her house.
> **§132** If a man's wife should have a finger pointed against her in accusation involving another male, although she has not been seized lying with another male, she shall submit to the divine River Ordeal for her husband.
> **§133a** If a man should be captured and there are sufficient provisions in his house, his wife [..., she will not] enter [another's house].
> **§133b** If that woman does not keep herself chaste but enters another's house, they shall charge and convict that woman and cast her into the water.
> **§134** If a man should be captured and there are not sufficient provisions in his house, his wife may enter another's house; that woman will not be subject to any penalty.
> **§135** If a man should be captured and there are not sufficient provisions in his house, before his return his wife enters another's house and bears children, and afterwards her husband returns and gets back to his city, that woman shall return to her first husband; the children shall inherit from their father [5, p. 105 – 106].

The corresponding articles of the *Law Code of Gortyn* are much more liberal, which can be explained by that they are quite later than the *Torah*. So, according to this code, the rape and sexual misconducts are punishable only with an appropriate fine:

> If a person commits rape on the free man or the free woman, he shall pay one hundred staters; and if on account of an apetairos, ten; and if the slave on the free man or the free woman, he shall pay double; and if a free man on a male serf or a female serf, five drachmas; and if a male serf on a male serf or female serf, five staters. If a person should forcibly seduce a slave belonging to the home, he shall pay two staters; but if she has already been seduced, one obol by day, but if in the night, two obols; and the slave shall have preference in the oath. If someone attempt to have intercourse with a free woman who is under the guardianship of a relative, he shall pay ten staters if a witness should testify.
> If someone be taken in adultery with a free woman in a father's, brother's or the husband's house, he shall pay a hundred staters; but if in another's fifty; and if with the wife of an apetairos, ten; but if a slave with a free woman, he shall pay double; and if a slave with a slave, five [8, p. 40].

By the laws of Hammurabi, a man is granted more by a privilege to declare divorce than a woman, but a woman with children can expect, first, returning her bridewealth and dowry or obtaining some shekels of silver if she had no bridewealth before, and, second, obtaining one half of the movable and immovable property ("her husband's field, orchard, and property"):

> **§137** If a man should decide to divorce a *šugītu* who bore him children, or a *nadītu* who provided him with children, they shall return to that woman her dowry and they shall give her one half of (her husband's) field, orchard, and property, and she shall raise her children; after she has raised her children, they shall give her a share comparable in value to that of one heir from whatever properties are given to her sons, and a husband of her choice may marry her.
> **§138** If a man intends to divorce his first-ranking wife who did not bear him children, he shall give her silver as much as was her bridewealth and restore to her the dowry that she brought from her father's house, and he shall divorce her.
> **§139** If there is no bridewealth, he shall give her 60 shekels of silver as a divorce settlement.
> **§140** If he is a commoner, he shall give her 20 shekels of silver.
> **§141** If the wife of a man who is residing in the man's house should decide to leave, and she appropriates goods, squanders her household possessions, or disparages her husband, they shall charge and convict her; and if her husband should declare his intention to divorce her, then he shall divorce her; neither her travel expenses, nor her divorce settlement, nor anything else shall be given to her. If her husband should not declare his intention to divorce her, then her husband may marry another woman and that (first) woman shall reside in her husband's house as a slave woman.
> **§142** If a woman repudiates her husband, and declares, "You will not have marital relations with me" – her circumstances shall be investigated by the authorities of her city quarter, and if she is circumspect and without fault, but her husband is wayward and disparages her greatly, that woman will not be subject to any penalty; she shall take her dowry and she shall depart for her father's house.
> **§143** If she is not circumspect but is wayward, squanders her household possessions, and disparages her husband, they shall cast that woman into the water [5, p. 107 – 108].

Also, it is well expressed that the woman of the *awīlu*-class can receive one half of the property produced by marriage:

> **§176b** If the woman of the *awīlu*-class does not have a dowry, they shall divide into two parts everything that her husband and she accumulated subsequent to the time that they moved in together, and the slave's owner shall take half and the woman of the *awīlu*-class shall take half for her children [5, p. 116].

In the *Law Code of Gortyn*, a woman after divorce can get her bridewealth and dowry back also and, additionally, she can receive one half of the property produced by marriage ("one half of the produce"), and she can carry away anything of the movable property ("anything else belonging to the husband") after paying five staters:

> And if a husband and wife should be divorced, she is to have her own property which she came with to her husband and half of the produce, if there be any from her own property, and half of whatever she has woven within, whatever there may be, plus five staters if the husband be the cause of the divorce; but if the husband should declare that he is not the cause, the judge is to decide on oath. And if she should carry away anything else belonging to the husband, she shall pay five staters and whatever she may carry away; and let her restore whatever she may have filched; but as regards things which she denies (the judge) shall decree that the woman take an oath of denial by Artemis, before the statue of the Archeress in the Amyklaian temple [8, p. 40 – 41].

Hammurabi established a protection of children's inheritance and property rights after the death of their father or mother. In the meanwhile, it is affirmed that the dowry of the died and childless woman belongs only to her father's house:

> **§177** If a widow whose children are still young should decide to enter another's house, she will not enter without (the prior approval of) the judges. When she enters another's house, the judges shall investigate the estate of her former husband, and they shall entrust the estate of her former husband to her later husband and to that woman, and they shall have them record a tablet (inventorying the estate). They shall safeguard the estate and they shall raise the young children; they will not sell the household goods. Any buyer who buys the household goods of the children of a widow shall forfeit his silver; the property shall revert to its owner [5, p. 116].
>
> **§162** If a man marries a wife, she bears him children, and that woman then goes to her fate, her father shall have no claim to her dowry; her dowry belongs only to her children.
> **§163** If a man marries a wife but she does not provide him with children, and that woman goes to her fate – if his father-in-law then returns to him the bridewealth that that man brought to his father-in-law's house, her husband shall have no claim to that woman's dowry; her dowry belongs only to her father's house [5, p. 112].

In the same way the inheritance and property rights of children after the death of their father or mother are protected in the *Law Code of Gortyn*, and the dowry of the died and childless woman is regarded also as belonging to her father's house:

> If a man die leaving children, should the wife so desire, she may marry, holding her own property and whatever her husband might have given her according to what is written, in the presence of three adult free witnesses; but if she should take away anything belonging to the children, that becomes a matter for trial. And if he should leave her childless, she is to have her own property and half of whatever she has woven within and obtain her portion of the produce that is in the house along with the lawful heirs as well as whatever her husband may have given her as is written; but if she should take away anything else, that becomes a matter for trial. And if a wife should die childless, (the husband) is to return her property to the lawful heirs and the half of whatever she has woven within and the half of the produce, if it be from her own property [8, p. 41].

> If the husband or wife wish to make payments for porterage, (these should be) either clothing or twelve staters or something of the value of twelve staters, but not more. If a female serf be separated from a serf while he is alive or in case of his death, she is to have her own property; but if she should carry away anything else, that becomes a matter for trial. If a wife who is separated (by divorce) should bear a child, (they) are to bring it to the husband at his house in the presence of three witnesses; and if he should not receive it, the child shall be in the mother's power either to rear or expose; and the relatives and witnesses shall have preference in the oath as to whether they brought it. And if a female serf should bear a child while separated, (they) are to bring it to the master of the man who married her in the presence of two witnesses [8, p. 41].

In the *Law Code of Hammurabi*, the male children should divide their father and mother property after their death rather equally:

> **§165** If a man awards by sealed contract a field, orchard, or house to his favorite heir, when the brothers divide the estate after the father goes to his fate, he (the favorite son) shall take the gift which the father gave to him and apart from that gift they shall equally divide the property of the paternal estate [5, p. 112].

> **§167** If a man marries a wife and she bears him children, and later that woman goes to her fate, and after her death he marries another woman and she bears children, after which the father then goes to his fate, the children will not divide the estate according to the mothers; they shall take the dowries of their respective mothers and then equally divide the property of the paternal estate [5, p. 113].

§170 <...> After the father goes to his fate, the children of the first-ranking wife and the children of the slave woman shall equally divide the property of the paternal estate; the preferred heir is a son of the first-ranking wife, he shall select and take a share first.
§171 But if the father during his lifetime should not declare to (or: concerning) the children whom the slave woman bore to him, "My children," after the father goes to his fate, the children of the slave woman will not divide the property of the paternal estate with the children of the first-ranking wife [5, p. 114].

§173 If that woman should bear children to her latter husband into whose house she entered, after that woman dies, her former and latter children shall equally divide her dowry [5, p. 115].

The same rule holds in the *Law Code of Gortyn* to divide the inheritance equally among the male children first:

When a man or a woman dies, if there be children or children's children or children's children's children, they are to have the property. And if there be none of these, but brothers of the deceased and brothers' children or brothers' children's children, they are to have the property. And if there be none of these, but sisters of the deceased and sisters' children or sisters' children's children, they are to have the property. And if there be none of these, they are to take it up, to whom it may fall as source of the property [8, p. 43].

It is prohibited to sell the inheritance of children as well as the same is forbidden by Hammurabi:

As long as the father lives, no one shall offer to purchase any of the paternal property from a son nor take out a mortgage on it; but whatever (the son) himself may have acquired or inherited, let him sell, if he wishes. Nor shall the father sell or mortgage the possessions of his children, whatever they have themselves acquired or inherited. Nor shall the husband sell or pledge those of his wife, nor the son those of his mother. And if anyone should purchase or take on mortgage or accept a promise otherwise than is written in these writings, the property shall be in the power of the mother and the wife, and the one who sold or mortgaged or promised shall pay two-fold to the one who bought or accepted the mortgage or the promise and, if there be any other damage besides, the simple value; but in matters of previous date there shall be no ground for action. If, however, the defendant should maintain, with reference to the matter about which they contend, that it is not in the power of the mother or the wife, the action shall be brought where it belongs, before the judge where it is prescribed for each case. If a mother die leaving children, the father is to be in control of the mother's property, but he shall not sell or mortgage unless the children consent and are of age; but if anyone should otherwise purchase or take on mortgage, the property shall be in the power of the children and the seller or mortgagor shall pay twofold the value to the purchaser or mortgagee and, if there be any other damage besides, the simple value. And, if he should marry another woman, the children are to be in control of the mother's property [8, p. 44].

Also, it is prohibited to sell father's property before his death:

If a son has gone surety, while his father is living, he and the property which he possesses shall be subject to fine [8, p. 47].

The children born to a free woman and a slave man are considered free by the Greeks:

(If the slave) goes to a free woman and marries her, their children shall be free; but if the free woman goes to the slave, their children shall be slaves. And if free and slave children should be born of the same mother, in a case where the mother dies, if there is property, the free children are to have it; but if there should be no free children born of her, the heirs are to take it over [8, p. 44 – 45].

The same rule in respect to a woman of the *awīlu*-class takes place in the *Law Code of Hammurabi*:

§175 If a slave of the palace or a slave of a commoner marries a woman of the *awīlu*-class and she then bears children, the owner of the slave will have no claims of slavery against the children of the woman of the *awīlu*-class [5, p. 115].

In the *Law Code of Gortyn*, it is affirmed that money for investment in a partnership venture should be divided equally and any court has to protect this right:

If one has formed a partnership with another for a mercantile venture, in case he does not pay back the one who has contributed to the venture, if witnesses who are of age should testify – three in a case of a hundred staters or more, two in a case of less down to ten staters, one for still less – let (the judge) decide according to the testimony; but if witnesses should not testify, in case the contracting party comes, whichever course the complainant demands, either to deny on oath or – [...], [8, p. 47].

An appropriate right to benefit from investment is well emphasized by Hammurabi, too:

§gap cc If a man gives silver to another man for investment in a partnership venture, before the god they shall equally divide the profit or loss [5, p. 99].

§gap ~ z If a man borrows grain or silver from a merchant and does not have grain or silver with which to repay but does have other goods, he shall give to his merchant in the presence of witnesses whatever he has at hand, in amounts according to the exchange value; the merchant will not object; he shall accept it [5, p. 99].

§107 If a merchant entrusts silver to a trading agent and the trading agent then returns to his merchant everything that the merchant had given him but the merchant denies (having received) everything that the trading agent had given him, that trading agent shall bring charges and proof before the god and witnesses against the merchant, and because he denied the account of his trading agent, the merchant shall give to the trading agent sixfold the amount that he took [5, p. 101].

By Hammurabi, each man can adopt a child, then he cannot rear this child without an inheritance, but the child can seek his father and mother to return to his father's house:

§185 If a man takes in adoption a young child at birth and then rears him, that rearling will not be reclaimed.
§186 If a man takes in adoption a young child, and when he takes him, he (the child?) is seeking his father and mother, that rearling shall return to his father's house.
§190 If a man should not reckon the young child whom he took and raised in adoption as equal with his children, that rearling shall return to his father's house [5, p. 119].

§191 If a man establishes his household (by reckoning as equal with any future children) the young child whom he took and raised in adoption, but afterwards he has children (of his own) and then decides to disinherit the rearling, that young child will not depart empty-handed; the father who raised him shall give him a one-third share of his property as his inheritance and he shall depart; he will not give him any property from field, orchard, or house [5, p. 119 – 120].

The same situation in relation to adoption is observed in the *Law Code of Gortyn*:

Adoption may be made from whatever source anyone wishes. And the declaration of adoption shall be made in the place of assembly when the citizens are gathered, from the stone from which proclamations are made. And if he (the adopted person) should receive all the property

> and there should be no legitimate children besides, he must fulfill all the obligations of the adopter towards gods and men and receive as is written for legitimate children; but if he should not be willing to fulfill these obligations as is written, the next-of-kin shall have the property [8, p. 48].
> <...> but if the adopted son should die without leaving legitimate children, the property is to revert to the heirs of the adopter. And if the adopter wishes, he may renounce (the adopted son) in the place of assembly when the citizens are gathered, from the stone from which proclamations are made; and he shall deposit ten staters with the court, and the secretary (of the magistrate) who is concerned with strangers shall pay it to the person renounced; but a woman shall not adopt nor a person under puberty [8, p. 49].

Thus, as we see, the only Greek law code, preserved until today, has evidently Semitic roots. Most probably, there was a direct Phoenician influence on establishing the Greek legal tradition. In any case, the Greeks knew deductions and other logical inferring within legal proceedings from a Semitic legal culture grown up, in turn, from the Akkadian *Law Code of Hammurabi* and other Old Babylonian codes.

4. Inference Rules in Trial Records

There are the following two most significant inference rules in Babylonian legal proceedings: *modus ponens* and *modus tollens*. They seem to us an evident tool in inferring. However, they are not so evident and easy even for philosophers. For example, one of the earliest "logical" treatises in India is represented by the *Kathāvatthu*, belonging to the *Abhidhammapiṭaka* of the Pāli Canon. It is a compendium of logical reasoning based, only at the first glance, on *modus ponens* and *modus tollens*. In reality, its author does not know how to infer logically by using *modus ponens* and *modus tollens*.

Let us consider an example from the *Kathāvatthu* consisting of debates between a Theravādin and non-Theravādins. One of these debates can be formalized as follows:

> Theravādin.—Is A B?
> Puggalavādin.—Yes.
> Ther.—Is A C?
> Pugg.—No.
> Ther.—However, 'if A is B, then A is C.' Then that which you say here is wrong, because you state that 'A is B' is true, but 'A is C' is false. But if 'A is C' is false, then 'A is B' is false.

Symbolically, it is a modification of *modus tollens*:

$$\frac{(A \Rightarrow B) \Rightarrow (A \Rightarrow C); \neg (A \Rightarrow C)}{\neg (A \Rightarrow B).}$$

So, the latter flow chart seems to be correct. But it is not, because the Theravādin believes that $A \Rightarrow B$ is false, while $A \Rightarrow C$ is true, and the Puggalavādin believes that $A \Rightarrow B$ is true, while $A \Rightarrow C$ is false. Hence, we face a sophism, not *modus tollens*: the Theravādin puts forward two premises, the first of them [$(A \Rightarrow B) \Rightarrow (A \Rightarrow C)$] is not valid, because its antecedent is false, and the second of them [$\neg (A \Rightarrow C)$] is false [namely, $A \Rightarrow C$ is true, so $\neg (A \Rightarrow C)$ is false], therefore the conclusion [$\neg (A \Rightarrow B)$] cannot be inferred at all.

Thus, the author of the *Kathāvatthu* does not know logic. Only one book of the Pāli Canon contains *modus ponens* and *modus tollens* with their logically correct applications. It is the *Milindapañha* written in Gandhāra at the time of the Greek rule and dated to from the 1st century B.C. to the 1st century A.D.

Among the Greek philosophers Chrysippus was first who correctly and explicitly defined *modus ponens* and *modus tollens*. His samples:

(i) *modus ponens*: "If it is day, it is light; but in fact it is day; therefore it is light" (Sextus Empiricus, *Against the Logicians* II, 224);

(ii) *modus tollens*: "If it is day, it is light; but it is not light; therefore it is not day" (Sextus Empiricus, *Against the Logicians* II, 225).

We do not know whether Chrysippus applied his propositional logic in a legal hermeneutics. But his prominent Roman follower, Marcus Tullius Cicero (106 – 43 B.C.), did it really well. Cicero wrote the *Topica* where he showed how we can use the *loci* (logical frameworks, Latin: "places") to draw out the consequences from legal propositions. His *Topica* is a unique sample of applying a symbolic logic in the Roman-Greek legal hermeneutics (see the commentary by Tobias Reinhardt in [3]). Cicero distinguishes 'invention' and 'judgment.' According to him, 'invention' is a logical investigation of differences among particulars and generals to introduce new concepts, and 'judgment' is a compendium of logical tools for reaching correct and true conclusions from different true propositions. By Cicero, Aristotle developed a system for both 'invention' and 'judgment,' but Chrysippus proposed a system just for 'judgment.' Cicero in his *Topica* tries to combine both approaches, i.e. the Aristotelian and Stoic ones:

> 6 Cum omnis ratio diligens disserendi duas habeat artes, unam inveniendi alteram iudicandi, utriusque princeps, ut mihi quidem

videtur, Aristoteles fuit. Stoici autem in altera elaboraverunt; iudicandi enim vias diligenter persecuti sunt ea scientia quam διαλεκτικήν appellant, inveniendi artem quae τοπική dicitur, quae et ad usum potior erat et ordine naturae certe prior, totam reliquerunt. 7 Nos autem, quoniam in utraque summa utilitas est et utramque, si erit otium, persequi cogitamus, ab ea quae prior est ordiemur. Ut igitur earum rerum quae absconditae sunt demonstrato et notato loco facilis inventio est, sic cum pervestigare argumentum aliquod volumus, locos nosse debemus; sic enim appellatae ab Aristotele sunt eae quasi sedes, e quibus argumenta promuntur. 8 Itaque licet definire locum esse argumenti sedem, argumentum autem rationem quae rei dubiae faciat fidem.

All methodical treatment of rational discourse involves two skills, invention and judgement; Aristotle came first in both, it seems to me. The Stoics on the other hand concerned themselves with one of the two skills only; that is, they pursued ways of judging (arguments) diligently by means of that science which they call dialectic. The skill of invention, however, which is called topice and which was both of more immediate practical use and certainly prior in the order of nature, they completely neglected. But since both skills are of the utmost usefulness and since we intend to pursue both, if time allows we shall begin with that which is prior. Just as it is easy to find hidden things, once their hiding-place has been pointed out and marked down, so we need to know the right Places if we wish to track down a certain argument; 'Places' [*A.Sch.—loci* in Latin and τόποι in Greek] is the name Aristotle gave those locations, so to speak, from which we can draw arguments. Therefore we may define a Place as the location of an argument, and an argument as a reasoning that lends belief to a doubtful issue [3, p. 119].

An example of inferring from a general considered by Cicero is as follows:

13 A genere sic ducitur: Quoniam argentum omne mulieri legatum est, non potest ea pecunia quae numerata domi relicta est non esse legata; forma enim a genere, quoad suum nomen retinet, numquam seiungitur; numerata autem pecunia nomen argenti retinet; legata igitur videtur.

From the genus an argument is derived as follows: Since all the silver was bequeathed to the woman, it cannot be the case that the money which remained at home in form of coins was not bequeathed; for the species is never dissociated from the genus, as long as it retains its name; but money in form of coins retains the name 'silver'; therefore, it seems to have been bequeathed [3, p. 123].

One of the main features of law codes regarded by Cicero is a full enumeration of particulars $A_1, A_2, \ldots, A_n$, related to one general B, i.e. a full list of implications $A_1 \Rightarrow B$, $A_2 \Rightarrow B$, $\ldots$, $A_n \Rightarrow B$ with the same B, as it was supposed in any law code. These $A_1, A_2, \ldots, A_n$ should be exclusive. It means that they should be connected by strong disjunctions "either ... or ..." (Akkadian: "*ūl* ... *ūl*...", symbolically: "... ⊗ ..."). In this case there is the following equivalence: $(A_1 \otimes A_2 \otimes \ldots \otimes A_n) \Leftrightarrow B$. From this we can draw the following conclusion:

$$\frac{\dfrac{A_1 \Rightarrow B; A_2 \Rightarrow B; \ldots; A_n \Rightarrow B; C \Rightarrow \neg A_1; C \Rightarrow \neg A_2; \ldots; C \Rightarrow \neg A_n}{(A_1 \otimes A_2 \otimes \ldots \otimes A_n) \Rightarrow B;\ C \Rightarrow \neg (A_1 \otimes A_2 \otimes \ldots \otimes A_n)}}{C \Rightarrow \neg B.}$$

Cicero formulates this rule thus:

> Tum partium enumeratio quae tractatur hoc modo: Si neque censu nec vindicta nec testamento liber factus est, non est liber; neque ulla est earum rerum; non est igitur liber.
>
> Next, the enumeration of the parts (sc. of the whole), which is handled in the following way: If someone has not been freed by either having his name entered in the census-roll or by being touched with the rod or by a provision in a will, then he is not free. None of these applies to the individual in question. Therefore he is not free [3, p. 121].

This logical rule implemented in any code may be named a *completeness of legal information*. This completeness means that if we take any factual verified case C of an indictment, then for any general B from the code, each court can announce either a verdict $C \Rightarrow B$ or a verdict $C \Rightarrow \neg B$ inferred from the code just logically.

Thus, each article of the code is formulated in the form of implication: "'If/when (Sumerian: *tukum-bi*) this or that occurs (A), this or that must be done (B)," i.e. $A \Rightarrow B$. Among different particulars $A_1, A_2, \ldots, A_n$, implying generals $B_1, B_2, \ldots, B_k$ there are some labels such as classes of personalities, e.g. some classes of people from the *Laws of Ur-Nammu* (ca. 2047 – 2030 B.C., Ur) are as follows: 'a free man' (Sumerian: *lû*), 'a wife' (Sumerian: *dam*), 'the first-ranking wife' (Sumerian: *nitadam*), 'the native-born woman' (Sumerian: *dumu-gi*$_7$), 'the widow' (Sumerian: *nu-masu*), 'a young man' (Sumerian: *guruš*), 'a male slave' (Sumerian: *arad*), and 'a female slave' (Sumerian: *géme*). These labels allow us to define whether our case C at a court corresponds to one of the particulars $A_1, A_2, \ldots, A_n$ or not. And due to this correspondence to one of $A_1, A_2, \ldots, A_n$, we can infer either a verdict $C \Rightarrow B_i$ or a verdict $C \Rightarrow \neg B_i$ for each general B_i.

In the Babylonian legal tradition, the law code must have been published at the beginning as a main source for legality. This publication was marked by erecting a stele with official inscriptions or by engraving these inscriptions on a wall. One of the best-known steles with such inscriptions belongs to Hammurabi and represents his laws cited above. Another example may be provided with the inscriptions on the wall in the agora of Gortyn representing the Greek law code cited above, too.

The law code was considered a set of axioms announced for all due to its publications on a stone. To the same extent, the Tables of the Law (Hebrew: לוחות הברית) inscribed, according to the *Torah*, by God were official inscriptions of the Judaic law code written on stones:

> And He gave unto Moses, when He had made an end of speaking with him upon mount Sinai, the two tables of the testimony, tables of stone, written with the finger of God (*Exodus* 31:18).

In the *Samaritan Pentateuch* it is stated more explicitly that the Israelites should have write down their code on stones:

> 14a And when Shehmaa your Eloowwem will bring you to the land of the Kaanannee which you are going to inherit it. 14b You shall set yourself up great stones and lime them with lime. And you shall write on them all the words of this law.14C And when you have passed over the Yaardaan you shall set up these stones, which I command you today, in Aargaareezem. 14d And there you shall build an altar to Shehmaa your Eloowwem, an altar of stones, you shall lift up no iron on them (*Exodus* 20:14, the *Samaritan Pentateuch*, translated by Benyamim Tsedaka).

This fragment is quite unique, because it is absent from the Hebrew Bible. The Tables of the Law were regarded here as made by human beings and put into the wall at the temple of mount Gerizim ('Aargaareezem'). Among other Semitic peoples it was a usual practice to write basic rules on stones for a public announcement of the law code.

We can assume that all the Semitic cultures directly influenced by the Akkadians had a kind of law code, even if this code was not preserved till now. For instance, we have no fragments of the Old Assyrian law code at all, but a publication of this code on stones is cited many times in some judicial records and letters, containing official verdicts, by references to "the words of the stele" (*awāt naruāim*), see for the details in [9]. In Akkadian a stele with laws was called *narûm* (Akkadian: "inscribed stone"). In Old Babylonian texts, 'a stele' is mentioned, for instance, in the following manner: "[F]or the shortfall which occurs one will treat him in accordance with the text of the **stele** (*kīma pī narīm*)" [9, p. 1721]. In Old Assyrian fragments, an appropriate mention is as follows: "To swear him with/by the three words of (variant: which are written on) the **stele**" [9, p. 1721] and "The creditors of Šukubum, from whatever Šukubum possesses, in accordance with the words of the **stele**, when it is confirmed by witnesses, (each) will take his silver in/at/from/by means of his …" [9, p. 1729].

According to the Neo-Babylonian cuneiform records (see [2]), we know that there existed a complex institution of royal judges (*dayyānū ša šarri*) who must have been experts in inferring trial verdicts from 'the words of the stele' just by deductions. The royal judges were organized in a bureaucratic hierarchy overseen by royal officials called *sartennu* or *sukallu*. The highest level in trial judgments was presented by 'the king's court of law' (*bīt dīni ša šarri*). In the Babylonian society, even the king was regarded as subject to the law. So, the royal judges were examined as social elite and, e.g., they were not removed from office when the king changed. Usually, each court consists of two judges, one of them handles a case and the second serves as a scribe/secretary.

Let us consider an example of trial. In the *Law Code of Hammurabi* there is the following rule:

> **§8** If a man steals an ox, a sheep, a donkey, a pig, or a boat – if it belongs either to the god or to the palace, he shall give **thirtyfold**; if it belongs to a commoner, he shall replace it tenfold; if the thief does not have anything to give, he shall be killed [5, p. 82].

For instance, "If a man steals X sheep and it belongs to the god (to an appropriate temple), then he must replace it thirtyfold (i.e. the amount of $X \cdot 30$)."

There is a trial record denoted YBC 3771, found in Uruk, and dated to 12.XII.3 Camb (22 March, 526 B.C.), see [2, p. 178 – 181]. In this trial record, two judges determine that Bēl-iqīša, who led away 5 sheep belonging to 'Ištar of Uruk and Nanaya' (a temple), must repay 155 sheep to the property of this temple, because 150 sheep is the **thirtyfold** penalty for five branded sheep and the five unbranded lambs are supposed to be born after steeling:

> (1–6) [1 ram 4 ewes] total 5 sheep branded with a star and 5 unblemished lambs, a total of 10 sheep, property of Ištar of Uruk and Nanaya, from the pen of Anu-šarra-uṣur son of Šarrukīn, which in Araḫšamna, year 2 of Cambyses, king of Babylon, king of the lands, Bēl-iqīša son of Ṣillaya led away (in payment) from Anu-šarrauṣur son of Šarru-kīn.

(7–11) In Addaru, year 3, Rīmūt and Bau-ērеš, the judges, wrote in a tablet and determined for Bēl-iqīša to pay 150 sheep, **thirtyfold** for the sheep branded for Ištar and 5 unbranded lambs, a total of 155 sheep, for repayment to Ištar of Uruk.
(12–14) On 25 Addaru, year 3, Bēliqīša son of Ṣillaya shall bring these 155 sheep, brand them in the Eanna and give them to the property of the Eanna.
(14–16) Arad-Nergal son of Mukīnapli descendant of Egibi assumes responsibility for the repayment of these 155 sheep.
(16–17) In the presence of Nabûmukīn-apli, the šatammu of the Eanna, son of Nādinu descendant of Dābibī;
(18) Nabû-aḫa-iddin, the royal official in charge of the Eanna.
(19) Witnesses: Arad-Marduk, son of Zēriya descendant of Egibi;
(20) Sîn-ēreš son of Nabû-šumu-līšir descendant of Ibni-ili;
(21) Bēl-nādin-apli son of Mardukšuma-iddin descendant of Bēl-aplauṣur;
(22) Nādinu, the scribe, descendant of Egibi;
(23) Arad-Marduk, the scribe, descendant of Bēl-apla-uṣur.
(24–25) Uruk. 12 Addaru, year 3 of Cambyses, king of Babylon, king of the lands [2, p. 179 – 181].

This trial record is symbolically represented as an inference by *modus ponens* as follows:

1. If a man steals *X* sheep and it belongs to the god (to a temple), then he must replace it **thirtyfold** (i.e. the amount of $X \cdot 30$) [the axiom from the code];
2. Ištar of Uruk and Nanaya is a temple [it is a fact, because 'a temple' is a generalization for the case of 'Ištar of Uruk and Nanaya'];
3. Bēl-iqīša son of Ṣillaya led away 5 sheep belonging to Ištar of Uruk and Nanaya [the fact established by the trial];

Then, Bēl-iqīša son of Ṣillaya must repay 150 sheep to Ištar of Uruk and Nanaya on 25 Addaru, year 3.

Another example of trial record is denoted BM 46660 (see [2, p. 43 – 44]) and tells us that Marduk-šarranu has accused Kīnaya of striking his son and, as a result, two siblings, a brother and a sister, guarantee that Kīnaya will appear at the court. If Kīnaya escapes, then the two must pay compensation to Marduk-šarranu:

10'. A-šú šá mBA-šá-a na-[šu-u ki-i]
11'. mki-na-a iḫ-te-[li-qu]
12'. ZI.MEŠ šá DUMU-šú sa2 md[AMAR.UTU-LUGAL-a-nu]
13'. mdNA3-NUMUN-MU u fiṣ-[ṣur]-[
14'. ú-šal-lim-mu lu2mu-kin-nu m[PN

(10’–14’) If Kīnaya escapes, Nabûzēra-iddin and Iṣṣur-[X] will pay compensation for the life of the son of Marduk-šarranu.
(14’–15’) Witnesses: PN
[2, p. 44].

Symbolically:

1. If a man strikes somebody, then he must pay compensation [the axiom from the code];
2. If a man cannot pay, his guarantors must pay [the axiom from the code];
3. Kīnaya struck Marduk-šarranu’s son [the proven fact];
4. If Kīnaya appears at the trial, he must pay compensation to Marduk-šarranu [the first conditional verdict];
5. If Kīnaya escapes, his two guarantors must pay compensation to Marduk-šarranu [the second conditional verdict];

Then, either Kīnaya or his two guarantors must pay compensation to Marduk-šarranu.

The next instance of conditional verdicts is taken from the text denoted BM 31162, found in Opis, and dated to 23.VIII.40 Nbk (5 November, 565 B.C.), see [2, p. 45 – 47]. In this trial record, Gudaya, the guarantor of a grain loan to Katimu’, testifies that he presented Katimu’ to Bau-ēreš (the creditor) to repay the debt. Bau-ēreš has pressed the charges that he has not been repaid by Katimu’. Gudaya must present two witnesses now. If Gudaya finds these witnesses for his claim, then he is clear. If Gudaya does not support his statement by witnessing, then Gudaya must repay the barley and the interest to Bau-ēreš:

(1–9) By 1 Kislīmu, Gudaya son of Ḫinni-ilī shall bring two *mār banî* (as) his witnesses to Opis and establish, against Bau-ēreš son of Nabû-bāniaḫi, that, at the time (of the termination of the loan), Gudaya brought Katimu’ son of Ḫagūru – for whose presence he (Gudaya) assumed guarantee to Bau-ēreš – to him (Bau-ēreš) and handed (Katimu’) over to Bau-ēreš.
(10) If he (Gudaya) establishes (the case) against him (Bau-ēreš), he (Gudaya) is clear.
(11–12) If he (Gudaya) does not establish (the case) against him (Bauēreš), then he (Gudaya) shall pay Bauēreš barley and its interest according to the debt-note.
(13–14) Witnesses: Silim-Bēl son of Balāṭu;
(14–15) Iddin-Marduk son of Nabûittiya;
(15–16) and the scribe: Nabû-aḫḫēiddin son of Šulaya descendant of Egibi.

(16–18) Opis. 23 Araḫšamna, year 40 of Nebuchadnezzar, king of Babylon [2, p. 46].

Formally:

1. If a man takes a loan, he must repay the debt according to the debt-note in the presence of a guarantor [the axiom from the code];
2. If a man cannot pay, his guarantors must pay [the axiom from the code];
3. Gudaya son of Ḫinni-ilī was a guarantor that Katimu' took a loan from Bau-ēreš [the documented fact];
4. If Gudaya has two witnesses that he presented Katimu' to Bau-ēreš to repay the debt, Gudaya is free [the first conditional verdict];
5. If Gudaya has no witnesses that he presented Katimu' to Bau-ēreš, Gudaya must pay Bauēreš barley and its interest according to the debt-note [the second conditional verdict];

Then, either Gudaya is free or he must pay.

Usually, any relationship between creditors and debtors was regulated by a legal proceeding that may be formalized as follows:

1. The creditor (*C*) has pressed the charges that the debtor (*D*) has not given back the *X* shekels taken from him.
2. This *D* is testifying at the trial: "The *X* shekels of *C* which I owed, I have paid to him in the presence of two witnesses: W_1 and W_2." In accordance with the words of the stele, it means that *D* is free.
3. If his witnesses W_1 and W_2 are confirming: "*D* has repaid the *X* shekels to *C*," then *D* must swear together with his witnesses and *D* is free and *C* forfeits his claims.
4. And if *D*'s witnesses do not confirm *D*'s statement, *C* must swear together with his witnesses W_3 and W_4 that *D* has taken the *X* shekels from *C* in the presence of W_3 and W_4 and *D* must pay *C*'s money back."

This legal proceeding has the following logical structure:

1. If a man takes a loan, he must do it in the presence of two witnesses W_3 and W_4 [the axiom from the code];
2. If a man took a loan in the presence of two witnesses W_3 and W_4, he must repay the debt [the axiom from the code];
3. If a man repays the debt, he must do it in the presence of two witnesses W_1 and W_2 [the axiom from the code];
4. If a man repays the debt in the presence of two witnesses W_1 and W_2, he is free [the axiom from the code];
5. There are two witnesses W_3 and W_4 that a debtor took a loan from a creditor [a documented fact];

Then, either the debtor must repay the debt or if he repaid it in the presence of two witnesses W_1 and W_2, then he is free.

Thus, each Neo-Babylonian trial record was a sophisticated syllogism, correctly constructed and based on true premises which are taken from the law code or verified by royal judges as documented facts.

To sum up, we can conclude as follows:

1. Drawing true and correct conclusions is not so easy and even philosophers can make mistakes or do not know how to infer at all. For example, the early Buddhist philosophers, such as the author of the *Kathāvatthu*, did not know correct forms of *modus ponens* and *modus tollens* and appealed just to sophisms.

2. Chrysippus was the first Greek philosopher who proposed a logical theory of inferring grounded on *modus ponens* and *modus tollens*. Cicero, the follower of Chrysippus, showed in his *Topica* that this theory is fundamental for the legal hermeneutics.

3. The logical analysis of Neo-Babylonian trial records allows us to affirm that the logical theory of conclusions based on *modus ponens* and *modus tollens* was established much earlier than it was done by Chrysippus; namely, this theory became a part of the Babylonian legal proceedings since the Sumerians.

Conclusions

In this paper, I have shown that symbolic logic was founded by the Sumerians and Akkadians within the legal tradition of the law codes. So, symbolic logic developed simultaneously with the legality.

References

1. Burrow, T. *A Translation of the Kharosthi Documents from Chinese Turkestan*. James G. Forlong Fund, Vol. XX. London: The Royal Asiatic Society, 1940.
2. Holtz, Shalom E. *Neo-Babylonian Trial Records*. Society of Biblical Literature Atlanta, 2014.
3. M. Tulli Ciceronis. *Topica*. Edited with a translation introduction, and commentary by Tobias Reinhardt. Oxford University Press, 2003.
4. Mukherjee, B.N. The Great Kushana Testament, *Indian Museum Bulletin*, Calcutta, 1995.
5. Roth, M. T. *Law collections from Mesopotamia and Asia Minor*. With a contribution by Harry A. Hoffner, Ir.; edited by Piotr Michalowski. Scholars Press Atlanta, Georgia. 1995.

6. Sims-Williams, N., and Cribb, J. A New Bactrian Inscription of Kanishka the Great, *Silk Road Art and Archaeology*. Volume 4, 1996, pp. 75 – 142.
7. Thapar, R. *Aśoka and the Decline of the Mauryas*. Delhi: Oxford University Press, 1997.
8. *The Law Code of Gortyn*. Edited by Willetts, Ronald F. De Gruyter, 1967, pp. 37 – 50.
9. Veenhof, Klaas R. In Accordance with the Words of the Stele: Evidence for Old Assyrian Legislation, *Chicago-Kent Law Review*. Volume 70, Issue 4, 1995, pp. 1717 – 1744.

Authors

Joshua Halberstam received his Ph.D. in philosophy from New York University, has taught philosophy at NYU, TC/Columbia University and currently teaches Philosophy and Communications at BCC/City University of New York. He has published widely in epistemology, ethics, legal theory, and philosophy of religion. He is currently working on a book on judgment and systemic confusion. He is also the author of the novel *A Seat at the Table* and has written several books in the area of Jewish Studies. His most recent book is *The Blind Angel: New Old Chassidic Tales*, a translation of Chassidic stories from the Yiddish.

Michael Chernick is Professor Emeritus of Rabbinic Literature at Hebrew Union College-Jewish Institute of Religion, New York School. He has authored three books on rabbinic hermeneutics, two in Hebrew:
לחקר המידות כלל ופרט וכלל וריבוי ומיעוט
and
לחקר מידת גזירה שווה
and one in English: *A Great Voice That Did Not Cease.*

Sergey Dolgopolski came to the Department of Comparative Literature and The Institute of Jewish Thought and Heritage in 2010. He holds a Joint Ph.D. in Jewish Studies from UC Berkeley and Graduate Theological Union, and the degree of Doctor of Philosophical Sciences from the Russian Academy of Sciences. His general area of interest is the variety of ways in which philosophy and literature interact creating new philosophical concepts and new literary forms. He specializes in the Talmud as body of text and thought seen from poetic, rhetoric, and philosophical perspectives, with a particular interest in mutual hermeneutics of philosophical, rhetorical, and talmudic traditions, and with an emphasis on mutually shaping engagements of poetic, talmudic, and philosophical thinking. He authors a monograph Rhetoric of the Talmud in the View of Post-Structuralism (1998, St-Petersburg and Jerusalem, in Russian). One of his books is *What is Talmud? The Art of Disagreement (Fordham U. Press, 2009).* His new book *The Open Past: Subjectivity and Remembering in the Talmud,* with Fordham University Press, was published in the Fall 2012.

Hany Azazy is a lecture of Methodology and Philosophy of Science at department of Philosophy, Ain Shams University. Main interests are Logic and its history especially Islamic medieval formal and informal logic.

Michael Nosonovsky is an Associate Professor of Engineering at the University of Wisconsin in Milwaukee. He got his Master's degree in engineering from St. Petersburg Polytechnic University (1992) and in Semitic languages from St. Petersburg State University (1996) as well as PhD in Mechanical Engineering (2001) from Northeastern University in Boston. Michael taught modern and Biblical Hebrew and participated in many field trips to Jewish sites of Eastern Europe studying Hebrew inscriptions on old gravestones.

Ely Merzbach is a Professor dealing with probability theory and stochastic processes and a member of the mathematics department and Gonda Brain Research Center at Bar-Ilan University. His research is focused on Set-Indexed stochastic processes, Levy processes, Fractional Poisson processes and spans numerous topics underlying important applications in areas spanning Brain Research, financial systems, Bio Systems, Complex and stochastic systems, Environmental and other systems. He served as Dean of the Faculty of Science of Bar-Ilan University. Professor Merzbach is also involved with connections between Science and Jewish philosophy. He wrote 40 papers on this subject and several books in hebrew, for example *The Logic of the Lottery*, Reuven Mass, Ltd., 208pp. (2009).

Moshe Koppel is a professor of computer science at Bar-Ilan University. His main area of research involves the use of machine learning techniques for text analysis. He is also the founder of DICTA, a research institute devoted to applications of computational linguistics to Jewish texts.

Andrew Schumann (University of Information Technology and Management in Rzeszow, Poland) worked at the Belarusian State University, Minsk, Belarus. His research focuses on logic and philosophy of science with an emphasis on non-well-founded phenomena: self-references and circularity. He contributed mainly to research areas such as reasoning under uncertainty, probability reasoning, non-Archimedean mathematics, as well as their applications to cognitive science. He is engaged also in unconventional computing, decision theory, logical modeling of economics.

www.ingramcontent.com/pod-product-compliance
Lightning Source LLC
Chambersburg PA
CBHW071155160426
43196CB00011B/2094
9781848902541